VIEWS from the FEN

JEACOCK GROUP

First published in Great Britain in 2008 by
The Jeacock Group, 11 The Hamiltons,
Newmarket, Suffolk CB8 0NF.

Typesetting by Cambridge University Press

Printed by Cambridge University Press

Cover photographs: Peter Dunne

A catalogue record for this book is available from The British Library.

ISBN 978-0-9558466-0-1

Contents

All profits from the sale of this book are to be shared between
St Nicholas Hospice, Bury St Edmunds and MacMillan Cancer Support

FOREWORD

AS well as being a dear friend and fellow sportsman, Michael Jeacock was one of the finest, unsung writers in the land. Luckily for East Anglians he was not 'discovered' by a national daily, although he had worked in Fleet Street, so for many years the people he loved most had the exclusive pleasure of his wonderful column in their local papers. He wrote about sport, natural history, eating, fine wines, leather bound books, old buildings, curious people, birds and animals, but mostly about Shakespeare's England with a perceptive joy that arrowed straight to the heart. His fan club was enormous, everyone knew him or knew of him: mention his name and people smiled.

He was a man that William Cobbett and Surtees would have recognised for his place was alongside Mr Soapy Sponge, Jorrocks and the larger-than-life characters of Handley Cross.

The first collection of Michael's evocative and rumbustious essays on rural life, *Views From the Fen*, proved hugely popular and here, posthumously, lovingly put together by Janet and the family, comes its sequel *More Views From the Fen*: he was so prolific that there is a vast body of his work from which to choose.

Revel in the pages that follow. Recall an England as it used to be and ought to be again, painted in glowing colours by one of its most eloquent, sharp-eyed and kindly spokesmen.

John Humphreys

A LABOUR OF LOVE

I BELIEVE that it is only right and proper that you, the readers, should be reminded occasionally of the extraordinary lengths to which I am obliged to go in order to bring you your weekly supply of snippets enshrined hereunder. Some might even agree that my lifestyle is one of, well, almost permanent sacrifice, of valour beyond the call of duty.

Take, for example, a recent four-day period when the sun was still shining from cloudless skies and in the garden the scent of roses hung provocatively on the still air as might the hint of eastern perfumes escaping from a seraglio window. And if you wonder whence cometh my knowledge about seraglios please just assume that I have a vivid imagination.

Anyoldhow, back to work. The first two of those four lovely days just happened to encompass the final two meetings of the season at the July Course in Newmarket where, as you might have gathered, I am wont to pursue my research into matters equine and financial, purely for your further edification, you understand.

Thus, instead of relaxing in the shade like any other half-sensible old codger who has been given his bus pass, there I was, flitting 'twixt bar and bookie endlessly ferreting for scraps of information about "good things" and "certainties" which might help to pay for next week's wine bill.

The result of my inquiries over those two days was purely a confirmation of what I have known ever since I lost my only two bob on a nag which fell at the first jump up at Flagg Races in Derbyshire when I was nobbut a lad. There is no such creature as a "good thing" amongst race horses. There is certainly no such beast as a "certainty". I rediscovered these eternal truths with a vengeance at the July Course and I am certainly the poorer due to my sterile research on your behalf. You should be grateful I didn't have time to pass on any tips.

I will not burden you at length with the details of my further trials and tribulations over the following two days except that they involved Herself and me having to loll our way through long hours of a splendid barbecue 'neath greengage trees groaning with weight in dear Lettie Gentleman's beautiful garden over in Dullingham. Still not sure what it was all about because it isn't Lettie's 90th birthday until later in the year.

But I worked hard on those plum trees during the afternoon, tasting one here, another there. Conclusion: don't leave your greengages on the bough. They are ready for the jampot – now!

Time to change and dash off to the magnificent Benedetto wedding reception in that posh Newmarket dining room, this time on the Rowley Mile.

Although by now the evening sky has purpled over and so have most of my research faculties I can report to you three observations arrived at with absolute clarity;

From the evidence laid out before our very eyes at this grandest of parties, Italians have the largest and friendliest families in the world.

They are the most generous people in the world.

Furthermore they give no quarter to their friends upon whom they impose their vast hospitality.

Three days down and one to go.....

And so to the 24th annual Fenland Country Fair at Stow-cum-Quy. Thousands of you were there (it seemed that most of you offered me a glass of beer) and you don't need me to tell you it is now one of the very best, real country fairs in the kingdom.

To explain I will pinch a couple of paragraphs from the welcome at the front of Fair catalogue (well, I did write it): "Here, over its two days – scarcely long enough to enjoy everything on offer – is to be found just about everything which touches upon the lives of those of us whose hearts are still in love with the traditions, sports and pastimes of a rapidly vanishing British countryside. The Fenland is even more than that, it is a great meeting place. It is an event where old friendships are renewed, new friendships are made, where ancient memories are re-kindled and where warm English beer can be drunk in the company of singing hounds, soaring hawks, twittering ferrets and the laughter of country folk at ease with each other."

I added another couple of lines to the welcoming message: "I have only one regret. I just wish I was half the man I was when I went to the first Fenland Fair."

After four days like that don't I just!

The Countryside

LIGHTNING IN THE FENS

OUT shooting one cold and grim day recently we fell to discussing old fenland traditions. I mentioned one which is still practised here and there. It is based on the firm belief that a child conceived during a thunderstorm will live a long, happy and healthy life. There were doubters among my listeners but I was able to assure them in my time in the fens, at the first flash of lightning and the first crack of thunder, I have seen farmers leaping from their tractors and others downing their hoes, as they dash off homewards.

Later I fell to a-thinking. Y'see on March 18th there is to be another great Countryside March in London to defend the future not only of traditional country sports but of the countryside in general. There will be upwards of a million of us in the capital that day. Much of East and Mid-Anglia will be drained of country-folk and fellow supporters from the towns.

But what, I asked myself, what on earth will happen in London that day if there is a thunderstorm during the great march? Verily, the mind doth boggle.

MARCH 1, 1998 — THE GREAT COUNTRYSIDE MARCH

TORRENTS normally start with a trickle. This was not the case with the Great Countryside March in London on Sunday. It was a tumultuous torrent from the very beginning. A raging river of mild-tempered, civilised countryfolk from every class, every political persuasion and, certainly, of every age. The torrent poured down the roads and railways of the country from every shire in the land to provide a spectacle of calm, dignified and peaceful protest on a scale the like of which has never previously been witnessed in London. It was a magnificent occasion and immensely moving. Herself and our son Simon and I were there and we walked without break for almost five hours. They were among the most memorable and amazing five hours of our lives.

For the record there were close on three hundred thousand of us on the march and I wonder how many more were there with us in spirit – the elderly, the infirm, those too busy to make the long journey; millions of course. One little boy had a placard on his back saying: "I represent my brother – he is working today." You see – and the antis who were doubtless infuriated by the fantastic success of the day will not accept this – we were there not just to defend countryside traditions. Deep down we were there to defend that most precious and hard-won of all British traditions. Its name is – freedom.

When our coach left the fenland farm where we had gathered early on Sunday morning all carrying our docky bags (if you don't know what they are ask the first fenman you meet) the paired-off partridges were flitting around the land we shoot over and imperious cock pheasants were casting lascivious looks over their harems of hens. In one field a husk of hares, six in all, frisked and frolicked. After all, this was the first day of March, a time for all hares to box, cavort and, above all, to go a-courting.

There was an odd feeling among the party – which included families with young children – aboard our coach for I don't suppose that any of us had ever protested in public about anything before in our entire lives. We were doing something so untypical, so out of character that I think we were almost embarrassed. This was not the way of countryfolk. On the other hand we knew the time had come when we needed to stand up and be counted. When we left the fen behind we could not have guessed that by the end of the day we would be counted not in tens of thousands or scores of thousands but in hundreds of thousands. We were not even to dream as we headed south that by the time of our evening return the countryside would have found itself a united and powerful voice, a voice which any government of any colour will, from now onwards, ignore at its peril.

Although there was a deep and underlying anger beneath the surface of the mile after mile, wall to wall torrent of marchers the whole affair was conducted with fantastically good humour. This caused the tiny groups of antis along the route to become incandescent with rage for their hysterical and obscene rantings were met with wave after wave of politely raised caps and cheery greetings. That was not the reaction they sought. At one point an anti shouted at our section of the vast concourse: "You're on the run, you........" To which the elderly Devonian farmer on my left shouted back: "No we're not my beauty. We're on the march at last."

What was particularly striking about the forest of banners and placards was the meekness of the messages they bore. Never in the history of demonstrations can there have been more "pleases" on view and fewer "demands". Here were people asking, not threatening. There was no "or else" about it. We were ordinary folk asking to be left alone.

The nearest the banners got to being political was one carrying the message: "Eat British lamb. Thirty thousand foxes do." Very, very politically incorrect, I suppose. But equally I suppose there was not a person on that great, that magnificent and that historic parade who gives a tuppeny toss for political correctness.

If nothing else the March in London on March the First 1998 showed how splendidly the British can still behave when they have their backs to the wall. It was a privilege to have been there.

DISTRESSED EELS

I WOULD like an honest answer to the following questions if you would be so kind – when did you last see a distressed eel? Have you ever seen a distressed eel? The two queries are posed in all seriousness because I believe they are symptomatic of the inane nuttiness of modern society.

They are prompted by a series of complaints published in a national newspaper from – wait for it – the Director of Advocates for Animals – an outfit of which, happily, I had not previously heard.

The Director, one Ross Minett, is seemingly much worried by the mistreatment of animals in that television show "I'm a Celebrity...Get Me Out Of Here". He is deeply upset, apparently, because insects and grubs were eaten alive on the programme and goes on to complain that "eels removed from the water were CLEARLY SEEN TO BE DISTRESSED".

Now I gladly confess that I did not watch one episode of that strange-sounding programme because I am an intellectual when it comes to televiewing and tend to restrict myself to those channels which show horse-racing, anything with John Wayne in it and recycled films of "Dad's Army".

On t'other hand, I have seen and caught many a dozen eels in my time but I have yet to come face to face with one which was clearly distressed. Some may well have been distressed but if so they managed to hide their feelings pretty damn well. The fact is your average eel is not the most expressive of creatures at the best or worst of times and is incapable, in my experience, of rendering visually or vocally its displeasure at being removed from its natural habitat. It can wriggle, of course, but that's in the nature of the beast.

Thus I find the Director of Advocates for Animals ability to recognise an abused eel on a television screen close to genius and he is to be congratulated upon his miraculous perspicacity. As for insects and grubs being eaten alive by the programme's contestants, I dunno. I suppose all insects and grubs are part of the food chain and are quite accustomed to being gobbled up by assorted birds, frogs, snakes, ant-eaters, iguanas, fish, aborigines and the like so I don't imagine they were too uptight about being scoffed by large-chested ladies or whey-faced male "celebrities".

Distressed eels my foot.

DANGER ALL AROUND

I SUPPOSE that what with the kingdom teetering on the verge of a severe nervous breakdown as it waits, breath baited, for the next twitch of a Beckham blanket, the fate of a clutch of warm eggs laid by an optimistic thrush at the top end of our garden is of little consequence. But it worries me.

The nest nestles amidst what will shortly be a cascade of honeysuckle intertwined with white, rambling roses and if you can think of a more heavenly spot for a family of nestlings to be introduced to our world then I would like to see it. The culture shock those little throstles face when finally they fly off to join in the menacing realities of our harsh society is uncomfortable to contemplate.

Except, of course, that they won't. Fly the nest that is. If they do, they will be very, very lucky thrushes indeed. Already their enemies are lurking in the neighbourhood. From where I sit now I see the slim, elegant outline of a lone magpie perched atop one of those pesky leylandiis not twenty yards from our garden and the nest. In his black and white uniform he is as smart as a ducal butler, but his heart is as black as his feathers. I would as soon shoot him off his perch before he works his voracious venom on the thrush's eggs but another half dozen would simply come flocking to his funeral. Magpies abhor a vacuum. I have said this before and I make no excuse for repeating myself – the magpie is a sickening creature and, despite what the do-gooders will insist to the opposite – is a colossal menace to our declining song-bird population. A severe national cull, as with woodpigeons, would be a most welcome and sensible addition to our annual countryside calendar.

DOOMED

THEY were doomed from the start, those blackbirds nesting in the high honeysuckle, and we knew it. Not that we didn't put up a fight on their behalf but the wretched magpie was not to be denied its wicked way. So now the twittering of the chicks has stopped and their nest is silently empty.

The final raid came at breakfast time and herself saw the hunter swoop into the honeysuckle. She hurtled across the lawn in flapping dressing gown clapping and hollering – a sight likely to frighten a regiment of well-armed Turkish foot soldiers but not, apparently, a voracious magpie. She was too late.

So the hunter has cleared our garden of young thrushes and blackbirds and for those of you who are still determined to defend this nasty creature just pause for a moment and think. There are millions of gardens in this country and uncountable numbers of magpies. Our experience this springtime has not been unique and it takes little imagination to realise the vast and horrendous songbird holocaust created by magpies. There is only one answer, only one way of helping our friendly song-birds. Magpies need a severe thinning out.

MURDERING MAGPIES

TO matters avian – to the magpie to be precise. There is an almighty brouhaha brewing currently over a group of people who have stumped up a £500 bounty to encourage a magpie cull. They hope the cull will arrest the very serious decline in the small bird population which they know is due in a large degree to the magpie which wantonly destroys the eggs and young of smaller birds

Inevitably into battle thunders that mega-rich and myopic charity, the Royal Society for the Protection of Birds. A major objective of this outfit seems to be the ever-increasing accumulation of massive funds and it relies largely for its staggering income upon the bequests of rich, elderly ladies. They might be deterred from leaving the RSPB so much as a groat should it be seen to agree with the culling of any bird no matter how vicious.

But the RSPB admits on its own website that there are now 650,000 breeding pairs of magpies. One of the cull supporters has worked out some horrendous figures ... if each pair destroys one nest of five eggs or five young birds the total number destroyed is 3,250,000. If, however, each pair destroys one nest a week over the breeding season, a very conservative figure, the number of eggs or young lost becomes 39 million.

Good luck, then, to the cullers. Our gardens have been too silent for too long.

A WARNING OF COLD WEATHER

JUST before that cold snap began last week with a flurry of snow, the bare treetops hereabouts were fairly crammed by rooks. Occupying the very highest branches, the big black birds sat unmoving and unusually silent staring out across the freezing landscape. I have always believed such a scene presages extreme weather though others will argue. All I know is that I haven't been proved wrong yet and the next time you see rooks sitting still as statuettes on the highest reaches of tall trees then put your rabbit skin liberty bodice in the airing cupboard. You'll be needing it.

ANTI'S DISGUSTING LANGUAGE

I CONTINUE to be saddened – well, sickened, actually – by the inability of the anti-hunting, fox-hugging brigade to express themselves during their public protestations without having to resort to the very foulest of foul language.

They do themselves and their ill-founded cause little good by their endlessly boring repetition on such occasions of the most nauseating words and phrases in the English lexicon. Why do they do it? Are they under some strange, twisted delusion that the filthier their language the more forceful their convoluted arguments become in the eye of the general public? They cannot have the slightest inkling of the disgust with which those uncommitted to one side or other of the hunting argument view their disgusting outbursts.

They were at it again in Newmarket last Saturday when the Thurlow met the day after the ban became official to exercise their hounds. More than 2,000 perfectly behaved citizens were there on foot to support the hunt's turnout, and another 200 or so were mounted. The antis mustered around 15 protesters. I was fascinated by one of them, a young lady whose shrill and hysterical screams would have worried a hardened psychiatrist. She was wearing a grubby white T-shirt upon which were daubed words of such scatological clarity as to leave not even the most innocent of by-standers in doubt about her feelings towards those who hunt.

She couldn't have been twenty years of age and her language as hounds and riders swept past still haunts me. She even managed to use the same gross invective as adjective, noun and verb in one sentence which takes a bit of doing. Then – and if it hadn't been sad it would have been funny – she screamed: "You blankety-blank blanks are just a bunch of blankety-blank obscene blanks." Young lady indeed.

WELL, WELL, WOULD YOU BELIEVE IT?

WELL, well! Blow me down, I'll go to the foot of our stairs, you could have knocked me down with a feather, whoever would have thought it – and any number of similar cries of astonishment and surprise!

I am brought to this state of incredulity by the results of an independent and scientifically approved survey just published which show that the ban on hunting with hounds has actually increased the suffering of foxes as more are now being shot and wounded and die lingering deaths.

A study carried out by Universities' Federation for Animal Welfare totally undermines the arguments of the RSPCA and the League Against Cruel Sports that hunting caused more suffering than shooting. The position really, as those of us who actually know about these things, is quite the reverse. The study shows and proves what many of us foresaw with certainty that up to fifty per cent of foxes shot with shotguns are wounded and not killed outright.

The study was commissioned by the Middle Way Group of MPs three years ago when pro-banners of hunting asserted that shooting was the humane alternative to hunting with hounds. A co-founder of the group, Lembit Opik, a Liberal Democrat, says: "The pro-ban groups were plain wrong. Many wounded foxes end up dying over hours, days or even weeks. With dogs it's all or nothing." Lady Golding, the Labour co-chairman of the group, was equally blunt. "The next Government must look again at the Hunting Act and replace it with genuine animal welfare measures."

Well! as we said at the beginning. Well, well! Just fancy that.

NAFFF

HAVE you noticed how the kitchen flies have slowed down overnight and are lethargic almost to the point of suicide? Only days ago, it took the skill of a hungry hunter to kill one. Now you can swat 'em into oblivion with the greatest of ease. It is a sure sign of impending winter so take five minutes off from slaughtering pesky insects and slip into the ol' rabbit skin liberty bodice a bit sharpish. Jack Frost is sharpening his sickle.

Oh dear! Was it wise to mention fly killing? I have not the slightest doubt that somewhere there exists a group of bearded ladies poised and prepared to form themselves at this very moment into the National Association of Fly Freedom Fighters (NAFFF), or some such organisation to protect innocent and persecuted flies.

THE MANEA METHOD OF KILLING FLIES

CAN we please address an urgent problem close to home? I refer to the common house fly which makes its unwelcome presence only too well-known at this season of the year in cottage and castle across the kingdom. It knows no barriers of rank or birth and is just as much at home whizzing around the left-overs on the ducal dining table as it is hovering over a take-home Chinky being scoffed in front of the telly.

It is a universally hated pest and not even the nuttiest of bunny-huggers has yet got round to forming a "Ban the Fly Swat" underground organisation. Its importance as a seemingly indestructible household pest has been underlined recently by a series of lengthy and erudite letters in one of the more serious national papers about the best ways of catching and / or despatching the obnoxious little creature.

Different theories abound, though it seems to be generally agreed that the ubiquitous fly swat is utterly useless, but I read all of the letters with a growing unease. Where had these people been all their lives? When it came to fly catching did they not know that there were no flies on fen-folk? Had they never heard about the Manea Method? The Infallible Manea Method to give it its full name. It is so called because it was invented by an ol' boy who lived in Manea and who regarded each and every plump fenny fly as a personal opponent.

It works like this. Assume that a swarm of flies is a-hovering and a-buzzing around the dish on the kitchen table with the bones from last night's rabbit pie waiting to go in the soup pan, a common enough sight up in the fens.

Answer? Simple. Just fill a bucket full of fresh pig muck and stand it in the middle of the sitting room. Wait until all the flies have transferred their affection for the kitchen to the delights of the sitting room then chuck a wet tea towel over the bucket, remove and empty the contents onto the midden in the garden. (Or, if you live in a flat, use the muck-heap on the balcony). I thought this little trick was common knowledge but apparently not.

Take it from me the Manea Method is absolutely foolproof. Anyoldhow, it has always worked for us

****

HAD a letter from a chap claiming to be the Mayor of Manea and complaining about my description of how the good burghers of that fenland community get rid of flies in the kitchen by placing a bucket of fresh pig muck in the sitting room. "Get your facts right", demands the Mayor who forgot to sign his letter. "We put the bucket of pig-muck in a bedroom during the day otherwise there would be a fair ol' pong when we were in the sitting room. We only put it in the sitting room when we go to bed."

He ends on a note of obviously high dudgeon. "What do you think we are in Manea? Uncivilised?" My apologies all round Mr Mayor. Only too pleased to put the record straight, your Worship.

WHO NEEDS COWS?

NOW here's a pretty kettle of fish or whatever the saying is. The Royal Society for the Prevention of Accidents (Rospa) advises walkers not to enter fields where cattle are grazing. This will have come as a considerable surprise to large chunks of our urban population who don't quite know what a field is and, even if they do, they'll be astonished to learn that big, wobbly, unhygienic beasts are still allowed to live in them. (For those who have forgotten a field is often covered with grass which is the same sort of material that grows on the edges of the Labour Exchange car park. Fields are very handy things for cows. Cows like grass).

Among those thus surprised will be the militant groups who have fought for decades for the right to roam over other people's land without considering for a moment the effect that such a right might have on those who try to derive a livelihood from that self-same land.

The footpath fanatics, the Sunday afternoon strollers, the countryside-is-our-playground brigade, will feel immensely cheered by Rospa's advice because it brings to the surface the most important of all questions concerning the modern countryside – what are fields really for?

Assuming that Rospa is worried about angry cows prodding noisy intruders carrying portable radios and mobile phones and not just pointing out the dangers inherent in tripping face down in a pile of fresh cow muck, then there is really only one answer. The freedom walkers won't give up their victories, the farmers will be terrified of litigation following a cow accident so – the cows will have to go.

After all, who needs cows in this day and age when, as we all know, milk comes out of Tescos?

All a bit different in my youth when it was a well-paid job (a tanner a day) during the school hols helping to lead the bull or the stallion around the farms to perform their all-important duties with the cows and mares. Everywhere up north the advice to the lad from the bull and stallion men was always the same: "Keep t'head to t'stack" and it was our youthful task to keep the females looking at the haystack. I never did quite know why. Was it the prospect of having a handful of hay as a reward which took the lady's mind off the proceedings or was the stack being used as a barrier to prevent her bolting away from a fate worse than death? What would Rospa have thought about all that?

A NATURAL DILEMMA

LET us look at the moral dilemma involved in the following tale of the wasp and the spider. It is a question of two parts and both answers are grisly. Do not let me put you off.

Early the other sunny morning on the outside of the bedroom window up in the right hand corner my little eye spies a late autumn wasp embroiled in the intricate clutches of a spider's web. The more the wasp struggles, the more lethally enmeshed it becomes. Its fate is plainly inevitable.

At this point in that cruel, hunting scene – that's precisely what it was – I begin to wonder what might be the reaction of those members of the fraternity who believe that all of God's creatures have an equal right to life? Would they lean out of the window and free the innocent wasp from the spider's trap so that it may continue on its useless way through life until the first frosts finish it off? But to do that would be to deprive the equally innocent spider of its supply of grub for the winter and itinerant, juicy wasps are few and far between these chill mornings.

So is one to be a Wasp Hugger or a Spider Hugger? To abandon the trapped wasp is to condemn it to death. To free it is to sentence the spider to slow starvation – either solution is a grisly one. So! Wasp or spider? Think about it – fox and chicken, hawk and rabbit; indeed any predator and its prey? Should mankind interfere? Answers from moral philosophers on a postcard or, in the case of Bunny Huggers, on 24 sheets of closely typed foolscap, please.

SILENCE

BRECKLAND is not only blessed by a strangely stark beauty with its sparkling silver birches bringing a feeling of Mother Russia's steppes to this corner of England, it is doubly lucky in remaining undiscovered by the developers. Its silence is audible. When we were there recently Herself and I realised there was something different about the walkers that we saw. They were not wearing those dreadful little wireless things in their ears. They were listening to the silence.

DANGERS IN THE COUNTRYSIDE

NOW here's some cracking news for those who love nothing better than mucking about with the countryside. Not IN it but WITH it.

The tale starts over the Easter hols with the Devil's Dyke, that extremely ancient earthworks which stretches from Reach on the edge of the fens, passing between the two Newmarket racecourses until it finally fetches up over in Wood Ditton. Or the other way round if you prefer.

The Dyke is one of the finest stretches of walking territory hereabouts, rising gently as it does above the surrounding low-lying land with enchanting views from every inch of its eight miles. But over the Bank Holiday someone, I know not whom, decided to close the wooded end of the Dyke at Ditton because it was too dangerous to use. It seems there are trees there which need felling and exposed roots of other trees causing a "trip hazard".

I know how vicious nature can be out there in the wilds what with falling conkers, bombarding pigeons and such-like but I had never before heard of the "trip hazard". In my peasant, yokelly innocence I had presumed that walkers always kept a wary eye on the path ahead.

Anyoldhow, I thought this such a splendid new form of nannying that I forthwith phoned the head office of the Health and Safety Executive, those world-renowned ginks responsible for the two-rung ladder and the death of the hanging basket. They were exceedingly miffed at not having thought up the "trip factor" themselves with its potential for closing thousands of miles of highly dangerous public footpaths which criss-cross the kingdom. They would act immediately, they said. But their problem was they didn't have a real guide to what terrible dangers are lurking out there. Could I help?

Thus: "The Jeacock Guide to the Hazards of the Country Stroll and How to Avoid Them".

1: When on a steep slope do not stand to attention, heels together, looking upwards and leaning backwards. You will topple over.

2: Beware of falling trees and branches. They rarely all fall down at the same time but should one decide it's had enough it will give warning with a series of creaks, groans and splintering crashes. Seek immediate sanctuary behind a silent tree.

3: Do not amble into an area of soggy ground in which gaseous bubbles rise to the surface. This is called a swamp or bog. If you stand in it first your ankles will get wet, then your knees and the damp will continue to rise. Do not confuse the rural "bog" with the urban variety and use it as such since this will bring murmurs of disapproval from other walkers.

4: Frequently, in the undergrowth, you will find recumbent couples, their arms entwined and seemingly trying to resuscitate each other. Do not worry. They are in no danger. Under no circumstance try to offer assistance as this will almost certainly lead to a punch on the schnozzle. You are merely observing a traditional and harmless bucolic pastime.

Sorry. Run out of space. For further details from my "Guide" log on to my i-pod on WHI 1212 – or something.

THE GRAND DESIGN

THE time: early in the last war. The place: a field under the lee of Longstone Edge, in Derbyshire. Present: a stoat, a rabbit and me, out rabbiting with my .177 airgun. Utter silence.

Neither creature knows I am twenty yards away behind a stone wall. The stoat, on its hind legs, dances gently, swaying like Kipling's cobra in my book at home. The rabbit crouches, head shrunk into its shoulders. I have never seen sheer, naked fear before. The stoat has petrified its prey into granite immobility. The old keepers' tales were true. Stoats can hypnotise. I know what the outcome will be. The rabbit's terror touches me. Shall I end its torture with one lead pellet?

The Church of England ran our village school and the Vicar told us infants that all God's creatures had their part to play in his creation. It was not for us to question His Great Purpose. Up there on the edge of the moors I am in a moral muddle. Why should the stoat starve? Why should the rabbit suffer? Who was I to interfere? It was all God's fault. The stoat struck. The rabbit died. I went home deeply troubled. I still am. Why did He weave cruelty into the tapestry of his Grand Design?

A MESSAGE LEFT BY A FOX

NOW here's a rum go, Master. I will keep the details brief since they are of a delicate nature. T'other morning we woke to find the garden bird table cleared of all food, as usual, but in the middle of the table there, alone in its, well, glory, was the dropping of a medium-sized mammal. Oddly, I am something of an expert in these matters, having studied the subject in biology at school, later in books in my library and in the wild. This offering was from a fox. No – not a cat, a rat, a squirrel or bird. It was a fox dropping. I know – I have seen more fox droppings in my time than Newmarket sausages. Why was it there? Because a fox leaves his sign to mark his territory high off the ground. How did it get there? Foxes can climb. Oh yes they can! Our bird table is alongside a fence. Easy-peasy for the fox. Jack the Cat is not going to like this.

Jack's Spot

Hi there, readers all!
I'm none too keen on this talk of a wandering dog fox in these parts. A couple of the lads reckon they've seen Charlie loping around in the summer moonlight – he's even been spotted sniffing out the dustbins where we hold our choir rehearsals. There is wild talk of forming a Defence Force a bit like Dad's Army. I tried to point out that most of us have had the operation and calling ourselves "Dads" would be like calling John Prescott a gentleman. They are determined and (naturally) asked me to take command. You will never see a cowardly whisker tremble on Jack the Cat's fizzog but I had to decline. I explained that as Choir Master my duties were already onerous, especially as I was re-writing my "Cats' Cantata", and I would be spending more time in the house of a night-time for the foreseeable future working on my great opus. My genius should not be wasted on a mangy fox.

A Gentle Farewell, Good People.

Jack the Cat

THE DEPRESSED MUSSEL

AS I was about to say, before I was rudely interrupted, you will be delighted to learn that between us we are putting the smile back on the shell of the depressed river mussel.... I will explain.

The river mussel, as you already know, is a mollusc of the bivalve genus *Mytilus* which lives – happily, I had always assumed – in our local rivers. Apparently not so. Well not so the happy bit. Anglian Water reckons they get depressed. That fact is tucked away in their publication called "focus", which arrived in the post with their most recent rates' demand. In it they explain how some of our money is spent on supporting conservation work among species with their different problems – including those of the river mussel, poor sad creature.

This is how A.W. puts it: "Anglian Water is supporting conservation work aimed to help prevent 48 species from extinction, ranging from otters to depressed river mussels..."

No, I didn't notice the mussel bit either until Herself pointed it out. (She likes to know how our hard-earned loot is being chucked about). We are both committed to helping nature's less fortunate creatures but "depressed mussels"? We are still debating whether this might be a mollusc slightly too far?

The mind doth boggle. How, for example, does an Anglian Water person recognise a 'DRM'? Do down-in-the-dumps river mussels frown? Are they frumpish? Do they clamp their shells as tight as a Yorkshireman's purse and refuse to pay their water rates? Or is it just that AW's exploding demands for water rates have the same effect on mussels as it does on us?

Whichever. I don't want a new battle with the Bunny Huggers and the Free Votes for the Oyster Brigade and I am all for healthy, happy, grinning river mussels but, to be cruelly insensitive, I would rather the BHs and FVOB footed the Anglian Water bill to pay for the trick-cyclists who specialise in nutty mussels and not expect me to fork out for them, thank 'ee.

WHAT DO YOU CALL A MUMMY-DADDY-LONG-LEGS?

MANY of you will have noticed that there is a plague of daddy-long-legs in this neck of the fens, most of which are gathered at our windows staring in at us like a horde of inquisitive and anaemic female models on a fashion catwalk. Their unwelcome presence prompts a number of questions which I ask myself every year at this time and which I have never been able to answer.

For example, since millions of 'em come dancing and prancing out of their underground dugouts in the autumn, they can't all be daddy-long-legs. Unless my school biology lessons were a mite wonky, the mummy-daddy-long-legs must appear in the equation somewhere. It is, as the teacher used to say, only natural.

But if so, why don't we give her a nice cuddly, female name. Lady-long-shanks, mayhap? Or, better, how about Mrs-spindly-knickers?

Actually, our local species, in youth, are called leatherjackets, live in the soil before they reach their dancing maturity and create merry hell by noshing the roots of the plants under which they shelter. And since this is Cambridge territory, let's complicate the issue totally by giving the young leatherjacket / daddy-long-legs / Mrs-spindly-knickers its Latin moniker: Tipula paludosa. It will do to your lawn what the sergeant major's first rude word did to my head – turn it bald overnight.

Jack's Spot

Where else but herein would you find a learned discourse on the daddy-long-leg? Not in the "News of the World" you wouldn't, mate. But I know something he doesn't. A Glaswegian tawny once told me that in Scotland the female daddy-long-legs is known as Jenny-Long-Legs. And that's my big scoop of the week, chums. Remember I was first with the news!

Jack the clever Cat

FISHING WITH A KING

BACK to birds for a moment, please. When I wrote about that kingfisher, the appearance of which down the distant fen so delighted me, I was astonished by the number of readers who contacted me to ask why it was they had never enjoyed a similar privilege. The best I could say was that it was all a matter of being in the right place at the right time. There is no such thing as an organised kingfisher-spotting tour.

Well, how about this for luck. Over by the medieval packhorse bridge at Moulton outside Newmarket t'other day Herself and I were with son Simon and his three little 'uns – Natasha, Abbie and Ben – and what did we see? Yes. Perched on a water-depth measuring pole by the little river was a kingfisher. It wasn't a dozen yards away from us, shoulders hunched, beak down, eyes reading the fast-flowing stream. Suddenly it dived, plopping into the chill water. Up it came, beak empty. Back to its perch. The children had eyes like organ stops, faces thrilled. Back in the bird dived. This time it surfaced triumphant, its beak carrying its lunch, a tiny tiddler. The flash of blue corkscrewed in flight upstream to enjoy its fishy repast on some distant, lonely bank.

The children, dad, granny and Bump Bumps were enchanted and that magical scene is indelibly etched on six memories.

But, as I say, it's all a question of being in the right place at the right time............

ROOKS AND ROOKED

AS the snow comes tumbling down there is one section of nature's society for whom spring has sprung – the rooks. They are in a noisy frenzy of nest building as if they are sure that balmier days are just around the corner and, who knows, mayhap they are right.

Now rooks are without doubt the most easily watchable of all birds for there they are, overhead, their every activity on view to any observer who wishes to observe. And, yet it's odd how few folk seem to be aware that the rook chooses live twigs with which to build its nest.

I was reminded of this only last week when I was watching a busy rookery through my new Christmas-present binoculars and there, larger than life in the lenses of my lovely Minolta, I saw one rook wrestling furiously with a half-tidy sized twig only a few feet below the nest.

For a full minute the bird tugged and twisted until finally, with a flick of its head the twig snapped and, as they always do, the rook flew around the tree in a circle before placing its hard-won trophy on the shallow nest with what I perceived to be a sense of triumph. The effort put into this operation is enormous and it is a perfect example of a ferocious natural determination.

In my unwisdom I had assumed that this particular trait in the rook's character was general knowledge but when I mentioned it in the pub later I was much scoffed at and general scorn was poured upon my acute observations. Why should rooks go to all that tiresome trouble, asked the ill-bred mob with whom I am obliged occasionally to consort, when the ground under the trees is littered with dead twigs? The general consensus was that I should cut down the amount of gin I pour on my Kellogg's of a breakfast time. Some people just will not be taught.

Anyoldhow, that particular lot in the pub are considerably more knowledgeable about the other use of the word "rook" (i.e., as a verb meaning "to fleece") especially when they are playing cribbage and darts as I am only too well aware from my own sad experiences in their company. As a man of honour I have always thought it demeaning and unsporting to take advantage of someone of a trusting nature but that principle does not seem to have entered into the murky philosophies of my so-called friends who continue to rook me unmercifully at every available opportunity. Their ability, for example, to exploit my inherent innumeracy when it comes to scoring at darts is often close to sheer genius and might well, I strongly suspect, considerably impress even the Lucasian Professor of Mathematics in the University of Cambridge.

People

EPITAPHS

WE started to laugh about death and its associated customs when one of our company told us, through tears of laughter, how recently an uncle of his had suddenly passed over in the most embarrassing of situations in the lee of a haystack on his farm in Suffolk. To put it not too finely the ol' boy was not alone at the time. The blokes in the village pub didn't stop guffawing for a week, said our friend, and he reckoned his uncle would have enjoyed the macabre joke as much as anyone had he been in a position so to do.

Anyoldhow, this set us off a-chortling about death's dafter side. One of us claimed that when his mother-in-law left them, the undertaker asked him whether he would like her cremated, embalmed or just plain buried? "Why take chances? Let's have all three!" said our mate.

Another of us was determined to have just one line on his tombstone. It would read, he said: "You Wouldn't Believe Me When I Said My Feet Were Killing Me". One of our group said he had arranged for his stone to carry the legend: "Here Lies The Only Englishman To Have Taken His Own Wife To Brighton For The Weekend".

Being a somewhat literary type of chap I told them about the poet John Keats (1795–1821 – dates are just about all I can remember these days), who wanted as his epitaph : "Here Lies One Whose Name Was Writ In Water". This, I explained was a line in some remote and esoteric play the name of which escaped me completely. Later in that century another chap from the bookish world adapted Keats' line slightly. Robert Ross (1869–1918) was Oscar Wilde's most loyal friend and, indeed, his literary executor. He decided at the end of his exceedingly stormy life that the only appropriate inscription for his tomb would be: "Here Lies One Whose Name Was Writ In Hot Water".

I rather fancy the epitaph Herself found in a churchyard up in Hunmanby where she went to school. That one reads: "No One Knows How Much He Suffered. From His Loving Wife". Oh! to have been the stonemason...

All very well, said the blokes. But what plans had I made for my own Great Departure? Simple, quoth I. My army-style proforma was already printed. It reads thus:

"Dear..........

I write to inform you that I backed my final loser on (date)......... and my funeral will take place on (date)...... at (church)........ at (time)..........

Your presence at the funeral is not obligatory. But if you don't turn up I shall seriously have to consider not attending yours. I trust we may meet again at the Heavenly Racecourse where tomorrow's winners are printed in today's papers.

Thanks and cheers.

P.S. Just in case you were beginning to wonder, I am writing this before the event and not afterwards, you understand."

Yea, verily, death can have its jolly side although not, alas, for those left behind – unless your uncle happened to be a very rich and rumbustious Suffolk farmer.

SORTING OUT THE NATION'S FINANCES

THE Chancellor of the Exchequer and the Governor of the Bank of England are said to be worried sick about the bottomless pit of personal debt into which the nation is sinking. As one who can scarcely spell the word ecconomics, let alone understand its finer meanings, you might be forgiven for feeling that I am the last person to come to their aid. Well – I am not.

We Brits are perfectly happy to pay the equivalent of a footballer's annual pay packet for a tatty two-up and two-down shanty and, having done so, we then re-mortgage the property and blow the extra spondulicks on holidays in faraway places where the beaches are littered with home-bred lager louts and local foreigners who can't stand the sight of us just because we've been obliged to hammer 'em in the occasional war down the centuries.

We all know it can't go on but the dozy Chancellor and his mate round the corner at The Bank can't for the life of 'em work out how to put a stop to the rot. Well – I can.

Only last week, quite accidentally, I discovered the secret of real econommics which, applied vigorously across all classes of society, will banish over-spending in a trice and, with it, over-borrowing. Perhaps the reason why the two fiscal bigwigs haven't rumbled my simple solution to forthcoming national penury is that they have never had to stand in a shop queue waiting to pay for a modest packet of brass screws as I did the other day. They should try it sometime then they, like me, might discover an eternal financial truism.

It came about thus: in the queue in front of me were an elderly couple, the husband clearly fed up with having to hang around dang-blasted shops instead of being down the pub with his chums. He was not in the best of tempers and when he noticed that his wife was carrying two smallish plant pots his face suddenly reddened.

"Why have you got two pots?" he hissed. "We only came in for one."

"Because", she whispered, "I've just saved £3.00."

He seemed slightly mollified. "How?" he hissed again.

"Well", said his missus smiling, "these pots cost £4.00 each but you can get two of them for £5.00. If I had bought them separately they would have cost £8.00. So I've saved three pounds by buying two."

It was clear the couple had been long married for the look on his face said it all. It was obvious he thought she was completely potty, to coin a phrase. He hissed slowly and clearly: "Y-o-u h-a-v-e n-o-t s-a-v-e-d t-h-r-e-e p-o-u-n-d-s." Then the words came spilling out and at this juncture I began to realise that I was listening to a mathematical genius. "You have not saved £3.00. You have wasted £1.00. We came in here for one pot which cost £4.00. You have spent £5.00. And before you say any more", he shouted, "we don't need two bloody pots."

Of course she won and they took the two pots home with them but that's not the point. I was left marvelling at the exquisite, simple, yet sheer genius of the angry husband's argument.

Firstly – if you don't need it, don't buy it. Secondly, you cannot possibly save money by spending it. Even I can understand that. But can the Chancellor and the Chairman get their puny intellects round what will come to be known throughout the world of lending and borrowing in due course as "The One Pot Principle"?

SUDOKU CHAMPIONS

HERSELF urged me to steer clear of subjects controversial this week and to refrain from mentioning angry bunny huggers, manic Cambridge cyclists, bearded lady vegans, whacky political correctees, clap-happy clergy who make you shake hands all round in the middle of Sunday service and all similar weirdos who intrude into the civilised echelons of our society. So be it. Won't even mention 'em.

Instead a compliment and one long overdue. It is addressed to the ladies. Recently, at The Times' national Sudoku championships, it was the ladies who thrashed the male competitors at this complex and esoteric game which is overwhelming the nation with its complicated attractions. Now the ladies' complete domination of the competition was a shocking surprise to those uncharitable male chauvinists of my acquaintance. Not to me, though. Oh no!

You see, throughout a long life I have held unswervingly to the belief that there just has to be something somewhere, some form of activity no matter how weird, how trivial, how totally useless at which women are better than men. Therefore, thank you, Sudoku ladies, thank you, for proving me right and confirming my unfaltering faith that one day the weaker sex would emerge triumphant in a battle with their superiors. Sudoku today!! The world tomorrow?

A QUESTION OF LOYALTY

THOSE questions designed to test an immigrant's suitability to be British are ludicrous and futile. Only one question is necessary to prove beyond a smidgeon of doubt whether newcomers should be welcomed to join us. It is this:

Immigration Question: In the final over of the deciding Test in Australia the English captain is 99 not out and last man in. England need one run for victory. You are the umpire. The ball hits his pad. Bearing in mind that the home crowd is in violent mood, do you answer the Aussie appeal for l.b.w. by:

a) giving him out

b) calling a belated "No Ball"

or c) running for your life?

To answer a) means you are a coward, b) you are a liar and c) means you are a True Brit and welcome.

AN UNSPOKEN UNDERSTANDING

I AM in Botolph Lane in Cambridge. An elderly couple precede me. Half way down, the ol' gel turns to her ol' man and says: "What are we walking down here for?" He says: "Because you started walking down here at the other end." She says: "That's ridiculous. Why should

I want to walk down here?" He says: "How the hell should I know?" She shouts: "Well, do you want to walk down here or not?" He is silent as they turn to walk back up Botolph Lane. He just shakes his head and looks at me with the sad eyes of a man who has been married long enough to know when it is best to shut up. He also knows I understand.

GEORGE BROWN'S SLIP-UP

SINCE the nation has got its moral attitudes in a twist over the drinking habits of Charles Kennedy, leader of the Liberal Democrats until forced out because of his over-fondness for the anti-flu vaccine of his native Scotland, perhaps I might be permitted a slight reminiscence. It involves one of the booziest of all 20th century politicians – Churchill excepted – and one of the most amusing, especially when he was drunk. It was Labour MP George Brown, and if you knew him as well as I did you will recall him with great fondness.

Alas, he only lasted as Foreign Secretary for two years – 1966–68 – long enough to endear himself to the laughing classes. His best moment? At an official reception in Peru when he tottered over to a tall, elegant "lady" to request a dance. The "lady" replied: "You are drunk, this is not a waltz, it is the Peruvian national anthem, and I am not a lady. I am the Cardinal Archbishop of Peru."

CAT'S EYES AND CANADIANS

I WAS was privileged the other day to escort a group of Canadian visitors across the border to Sandringham House in Norfolk and what a lovely day it was. Norfolk is one of the last of our unhurried counties and on a hot summer's day like ours when we were there you could almost touch the stillness.

However, there was one very curious moment during an otherwise blissful outing. The second we left the coach an extremely agitated Canadian lady took me to one side. She was clearly upset. What, she demanded to know, what was the meaning of those terrible advertisements along the side of the road a few miles back?

Puzzled, I explained that we don't normally allow advertising on our country roads.

She was not only adamant she was patently angry. She had seen them clearly for mile after mile. Terrible, she said. Dreadful. Somebody, she said, was offering to remove cats' eyes. Why?

I realised I had indeed seen her "advertisements". They were road signs where workmen were repainting white lines. "Cats Eyes Removed", they said. It was a statement, I said, not an offer.

Having explained what they were she was hugely and obviously relieved that there wasn't some sort of sinister trade in real cats eyes being carried out in deepest Norfolk. In Canada, she said, they called the shiny little things down the middle of the road "markers" and with that we all marched off to inspect her Majesty's personal treasures.

I always find it easy to feel at home at Sandringham, in fact I could quite happily move in tomorrow without the slightest difficulty though Herself might moan somewhat at having to light all those fires.

(I was there a year or two back when a young lad and his father were walking around the House in front of me. The boy, obviously city-bred, asked why all the big baskets near the fireplaces were filled with pieces of wood? They were for burning on the fires in winter, said his father.

"Can't they afford electric fires?" asked the lad).

SIMON H GOES TO JESUS

HERSELF came in for a nasty shock the other day. She phoned St John's College in Cambridge and asked to speak to our friend Simon Hawkey, the college's extremely talented conference and catering manager. She was utterly horrified when a serious voice at the other end of the phone informed her: "I'm terribly sorry but Mr Hawkey is no longer with us. He has gone to Jesus."

Herself was therefore considerably comforted and relieved to learn that Simon Hawkey was well and thriving in his new position with.......Jesus College.

'GOD' IN BED

AT the other end of the world – well, down on Exmoor actually – the hunting world has been mourning the death of Captain Ronnie Wallace, probably the greatest Master of Foxhounds ever. He was 82 and he spent 58 consecutive seasons as a Master of Foxhounds.

I met him a couple of times socially (don't bother writing, dear antis, I don't ride to hounds – unfortunately) and I found him a splendid character straight out of the 18th century. He married four times and boasted that on one particular day all four wives hunted with him on the same day. He was known throughout the hunting world as "God" and he never denied the story that when one of his wives complained: "God! It's cold in this bed", he replied: "I think, my dear, you may call me Ronnie when we are alone together."

DR WILLIAM HARVEY

MY moments of intellectual glory have been sparse to the point of non-existence but I did shine brightly t'other evening to the astonishment of the old codgers in whose company I frequently find myself in The White Lion atop Newmarket High Street. We were watching "Who Wants to be a Millionaire" on the telly in the pub and one contestant was on the half a million quid question – which of these scientists was credited with the discovery of the circulation of the blood?

William Harvey, I shouted in glee – this being about the only question I have ever been able to answer on the programme. I was, of course, correct. And so I should have been. Most days of my life I walk past Harvey's statue on the wall of the building opposite Gonville and Caius College in Cambridge where he was a student in the 1590s. One old codger was so startled by my unprecedented flash of brilliance that he almost bought me a drink.

I once explained to a group of Chinese tourists the importance of Harvey's discovery. One of them shook his head. "No", he said. "We knew about blood circulation 2000 years ago."

"Then why didn't you tell us?" I asked. He smiled: "To tell the truth we had never heard of England at the time."

FUNNY FENNY FOLK

ALWAYS been a mite worried about fenny folk. Still am. Take, for example, Mrs Dorothy Matthews of Canute Crescent, Ely. After a service in the Cathedral recently she sidled over to Herself and wondered if I knew how to count accurately a large skein of geese passing overhead. Probably not, said Herself. Fenfolk knew the answer, said Mrs Matthews. Simple. Count the wings and divide by two.

Example number two – Mrs Isobel Bryant of Swaffham Prior. As a Cambridge Blue Badge guide she was showing four charming Americans around Cambridge and they popped into The Eagle for lunch. The date was March 20, the day of the Vernal Equinox. One American borrowed a raw egg from the pub. He waited for the propitious moment of 1.31 p.m. and proceeded, to the astonishment of onlookers, to balance the egg on its end on the dining table. He swore it wasn't a trick and said it can only be done at that time on the day of an Equinox. Our friend Isobel assures me there were plenty of witnesses. Is it true? Is there an explanation? Or had Isobel broken the habit of a lifetime and had a second glass of wine?

OLIVER CROMWELL'S HEAD

WERE you aware, perchance, that Oliver Cromwell would have worn a hat measuring six and seven eighths in the days when he was dashing around England and Ireland knockin' fings abaht a bit? Mayhap this vitally unimportant detail has managed to escape you until now but for reasons I cannot explain it has been rooted firmly in the nether regions of my memory these many years. Perhaps it is because I possess a strange brain which is stuffed with utterly useless information, facts and figures, garnered during a long and misdirected life from books which the rest of mankind has managed to ignore without doing itself the slightest intellectual damage – information which I have squirreled away because, as they say, it might come in handy one day.

And it did. For those of you who don't know this, Oliver's skull now lies buried in a secret place under a flagstone in the ante-chapel of his old Cambridge College, Sidney Sussex. It was secreted there in

1960 at dead of night so that it cannot easily be found and removed by any passing fanatic.

Pause, here, for a macabre little tale. Some time ago I was escorting a group of delicious Irish ladies around Cambridge and took them into Sidney's ante-chapel to show them the Cromwell plaque therein. Cromwell is scarcely a folk-hero in Ireland and before I could stop the lovely ladies they started to perform a vigorous Irish jig upon the flagstones under which the skull of their oppressor lies. The wild jig was accompanied, to my horror, by whoops of joy. I managed, with great difficulty, to restrain my guests and to usher them out of the college before I was garrotted by the Master and Fellows for my lack of control over my group. At this point one of the party gave me a big smacking kiss. She said: "Michael me darlin', thank you, thank you. We've always wanted to dance on the auld divil's grave."

NEWTON WHERE ART THOU?

SOME of the simplest inventions are of such staggering importance to mankind that in my view the inventor should be awarded an instant Nobel Prize by a grateful world with maybe a salaried dukedom chucked in for good measure.

I came across such a person only last week. I stopped the car to ask directions of a bloke of mature years and an even maturer waistline who was half-sitting, half sprawling on a log at the edge of a field of set-aside over near Huntingdon. He had a tennis racquet in his hand. He bade me a friendly greeting and I responded by asking if he was waiting for his partner for a game of tennis. At which point a scruffy lurcher bounded into view, a tennis ball firmly clenched between its teeth. "Nope", said the stranger, "I plays tennis every day with me dog." With which he took the ball from the dog's mouth and thwacked it with the racquet into the middle of the field. The dog raced off to retrieve it and the game went on like this for some minutes.

"Got fed up years ago walking the damn dog every day so I decided to exercise her this way. Keeps her fit and me fat", he said and rumbled with laughter.

He sauntered off slowly to what I assumed was his home, a cottage a good sixty yards away, both dog and master sated with arduous exercise. I raised my cap and wished them both well. It is good to be in the company of a genius just now and then.

GIVE ME A DOG ANY DAY

A CHAP I know slightly greeted me in Newmarket High Street t'other day and said, completely out of the blue: "Why is a dog better than a woman?" I shook my head. He went on :"Because when a dog gets old and starts snapping at you endlessly you can shoot it." With which he disappeared through the front door of The Bushel.

Two days later I bumped into him again. His latest offering, "Dogs don't notice if you call them by another dog's name." He slipped into The Waggon and Horses and almost immediately popped out again. "Furthermore", he bellowed down the street "It's legal to keep a dog chained up." God only knows who he is. I'd quite like him to meet Herself. Strange place, Newmarket High Street.

COWARDICE OR WAS IT GUILE?

TO Lowestoft which, for the benefit of newcomers to this area, I should point out, is not pronounced by East Anglians as it is written. You say it thus: Looostft. Anyoldhow, there I was on business in the aforementioned Looostft t'other day when I was accosted close to the sea-front by two of the largest, toughest drunks I have ever had the non-privilege of meeting. Their demand for money was accompanied by considerable menace. The louts were not to know that the man they had picked on was no less than the President of the British League of Cowards himself (and hon. treas. also should you wish to join). Struck rigid with fright the President summoned up his only line of defence – guile. "I apologise, gentlemen", quoth he, "but I fear I have left my money on the coach." Which so-and-so coach demanded the taller of the two? "The one over there with the Metropolitan Police bowls club on board", said the quaking President. The varmints vanished sharpish. The President of the BLoC turned sideways into a hostelry equally sharpish and ordered two large scotches. "Who was the other one for", asked the landlady? "Me", said the President.

CHINESE NEW YEARS

LUNCHED the other day with a small group of Chinese visitors. Their spoken English was impeccable, almost Queenly, their knowledge of our customs, history and manners, remarkable. A humbling occasion. I asked what this new Chinese Year of the Ox meant to them. A year of very hard work they said. I was about to ask if they had a Year of the Rabbit and if so...... but, happily, the wine waiter arrived and we changed the subject.

A CHEESY TALE

PLACE your hand over your heart and answer me with total honesty: when were you last offered a piece of smoked yak cheese on King's Parade in Cambridge?

I pose the question because, in my own case, it happened to me at precisely 11.15 am last Saturday and I dare lay odds of 1000–1 that it will not happen to me again, ever.

And it is to my eternal shame that I declined the offer. Now, I shall never know what smoked yak cheese tastes like. The trouble was, I had been forewarned. You see, I was showing a mixed group of foreign students around the Cambridge colleges and one of their English teachers was having difficulty talking to me. Great difficulty. His upper and lower jaws seemed clamped together. From between gritted teeth he explained that one of his students had offered a piece of the aforementioned cheese and he had been chewing it for the previous half hour and he still couldn't get rid of it. "For Godshake don't acshept anyft", he spluttered. Sadly, I took his advice when one charming student from Bhutan proffered a piece of the yellowy-green substance. I probably offended him terribly but I just didn't dare try it since I was obliged to talk to the group for another hour and a half.

There were six of them in the group, Bhutanis, that is (if that is the correct term), and they were on their first trip away from home in that remotest of Himalayan kingdoms. Apparently the bulk of their luggage was made up of cheese and a good job too for I suspect our homogenised, plasticised, tasteless western food would have destroyed their digestions for ever.

They were lovely, lively people, inquisitive and full of fun. When I took them into Trinity College and showed them where their king had lived when he was a student at Cambridge they were silent and deeply moved. "His Majesty will be pleased to know his people have been here", one said quietly. I think they would have stayed on the spot all day if I hadn't urged them on.

When we parted I suggested that a party of six Bhutanis was rather a large group to all be away from such a tiny country at the same time and asked jokingly how many they had left at home. One replied, with a straight face: "The other six." At which we all burst into laughter and parted the firmest of friends. I shall always remember them but I shall die sorrowful at never having eaten a piece of smoked yak cheese at 11.15 of a Saturday morning on King's Parade, Cambridge.

WHAT'S IN A NAME?

DID you perchance read that story in the national papers the other day about the defendant in a London court who turned up for the hearing of his case so drunk that it had to be adjourned until he sobered up? It took me back to that delightful and (allegedly) true story of a similar case when the defendant was asked by the judge why he had committed the offence with which he was charged. "Because", said the defendant, "I was as drunk as a judge." "Surely", said the judge, "you mean as a drunk as a lord." The defendant answered: "Yes, my lord."

TIME TO RELAX

OVERHEARD by me in Cambridge Market Place........a group of scruffy young beggars complete with dogs are talking. One is asked where his pitch will be. He replies: "I'm not working today. It's my day off."

CANVASSERS AT ELECTIONS

ANY time now there will be the dread knock on the door. It will announce the arrival of a small knot of people wearing false smiles and oozing ersatz sincerity. One of 'em will be the candidate desperate for your vote in the general election. There are a few hard rules to be observed at this point. Keep your door firmly closed lest they see your framed portrait of Karl Marx. Do not allow your tiny offspring to be kissed by the politico otherwise the babe will be intellectually scarred for life. Refrain from entering upon a political argument otherwise the candidate will breathe whisky fumes all over you whilst promising to show you the kingdoms of the earth and the treasures therein which are yours for a pencilled cross.

Many voters will resort to crude imprecations when the political circus arrives suggesting, for example, that they all go forth and multiply or that they "shove off" and "clear off" or words to that effect. A mistake. Be more subtle. I have discovered a totally obscure but highly efficient word for the occasion. It is: AROINT.

Shakespeare uses it once in Macbeth and once in King Lear otherwise it scarcely exists. It means – be gone, hop it and, yes, shove off. When you answer the door simply fling an arm out and shout in your best Stratford voice: "AROINT THEE". They won't understand it but they will aroint themselves p.d.q.. They'll think you are barking mad.

TAKING THE MICKEY OUT OF OLD PEOPLE

SO I'm sitting in the waiting room at hepatology in Addenbrooke's ruefully reviewing the lifetime of splendid debauchery which has led me thither and coming rapidly to the conclusion that the pleasure was worth the pain when the ancient bloke next to me digs me sharply in the ribs.

So sharp indeed, that I fancy an immediate transfer to accident and emergency. He looks up from his paper and inquires: "Do you have a problem about people taking the Mickey?" though his language is more suitable for urology than hepatology.

I humour him by saying that if I worried about people taking the, er, Mickey out of me I would be a gibbering, nervous wreck. But why does he ask, I ask?

"Because", he replies, "it says here that those bloody Europeans are going to make it illegal to joke about old age. Soon we won't be able to tell oldie jokes, send oldie post cards and, in general, say, write or do anything which might offend us boys of the old brigade without being hauled up before some damn court in Brussels or wherever."

Apparently, our continental rulers are drafting legislation which will outlaw any form of disrespect to those of us of advanced maturity. At first the new ageism law will apply in the workplace but as my belligerent neighbour so rightly points out, it can only be a matter of time before it applies in all walks – or, in our case – dodders – of life.

"Do they think we can't take it", he says giving me another jab? "Do they think we can't dish it out? We're not finished yet, mate, you and me, and I'm as good a man now as when I was last in Brussels pointing me bayonet with intent. If I could take that I'm damn sure I can take a joke."

Before I am ushered into the haven of the consulting room I hear him bellow something about the whole world going bloody mad. "Where will it all end?" he roared at a passing and bemused nurse.

ENTENTE CORDIALE

OVER in Oxford on Sunday with a group of charming Chinese guests of the University of Cambridge showing them the sights of "the other place". We saw a magpie. Naturally, I said: "Good morning Mr Magpie and how are you today?" They did not understand. Their interpreter was puzzled. I tried to explain that it was bad luck not to speak to a passing magpie. They were bemused and did not quite grasp what I was saying. Some of them spoke a little Russian as do I. I tried to explain our strange magpie custom in Russian. Finally they understood and we all laughed. On the way home I laughed again to myself. Perhaps only in Oxford or Cambridge are you likely to find some twerp like me explaining in Russian to a group of Chinese why the English say good morning to a magpie.

Gardens and Things

WHEN MY TROUSERS FELL DOWN UP A LADDER

I SHALL long remember the afternoon my trousers fell down whilst I was half way up – or down, it matters not – a ladder. It was at the beginning of last week's heat-wave and the languid air was tinged with a mixture of those most genteel of English summer scents, rose and lavender. Tranquility flooded this little corner of our world. I decided to dead-head the climbing roses hanging in decaying profusion on the tall wall at the end of the garden. I was unprepared for what was to follow.

Happily snipping and sniffing simultaneously the very last thing to enter my mind was a desire to remove my trousers. As it transpired I was about to have no choice in the matter. They simply slipped to my ankles of their own accord and without so much as a by-your-leave.

Y'see, I had not considered the combination of my fairly substantial loss of weight during my recent poorly patch and the effect of reaching skywards to remove a faded bloom. Arms raised in apparent supplication I am suddenly trapped on the ladder by my over-large, pre-illness summer slacks which are now supported by ankle rather than waist.

Trapped? Well, you try to climb down a ladder under such conditions. Nothing in life prepares one for such a predicament. From creche, through school, the army and decades of varied adventures not once, ever, did anyone take me to one side and tell me: "Now, should you ever find yourself half way up – or down, it doesn't matter – a ladder with your trousers round your ankles, the following rules should be followed..."

It is impossible to bend down to hitch 'em up. Nor can I kick them off because one cotton leg is now inextricably enmeshed in the thorns of a rather splendid red climber. It is as though I am pegged to the wall by the will of some mischievous garden imp. I find myself murmuring words which I first heard on the barrack square and have used only rarely since.

Meanwhile, I am faced with two major concerns. The first is a question of maintaining some degree of dignity. Are the neighbours watching? Being so high up I am feeling extremely exposed, if that is the right word. On second thoughts, to hell with dignity, says I to myself, because it rapidly becomes apparent that, so far as I am personally concerned, there is the somewhat vital question of my own physical safety. Finding oneself trouserless among a mass of thorny roses presents, shall we say, a delicate problem. Any precipitate move on my part is likely to lead to an unfortunate wound. Or, indeed, several.

Thus, slowly and with infinite care, I descend, trousers ripped to bits but the rest of me happily thorn-free. I try to muster a modicum of nonchalance as I stroll back to the house, trousers 'neath my arm and shirt tail flapping in the balmy breeze.

So far the neighbours haven't mentioned the episode so I assume they either missed the spectacle or they are too refined and well-mannered to mention it. They won't get another chance. The ladder is stowed away and I have bought a pair of long-handled secateurs.

GROWING OLD IN THE GARDEN

THEY do say that to plant is to pray and that is what I am doing in the garden as of now. There are only two ways in which a small garden can be extended and they are to widen existing flowerbeds or to grow upwards. I am in the process of doing both. Thus next year will see more rambling roses and honeysuckle going aloft and there is now enough room down below for extra daffs and swathes of snowdrops, bluebells, crocuses, anemones and anything else which feels like joining the party. All the work wears me out but I am rapidly learning the art of growing old disgracefully. The recipe is simple. Bit of effort. Long pause. Glass of cold cider. Bit more effort. Long pause. Platter of Stilton and raw onion. Another glass of cider. Decide to do a bit more tomorrow. Go to The Boot. Tell 'em how hard you've been working in the garden. "You'll be needing a drink then", ol' Hookey will say. "Phew!" I'll say. "Not 'alf".

TERROR

AT breakfast time, our garden was not so much unnaturally quiet as sepulchral – not a bird in sight, the bread and nuts untouched. Normally by now, the "regulars" would be tumbling over each other in their haste to grab the tastiest-looking morsels. Now, nothing. Odd, said I to myself. Distinctly odd.

However, there was movement aplenty in our neighbours' garden. There, in the middle of their lawn and bold as brass, a stately sparrow hawk was busy plucking and eating its own breakfast. The predator had its back to me and I couldn't make out what sort of prey it had killed but there was the reason for our silent and bird-free garden. Terror. Our lot knew there was a ruthless killer just the other side of the garden fence so to hell with the crumbs. Breakfast for them would be late that day.

And so it was. The hawk ripped and gobbled, supremely confident of its own invulnerability and, I suppose, not caring two hoots about upsetting the eating habits of the cowering local bird population.

Finally, the hawk, clearly gorged, shoved off clutching a piece of its prey in its talons. Elevenses perhaps? It was a good ten minutes before the first of our craven brood dared to show its beak. A male blackbird, actually, and he didn't dally. Gradually they all grew braver and our offerings were cleared with astonishing rapidity as though the birds still were not sure that the all-clear had been sounded. Then they, too, were gone and soon all that was left to remind the world of that brief – and to some – terrifying breakfast-time drama were a few scattered feathers on our neighbours' lawn. Looked like dove feathers, I thought to myself as I made a cup of coffee.

BULBS ON THE MOVE

OVER recent weeks I have spent much time and effort on planting springtime bulbs, many of them in our huge array of pots. I am somewhat stuffy and meticulous in these matters and I like good order and discipline in the ranks of bulbs when spring arrives. Thus, with infinite care, I compose artistic designs of circles, squares and whirls of daffs, tulips and whatever comes to hand. A ring of black tulips here, encircled by a white variety, massed wallflowers intersected by dwarf narcissi – all very arty-crafty, you understand, and extremely easy on the eye come the hey-ding-a-ling season.

Well, that was the plan. Now, those dang-blasted marauding squirrels have made a total nonsense of the whole immaculately-planned campaign. Not only have they discovered the whereabouts of the bulbs, they have clearly taken a liking to the taste of 'em. Before I realised what was happening, they had ransacked all the bigger pots, leaving bulbs lying about all over the place. Between them they have spirited heaven knows how many into the Prevosts' garden next door where they have re-interred them. I reckon the Prevosts have now got more of our spring bulbs than we have. (In fact, and I wouldn't want them to hear about this, I'm half inclined to suspect that they have been secretly training the damn squirrels).

Anyoldhow, the bulbs that haven't been nicked are lying around the place in complete disarray and I'm shoving 'em back in haphazardly which wasn't the idea at all. So should you come a-visiting in the spring I shall be much obliged if you would kindly hide your mirth when you see the mish-mash of colours in what was until now the most perfectly planned of patio gardens.

Meanwhile, if those pesky little beasts come scrapping about round here any more they can abandon all hope of a Merry Christmas. Indeed, they can simply abandon all hope. I'm not having it.

Upon reflection, it does make you wonder how they know where to find the bulbs. Is it by smell? Or do they squat furtively in some distant tree watching the gardener's every move, smiling cunningly and licking their little lips in greedy anticipation of the feast to come.

CHRISTMAS CAKE – NO THANKS

PAINFUL, indeed, distressing, though it may be for a Certain Party I feel I have to ask the following question – why should a Robin Redbreast turn up its beak at the leftovers from my wife's Christmas cake?

For decades Herself has turned out delicious Yuletide cakes which have delighted family and friends with their mixture of intense richness and the TLC with which she makes them. Always the icing is decorated with at least two or three robins, together with Father Christmas, numerous Christmas trees, snowmen, reindeer, cherubs and, for some reason, a red letter box – in fact it's almost impossible to insert a knife into the damn thing without dismembering one of the precious decorations. Which may be why some of the cake went uneaten this year. But I digress.

When the snow finally arrived last week I decided to give the garden birds a special treat by offering them what was left of the cake. A rook snatched a piece immediately, starlings nibbled greedily and then the robin arrived. It strutted round the remaining crumbs and there before our very eyes was the perfect wintry scene – real snow, a real robin and real Christmas cake.

If it is possible for a robin to wear a look of disdain this one did. The creature completely ignored the luscious offering, not even bothering to risk a brave little peck. Instead it concentrated on a piece of mouldy bread on the bird table.

Herself watched this icy tableau with some dismay. What, she wondered, was so wrong with her recipe? There had been not a single complaint over the past 40 years. The other birds clearly loved it. And of all the birds of the air surely a robin should have been first in the queue?

I felt obliged to comfort her in her obvious distress by suggesting that maybe real robins had become so brassed off with seeing their own plastic effigies stuck into millions of Christmas cakes over the years that this was their one chance of giving a two-clawed salute to the cooks.

I did not mention that this year I had noticed a distinct lowering of the brandy content in her cake or that maybe the robin was trying to tell her something I dare not.

REPRIEVE FOR A ROSE

EVEN as I write, the encircling gloom of a miserable January day is pierced by a pair of glittering yellow roses which hang from the very top of a climber outside my study window. This particular climbing rose (I can't remember the variety) winds itself around one of those metal pergola thingamajigs and, frankly, put up rather a poor show during that long hot summer; so much so that I harboured strong thoughts about digging it up – the rose, that is, not the pergola. But now it positively glisters. Furthermore, the blooms point themselves towards me, heads hanging down slightly as though in supplication. Has the rose read my thoughts about its future? Is it trying to tell me something? Again, I know not. What I do know is that it is blooming at absolutely the wrong time and brings a rare and delicious beauty into a darkening winter world. It stays.

A BUTTERFLY TO REMEMBER

TEN minutes ago, having just seen the first butterfly of the season, I dashed from the garden into my study to answer the phone. I tripped over a loose piece of carpet, measuring my length as my head bounced, ping-pong-ball-like, from desk to door and I ended up, as they say where I come from, lying all of a muck heap.

Having little better to do other than to check protesting ribs and a moaning bonce and nobody around to help, I lay there for a few minutes and fell to pondering about the butterfly. I only caught a brief, albeit thrilling, sighting of this delicious harbinger of spring as it fluttered over the daffs and early tulips. Perhaps it was the effect of the fall but somehow I thought of it as being an early Cabbage White. Then, as my left knee began to double in size, I was stricken by the simple truth that Cabbage Whites are definitely not yellow otherwise, I said to myself, we would call them CabbageYellows.

My butterfly, which had enlivened a hitherto uneventful morning, was, upon reflection, most certainly of the yellow variety and, in any case, at this time of the year the large white's staple diet of cauliflowers, cabbages, radishes and such-like, is still no more than a twinkle in the average gardener's eye.

By now I have dragged myself into the chair at my desk and, satisfied that nothing is broken, I ponder further. Undoubtedly, the delicious creature which had graced our garden ever so briefly had been a Brimstone, for not only does it hibernate but it leaves its winter shelter early in springtime and has even been seen on the wing whilst the remnants of the final winter snows clings tenaciously to sheltered corners.

So – welcome fluttering Brimstone, beautiful herald of the delights of spring and summer just around the corner. I shall long remember your arrival today as, indeed, will my unhappy and oversize left knee, my protesting left rib cage and my aching cranium.

OH TO BE A GARDEN...

MOWED the lawn, dead-headed faded daffs, dug in new lavender plants, tied back some meandering climbing roses, hoed every inch of free bare soil, potted the first of the geraniums, poured a mug of camomile "tea", sat in a favourite garden chair for a five-minute breather and woke up two hours later, the air bathed by the soft scent of tall wallflowers and warmed by a sinking sun, tea untouched. That is what I call true pleasure and, yea, verily, I pray I may be reincarnated not as a gardener, but as a garden itself for the garden is pampered beyond the dreams of wealth and idleness. It is lovingly tended, watered, fed, manicured, carefully put to bed in autumn and teased into new and vibrant life come springtime. Frankly, all that a garden has to do is to lie back and enjoy it.

HEAVENLY ASPARAGUS

WHEN I am canonised – and it can only be a matter of time – I intend to take as my saintly symbol the English asparagus. That truly heavenly vegetable has escaped the attentions of existing saints so far as I can discover. I suppose that since most of 'em are foreign they may not have heard of that most glorious of springtime offerings to the Englishman's table so I intend to take a bunch of fresh-cut Cambridgeshire asparagus as my eternal badge. Well, why not? Lots of saints have their symbols. St Malachy has the apple, St Elizabeth of Hungary a basket of roses, St Arnold of Soissons grabbed the hop as his badge, St Elpidius the vine, St Gertrude of Nivelles the rat and St Pharaildis the gosling. That's just a few of 'em. The asparagus is waiting to be adopted by an up-and-coming saint, beatified and canonised for his sacrifices upon the high altar of abstinence. Moi.

Meanwhile breakfast awaits. Two duck eggs, softly boiled, with cold asparagus for soldiers. Excuse me.

THE APPLE HARVEST

LAST year our entire apple crop was eaten by a squirrel. One squirrel? Well, actually yes. We have but the one espaliered apple tree and last year it produced one apple. The squirrel plucked it and, sitting on the garden fence, munched it a few feet away from the window through which we watched with mounting fury. This year we had a magnificent crop of nine apples. Not a squirrel in sight, ho ho. Instead a plague of wasps. They did for 'em good and proper – apart from two unripe ones which I rescued. Sour enough to give the wasps bellyache, I'm happy to report.

BREAKFAST PRESENT FROM A ROBIN

ALL of which brings me to a pair of friendly robins whose company provides me with much of that simple pleasure to which I am now committed. I have mentioned our local robins before. They make their home in our neighbour's garden but prefer to dine out in ours which proves to me that we have a higher quality crumb than the couple next door. It's all a question of upbringing, you understand.

Well, anyoldhow, I love to start off the day – weather permitting – having breakfast in the garden at the old marble slab we call our outdoor dining table. On most such occasions I am joined by the robins and, with endless patience, I have gradually encouraged them to approach my breakfast platter without fear. They will fly off with a proffered crumb but return almost instantly for more of the same, thank you very much.

So there we were the other rare, sunny morning, just the three of us. There was smoked salmon and scrambled egg on my plate (unaccompanied, alas, by that glass of chilled champagne which would have been its inevitable consort of yesteryear) and crumbs scattered on the table. The Buddleia bowed over us, its purple candles as heavy with perfume as an incense-laden church. A scene of utterly simple charm. Then one of the robins, the more daring of the two, hopped onto the side of my plate. I was still and quiet and delighted. At which point that dangblasted robin performed a totally uncivilised act which, suffice it to say, instantly rendered the remainder of my salmon and eggs quite inedible. Mayhap this is a robin's way of bidding 'farewell and thanks'. If so then I think that in future they might have the common courtesy to wait until I have finished the goodies on my plate.

A DIFFERENT ROBIN – I HOPE! – JOINS ME FOR LUNCH

THE heat of the sun lured me into the garden t'other day to eat my lunch of fresh bread, crumbly Lancashire cheese and a scattering of those fiery pickled onions which Kevin McDonnell makes at his home in Dullingham. Suddenly a thirst came upon me and I felt obliged to fetch a flagon of chilled Norfolk cider. 'Pon my return I found I had a guest. Our friendly robin was helping itself to my bread. When I sat down the bird neither flittered nor fluttered but carried on pecking, utterly fearless. Thus we ate lunch together though I hope Kevin will not be upset when I tell him that the robin viewed his pickled onions with obvious and haughty disdain.

GARDENING IN THE SPRING

PERHAPS it is a phantom spring but there is definitely a touch of change in the air. Rooks are building high, the daffs are popping up like searching periscopes, buds are bursting with enthusiasm, catkins hang heavy on the bough and the garden beckons enticingly and irresistible as a wanton siren.

And that, I suppose, just about sums up the garden. For us blokes it is a powerful mistress, endlessly demanding attention, a greedy seeker after embellishment, mulish if not well-fed and downright moody and sulky if ignored. Yet we are willing victims as she woos us with her wiles and hints of future pleasures. Be generous now, she seems to say, and I promise you a long summer of soft-scented delights.

Well, anyoldhow, I keep on falling for it which is why, despite the sabre-sharp March wind the garden dragged me out the other day to give her an early face-lift – a gentle bout of lawn mowing, edge-trimming, hoeing and careful pruning followed by a fairly vicious attack on the dead detritus of winter. I love it – gardening, that is – and I remind myself once more that, family aside and despite the fact that I'm still an amateur, gardening has been one of the ruling passions of my life.

At which point I detect a chortle from that Inner Voice of Conscience of mine which pipes up – when I have said something daft; and that, as you might imagine, is fairly frequent. 'Ere, says my

IVoC, what about all your other ruling passions? Such as what, says I? Well, says the IVoC, how about....shooting, racing, cavorting, gambling, pub-crawling, books, music, idling, cooking, noshing, walking, whittling sticks, cricketing, baiting bunny-huggers, kipping after lunch.....

I inquire of the IVoC if it has quite finished? No, it replies, but that would do for starters. Then it adds that once upon a time it might have included the grape, the malt and the hop but due to my enforced teetotalism it thought it politic not to mention them.

Back to the garden. Somebody, and I'm blowed if I can recall who it was, wrote that he valued his garden more for being full of blackbirds than of cherries. The mystery author certainly lived before the magpie proliferated and helped put an end to that idyllic concept.

Often, down the years, I would quote Kipling to Herself and our brood hoping for a bit of help with the digging and the dobbing. You know, the bit about "For the Glory of the Garden glorifieth every one". It fell on deaf ears. Maybe it was because I went just that bit too far once when I added his following lines:

"And when your back stops aching and your hands begin to harden.

You will find yourself a Partner in the Glory of the Garden."

Aching back and hard hands indeed. Leave that to the old man.

MOTHER NATURE

THE lawn is spattered with yellow, crimson and white rose petals, all dashed to the ground by a furious July storm. This causes me to ponder. I have been puzzled these many years as to why we always refer to nature as a feminine entity – we never speak of Father Nature. The evidence on the lawn provides the answer. Only some streak of feminine perversity can design early summer roses to reach the point of perfect maturity in order to coincide precisely with the first of the inevitable and destructive July thunderstorms. Mother Nature? More of a Wicked Step-Mother Nature methinks.

NO TIME TO BE ILL WHEN THERE'S GARDENING TO DO

AT this rampant season our vegetables come to us straight from the soil. Not our soil, unfortunately, but that which is to be found in the immaculate garden to the side of "Uncle" George Gentleman's bungalow in Dullingham. These many years Uncle George's blessed plot has been the envy of gardeners from miles around, especially me. For reasons best known to himself he regards me as a friend and each weekend at this time there is always a couple of bags of freshly-dug taters, beans – broad, French, runners – carrots, cabbage and anything else that's ready, waiting for me in his lop-sided old shed. I can declare without fear of contradiction they are tasty beyond the dreams of Lucullus.

But there is more to Uncle George's garden than mere perfection. Y'see, George is getting on a bit and last year he was decidedly unwell, so much so that when he went off to hospital I'm afraid many of us shook our heads in the sad way that folk do when they fear the worst for a friend.

George had other ideas. He insisted on going home. There was the question of his garden, you see. This spring and summer it has never looked better and nor has he. All of which is more than somewhat remarkable because Uncle George – not my uncle, everybody's uncle – is 89 years of age.

I called on him the other day for his weekly gift of garden goodies. There he was, not merely whip-thin but little taller than his tater plants, splitting logs with the aid of two axes and a huge wedge. I dare not chide him. He looked at me and, knowing what I was thinking, explained almost apologetically: "Just getting ready for next winter. I like a good fire." Then he laughed. "You gotta keep a-going, boy", he said.

ODE TO AN ENGLISH LAWN

ARE we to be the last generation of our people to worship at the high altar of the Great English Lawn? Are our beloved green vistas, cottage or ducal, to become dusty and pebbled like the sad plots which our continental cousins laughingly refer to as gardens?

Well, what with the threat of water rationing and with hosepipe bans top of the list in just about all parts of the south of England many of us could be forgiven for digging up the thirsty greensward and calling in the men with concrete slabs and barrow-loads of dreary, lifeless, undemanding shingle.

Such a prospect has a touch of doomsday about it for how many of us, abroad for too long on pleasure or duty, have not longed deeply for the inexplicable balm of "some wet, bird-haunted English lawn"?

The striped English lawn, its edges manicured with greater care than any starlet's nails, its boundaries boxed by sweet-scented English lavender, its neighbouring beds a triumphant display of proud English roses, is at the sacred heart of our national obsession with domestic soil. It is not garish nor is it sumptuous. It is the only possible home of the deckchair. The well-bred cucumber sandwich would droop with shame if eaten on a bed of shingle and an England without the traditional summer cacophony of the neighbour's lawn mower would be a poor place indeed.

Sadly, to attain their full glory lawns need water – in vast quantities. Try using the sprinkler this summer and you risk the lethal wrath of the water companies which, despite their long experience, still have not realised that if they let their pipes leak our water simply runs away.

But do not despair, do not surrender. With luck, as from April until just before the harvest, the heavens will open and the lovely drumming of huge downpours on parched lawns will be loud in the land. The Great English Lawn may yet be saved.

LEARNING ON THE JOB

AGED thirteen, my father left school to work for the Duke of Portland as an under-gardener. Scarcely schooled, he soon knew the Latin names of all the plants he tended. He never forgot them. Odd, that.

WHY SPOIL A PERFECT WORLD?

SEVEN o'clock of a June morning. An English garden. Cool, clear air sweetened by honeysuckle, roses, early lavender. Just one week of sunshine has transformed the garden into a gaudy jigsaw of vibrant colours. The first visitors drop in for breakfast at their already-laden table. Blackbirds, hugely welcome. They are followed by a pair of magpies, outwardly sleek as elegant headwaiters, inwardly murder-minded. Most unwelcome. Smaller birds flock in – finches, robins, sparrows. I am no longer alone in my tiny pocket of peace and perfection.

Suddenly I am seized with a pang of desire. I haven't smoked for full 40 years. Back then, though, the best smoke of the day was always the first fag in the morning. For the briefest of moments the urge returns. It is quickly borne away on a wave of self-disgust. Why on earth would I want to pollute a scene of such natural beauty? And that, perhaps, is a question which all of us might ask ourselves when we look round at the sins we have heaped on our innocent world.

HOW BIG?

THERE we were, the others getting stuck into pints of Greene King whilst I toyed with a bottle of ginger beer, and, as always, we got round to gardening or, rather, to talking about it. Some said they had too much land, others too little. I said I missed my vegetable garden. I asked a newish member of the fraternity about his garden and he said it was massive. Well, I know where he lives and I couldn't imagine him having enough space for a big garden. He explained: "It's fairly small on the surface but it is four thousand miles deep." I think he'll get on well with the other ol' boys.

GALVANIC LETHARGY

A LOCAL lawyer, equally well versed in loquacity and the law, demanded of me recently why my garden seemed to produce so much wildlife drama? He could scarcely glance at my weekly offerings without finding references to strange ornithological happenings within the confines of my smallish garden. Why did my birds get up to weird tricks when his never did?

We were strolling in a leisurely manner towards one of the racecourse nosheries at Newmarket near the end of the season and since he had broken the habit of a lifetime by offering to pay for our repast I felt it only reasonable to let him into my secret.

It was not, I explained that my garden birds behaved any differently from his – or, indeed, those of anybody else. It was simply that I was able to spend vastly more time watching birds than any £200-an-hour lawyer because I had mastered the art of indolence. Exactly similar shenanigans were being performed in his garden. It was just that he was never there to observe them.

How, then, he wondered, did I manage to have so much spare time on my hands? At which point (we were now well into his claret and I was feeling especially benevolent towards him) I decided to expound to him the principles of a natural law which have guided me through my long and gloriously inactive life.

I call it the Law of Galvanic Lethargy.

Quite simply it requires the practitioner to appear to be extremely busy whilst in reality nothing could be further from the truth. It involves the crafty use of subterfuge and disguise so that casual observers can be lulled into believing that effort is being expended where it most certainly ain't. I realised how easy it was at an early age when I would sit at my school desk, head in hands, seemingly deep in intellectual thought, whilst actually having a quiet zizz. On school cross-country runs the trick was equally simple. Just fall to the rear of the runners, take a pre-determined short cut, and fall in behind the other exhausted runners close to home. I never won any silver cups for that particular sport but I never wore myself out either.

The army, I went on, was an even bigger doddle. All that a soldier needed to galvanise himself into a fit of lethargy was to arm himself with a clipboard. Nobody ever queried a man carrying a clipboard and there was always a spare bed in an empty barrack room where a chap could repose after lunch to the sound of barked orders and marching feet. Thus did I while away many a languorous afternoon during my seemingly arduous days of service to the Crown.

But what on earth demanded the legal eagle, had all this to do with watching garden birds? 1 thought he might have twigged this by now since he knows that my study at home is at ground level and looks straight down the garden. I reminded him of this and he began to see the light.

"So", said he, "when not actually working you can look up from your desk and glance at the wildlife outside the study windows?"

I did not quite like the way in which he automatically established a link between my study and work and told him so emphatically.

"My study", quoth I "is where I pretend to work. It is where Herself firmly believes that I spend endless lonely hours each week writing. re-writing and polishing the flashingly brilliant phrases of my great novel, an opus of startlingly original genius upon which I have laboured lovingly down the long corridors of time. Or, indeed, not as the case really is."

"You mean", he said incredulously, "that you just sit there watching the birds?"

"Yup", said I "beats slaving over a hot quill any day. I love it."

He killed off the last of the claret in unaccustomed silence. On the way to watch the next race he inquired of me in the sly, cunning manner of the £200-pounds-an-hour lawyer: "How many chapters of the great novel have you actually written?"

"I might start on chapter two next week", said I, "depending. But not a word to Herself."

PULLING THE BIRDS

IF you will forgive my use of a slightly inelegant phrase I should inform you that I am having increasing difficulty pulling the right sort of birds. I have no problem attracting the larger, coarser varieties but I have long lusted after the more petite and prettier types and these are the ones which are now spurning my advances.

It's like this. The word has got round the wood pigeon world, the rook community and now, dang-blast it, even the magpies are in on the secret – that Herself and I are hugely generous with our bird breakfasts of leftover loaves and such like. For ages, and to our great joy and pleasure, our offerings brought song birds, robins, sparrows, tits and similar charming little birds into our garden. Even the occasional lustrous starling was welcome as indeed were the gentle, cooing doves.

Then suddenly, in moved the heavy mob, rough bullies all and now they have taken over. Before the little 'uns can even get a look in never mind a beakful of crumb, their larger, greedier cousins have swooped and nicked the goodies in a furious flurry of flapping grey and black and white wings. When the grub is laid out for breakfast our little garden is like Trafalgar Square of old – a cacophony of whirring feathers. As a result the pretty ones have almost deserted us.

This has only happened recently and it angers me because I know not what to do. You can't single 'em out like a bouncer at a night club. If you shoo the big ones away you startle the little ones, nut cages get destroyed by squirrels and now sadly the delightful warbling and singing of former times has been replaced by the harsher calls of the big bird bully brigade.

The sophisticated, well-mannered little birds always trilled their thank-yous. The big, brutal, uncouth creatures don't even look grateful.

How can I separate them? I want the little 'uns back! Help!!!!!

WHY I DON'T LIKE WOOD PIGEONS

A PERCEPTIVE psychiatrist might sometimes wonder if there is anything deep within my contorted psyche which makes me so dislike the greedy wood pigeon. Well, yes, there is. It goes back many years to when we were living in the lovely old Merchant's House in Swaffham Bulbeck with its large garden. Each year I planted a long row of cabbage plants in the kitchen garden. Each year the pigeons demolished 'em. Once I thought I would get my revenge. I waited for several of them to attack the row of succulent young plants at the same time, then crept round the corner of the house and with one shot from my twelve-bore put an instant end to the varmints. Alas, it was more a case of the pigeons' revenge for although I bowled them all over my shot also ripped out each and every one of my burgeoning and treasured cabbages. Never have forgiven 'em – the birds, that is. Not the cabbages.

PRICKLY QUESTION

ACTING upon Jerome K. Jerome's splendid thesis that it is impossible to enjoy idling thoroughly unless one has plenty of work to do I have spent the winter with some pleasure watching the unswept leaves of autumn a-mouldering on lawn and border in the garden. I do not have the time, inclination, or, let's face it, the energy, to bother with a mountain of perfectly innocent leaves which, in my opinion, are as entitled to a long winter's nap as is their willing host.

Alas, all idylls falter and fall and come that balmy first day of spring last Sunday Herself's harsh rebukes woke me from my winter's lethargy and, like a fearful recruit obeying the stern commands of his sergeant-major (why does that analogy always leap to mind when herself addresses me?) I sallied forth with rake and fork.

I wish hugely that I had not. Beneath one drifted pile of leaves under some collapsed clumps of honeysuckle (I'll deal with 'em shortly, my dear) I turned a hedgehog out of its winter bed. As one professional idler to another I looked it straight in the prickles and apologised. It waddled off, stiffly, sadly, At this point I thanked the Creator for producing such a gentle creature as the hedgehog, happily lacking all the nastier virtues of man – fury, spleen, vicious revenge. Because, if I had been that sleepy little hedgehog, I would have reared up on my hind paws – all nine inches of me – and prickled to death the swine who had raked me out of my comfy, warm, leafy kip a full month before I was ready to wake up.

Meanwhile I should tell you that we have all of two snowdrops in our garden this year. Two. Previously we had them in swathes. Is this some local ecological disaster, some hitherto unknown bulbiferous disease, which has been visited upon us, you may ask? The answer is: yes, The scientists may not know its name. We do. The name is Maj, our utterly useless, clumsy, mad, dashing-about-but-totally-lazy little black bitch. Her long-buried bone was beneath the snowdrops. It is no longer buried. But the surrounding area is a pock-marked battlefield. If I could train startled hedgehogs to chastise daft dogs then we could all live happily ever after.

Our first daffodils are out as well. Or, rather, in our case, squashed. Maj hurtled through a patch of 'em under the cherry tree in useless pursuit of a grey squirrel. I give up. The dog can have the whole blasted garden. Though, on second thoughts, perhaps she's entitled to it. She certainly digs it up more often than I do.

A GREAT DEFEAT

I WRITE this on the morning of the 250th anniversary of Culloden – what all historians would have us believe was the last battle to be fought in Britain. It was not. There is a fierce battle being fought without the very walls of our domiciliary residence even now. The field of conflict is what we call our garden. The fight is bitter and, I fear, increasingly one-sided. Violence erupts annually for, hey nonny no, 'tis merry springtime with all the horrors that season brings with it.

The battle lines are drawn up thus: the invaders are faced by one who is cowed by years of humbling defeat. Armed only with fork, spade, hoe and a little spraygun, he (me, that is), is faced by massed battalions....... slugs, caterpillars, weevils, leatherjackets, mites, red spiders, thrips, greenfly, blackfly, whitefly, mildew, fungus spots, viruses, drought, frost, heat and storm. Now, however, this marauding army, not content with its obvious firepower superiority, has enlisted as allies a group which will bring about my complete and utter rout – my grandchildren.

With the garden looking tolerably neat they (the little darlings!!) descended upon it at the weekend and havoc was unleashed. Lydia, Tom, Natasha, Megan and Abbie – were ever invading Goths and Vandals so misleadingly named, so cutely fashioned? They came armed with trikes and bikes, prams and fire engines. They attacked lawn and border with screams of joyful ferocity. I retreated behind the ramparts of cowardice, shrouded in defeat. Compared to all this Culloden was a children's picnic.

AUTUMN IN SUFFOLK

OVER in Suffolk in the hinterland between Newmarket and Bury St Edmunds where the narrow roads lead nowhere and a hushed peace lies upon the land. Golden stubble clothes many a broad acre, conkers are falling early and, already, blackberries glisten in the dense hedgerows beneath blushing crab apples. Here a manor house in parkland mown short by hungry sheep. Everywhere cottage gardens ablaze with colour, thatches patched for the winter, muffled laughter sneaking out of open pub doors. My destination was a deep wood where oft-times I shot high pheasants curling over the tree tops. I thought I would go there, alone, just to remember. It hasn't changed. The same heavy silence is broken only by a flutter of pigeon wings, a twig snapped by a disturbed deer. The musky smell of dog fox explains why the pheasants are cowering in thick cover. He won't last long when the keeper sniffs him out.

In every snoozing village the parish church stands square and squat, repositories of centuries of prayer. No hysterical clerics spouting messages of hate and violence ever desecrated these holy places. Love and tolerance yes. Hatred no.

At home a shady lunch (Uncle George's cold potatoes with butter, runner beans and a thick slice of Suffolk ham) in the garden. The Buddleia was seducing an endless stream of butterflies with its perfumed charm. Appalling to realise that London and terror is but a fast ninety-minute drive away from that magical Suffolk wood, Uncle George's verdant vegetable patch and our pleasant garden. Yea, verily, we are a much divided nation.

A WHITE CHRISTMAS

THE long-range weather forecasters tell us that we are in for a particularly hard winter but, since most of the experts couldn't forecast what happened yesterday, I shouldn't panic if I were you. Howsomever, their prognostications encourage me to make one very last stab at getting my own annual forecast right. Those of you who have followed these weekly notes of mine faithfully over the past thirty years or so will be able, from long experience, to anticipate what I am about to say. Yes! Right first time.

It is this. We will definitely have a white Christmas this year. This promise is not based upon minute and scientific observations of the local flora and fauna but rather upon the admittedly irrational mathematical law which states that if an assertion is repeated often enough it is bound to come up trumps in the end. It is the law behind which successive governments of all political shades hide at election times – we will make the streets safe, the trains will run on time, there will be no hospital waiting lists and, if you promise to vote for us, we'll tell you the name of the winner of next year's Derby.

The odds against me getting the Dickensian Christmas scene wrong yet again must be increasingly narrow. Anyoldhow, this is the last year I shall make my forecast and if a cold nor'easter fails to come a soughin' across the snowy fenland fields this Yuletide then I shall pack the game in. Just as I threatened to last year.

Meanwhile, Herself and I have been rummaging about trying to find those ol' fenland ice skates we haven't been able to enjoy for many a warm winter. The rabbit-skin liberty bodices are in the airing cupboard along with hand-knitted scarves, knee-length socks, sweaters with holes at the elbows and woolly under clothes guaranteed to tickle those parts which modern man-made fibres seem unable to reach.

These latter garments are doubly useful in real winters for not only do they defy the cold to penetrate important areas but they force the wearer into constant, warming motion in order to find convenient corners where a good ol' fashioned private scratch can be enjoyed. I even propose to rescue my hip flasks from their enforced state of retirement and to fill them with life-saving potations such as sloe gin and raspberry brandy. I may no longer be allowed to drink such nectar myself but that doesn't mean I cannot offer succour to a mate stuck in a snowdrift. I fancy myself rather as an English St Bernard. After all, you never catch one of those swigging brandy from that little barrel they carry tied round their necks as they pad from mountain to mountain in search of poor peasants trapped up to the icicles by an avalanche. So – snow, frost and wintry winds – let 'em all come. Herself and I are all geared up.

COLD WEATHER FORECAST – AGAIN!

AT this time last week (which is when I am writing this) I was convinced that by this time this week (which is when you are reading it) we would all be up to our fetlocks in a severe Siberian freeze. In other words, last week the pointers were all towards that vicious winter with which we were threatened by those townie weather forecasters at the end of the summer which never turned out like they said it would anyway. The summer, that is, as well as the winter so far.

But a few days ago it looked as though their turn to be right had finally arrived. For one thing, Muscovites were friz up to their fur-lined liberty bodices in the worst Russian frosts for decades. And secondly, when I was out in the fens watching a flock of lolloping lapwings, I swear I could hear the Troika bells tinkling as the horses pulled their sleighs across the ice on Red Square, their breath freezing in their delicate nostrils while Mr Putin and his comrades were busy necking the hot vodka to ward off the Kremlin chill..

And when you can pick out the gentle bells of Moscow whilst standing on the edge of the black fen, you know that the soft southerly wind has veered and is now screaming straight out of the heart of Mother Russia – so be prepared. Anyoldhow, come to think about it, if what I was forecasting at this time last week is happening at this time this week you already know about it and I am wasting your time and mine. So – I'll leave you to prepare a cauldron of "schee ee kasha" which, if you didn't know, is the foul shredded cabbage potage which keeps the Russkie peasants going through their winters. Do you all good.

There is one certain sign of really bad weather and that is when the fieldfares start bunching up in the shelter of a tree, all facing one way. Then – take it from them – it'll be as cold as a nagging mistress.

WIPE FEBRUARY FROM THE CALENDAR – OR ELSE

EITHER they erase February from our calendar next year or I'm going to emigrate. Of the many useless inventions in life – wasps, Chancellors of the Exchequer, loose-fitting wigs, most Europeans, social workers, statistics, three-legged racehorses (there are, you know, there are!) and such like – the twenty-eight days of February come top of the list.

OK, if you've been mucking about I grant you there is the Feast of Purification on the second and if you feel like mucking about again, there is St Valentine's Day on the fourteenth, but now I live a life of such enforced purity that both days are superfluous to my requirements. As for the other 26 days, there is absolutely nowt to recommend them. Shooting finishes on the first, cricketers flit off to warmer climes, the garden is climatically out of bounds, horse racing is a squelchy farce, plump publicans fill us with furious envy by spending our cash holidaying until March on expensive, sun-drenched islands while those of us left behind daren't turn the central heating on for fear of bankruptcy.

So, emigration? Mmm. Yes. Well. As many a grandparent knows it is an idle threat. Freedom of movement is not a choice for us because we are the happy victims of the glorious tyranny of grandchildren. For us, the allure of scorching February days under some foreign sun would be forever secondary to the worry of how the little ones were getting on back home. Even a month away for some of us would be a tiresome sacrifice.

There are only three answers. Accept the English February with a stiff English upper lip is one. Commit some pleasing misdemeanour which warrants a bit of Purification is another. The third is to try to remember why February 14th is so special.

PLEASING SOME OF THE PEOPLE SOME OF THE TIME

FOUND myself in Cambridge t'other day with a group of visitors from the deep south of America. It was as cold and damp as a fen dyke in January and I apologised to the Americans for our dreadful summer weather. They regarded me as though I had just dropped in from a distant planet. This weather, they explained, was their idea of heaven. Back home they had left drought and endless, unbearable heat. They looked longingly at the brooding grey sky and I could see they were praying for rain. When they saw the perfect, green-striped lawns of King's College, a side-product of this wet summer, there was a round of spontaneous clapping. Some of them called into The Eagle and took their drinks in the open courtyard exulting in the dank chill while the sweater-clad locals cowered inside complaining of the draught every time a door was opened.

Mates and Muckers

COMRADES IN ARMS

SUNDAY morning and the centre of Cambridge is bustling with the first of the year's new students. The rain has gone and there is that brittle chill in the air which comes when the wind drifts in from The Steppes. The fresh undergrads look younger each year but their aura of excitement and expectation is unchanging.

The previous evening a group of us had celebrated the day when we too began what was to be our "university" careers nearly half a century ago when, as soldiers and airmen we had joined the first intake of the Joint Services School for Linguists down in deepest Cornwall. We were about the same age as the Cambridge freshers and many of us, like them, were straight from school. We studied hard, day and night, like the Cambridge youngsters and rapidly mastered our subject – the Russian language. But there was one major difference between our studies and theirs. Our linguistic endeavours were constantly interrupted as we were taught how to kill the very people whose lovely language we were learning. All these years on I can still recall the mixed emotions which sprang from spending the morning being taught the skills of slaughter and the afternoons reading the exquisite literature of our potential victims. (Some of us weren't that skilled! One chap, Eric Lowe, completely missed the target and put a bullet through the warning flag flying high on the firing range. The sergeant instructor looked at him in despair: "Never mind, lad, you'll just have to use your bayonet.")

Our reunion in Cambridge had brought us all together again from all around the world. Now we are greybeards and granddads and our Russian is half forgotten though we did manage a verse or two of "Volga, Volga, Mother of Russia" in the original after the reunion dinner much to the bemusement, I suspect, of our wives.

We recalled how we were sworn to absolute secrecy about our work – all to no avail because wherever we went in Cornwall the locals would say: "Ah, you'll be from that Russian school in Bodmin." Odd things come back. Somebody reminded me how we were still gentlemen even in adversity. On manoeuvres one night our lorry plunged into a ravine. In the silence after the crash apparently I said: "Would somebody kindly remove his boot from my mouth!"

But what is it which brings together a group of men some of whom hadn't met for nigh on fifty years?

Of course, bonds of friendship or, rather, comradeship (and there is a world of difference between the two), are forged strongly in the armed forces especially at an early, impressionable age. But I believe there was something else which brought us all to Cambridge at the weekend. It was something we learned unconsciously alongside our Russian and our skill at arms. Something called "pride". It may be a difficult expression to understand these days for pride is an unfashionable concept, but to us in those long-gone days it was inseparable from our way of life. We took pride in our unit, pride in our uniform, pride in our appearance, pride in our marching and pride above all in being of some slight service to our country.

I looked around at the weekend at the men who were boys when I was a boy and I am happy to report that they were still stamped with an unmistakable pride. As they say, you can take a man out of the service but you can't take the service out of the man. I for one am proud of our pride.

Having got that off my unbemedalled chest I can tell 'ee with absolute certainty that I am no longer the man I once was and spending a mere three days in their company has left me feeling as though I have just climbed the north face of the Eiger in full field service marching order with a Bren gun strapped to my back. They talk about another reunion, down in Cornwall in a couple of years time, if any of us are still around. I shall take my own ambulance.

WHEN IS ENOUGH ENOUGH?

I AM off to another of our army reunions, yet another of those intimations of mortality with which I seem to be reminded almost daily. There isn't a decent fight left in any of us who might manage to stagger with our wives to the gathering where we will talk of the robust days of more than five decades ago when we could just about muster a degree of belligerence. The question always arises at our infrequent reunions – how long do we carry on with 'em. Until the last two of us shake hands over a final decanter of claret each wondering who the hell is the other bloke, says I. Until then, tally-ho.

It is the strong pull of nostalgia drags me to a reunion of the young men I "joined up with" half a century ago. Is this, I ask myself, a good idea? Going back anywhere can be a dispiriting experience. Our camp of freezing wooden huts is now, apparently, an industrial park and our parade ground where bellowing sergeants transformed us almost overnight from slouching lads into shoulders-back, chest-out, chin-in, thumbs-by-the-seams-of-your-trousers full-blown men is probably now the site of a rest home staffed by counsellors for sad, stressed-out policemen.

The fact is, of course, that the few of us who are left will have a magnificent jolly for one of the ineluctable truths of nostalgia is that time not only heals wounds but also dims the memories of hardship. Looking back the sergeants didn't bellow, they whispered encouragements. The regimental sergeant major was not a towering tyrant, merely a guide and mentor who happened to be blessed with a colourful turn of phrase. The slops the cookhouse served us were, upon reflection, Lucullan feasts fit for hungry princes.

Whatever is the point of growing older if we remember only the bad times, the hard times? Perhaps nostalgia was designed for those of us who enjoy the unreality of the past. Those of us young soldiers whose lovely, kind sergeant majors tucked us up in our little wooden beds each night.

TIDDY OGGIES

I HAVE a heavy heart for I have left undone that which I should have done and not once but twice. Y'see, I have just returned from an army reunion down in distant Cornwall and due perhaps to the endless proliferation of jollifications I never did get round to addressing myself to a tiddy oggie.

For the unluckily uninitiated I should explain that a tiddy oggie is a Cornish pastie and half a century ago us young servicemen scoffed 'em morning noon and night and they helped to put some brawn onto our scraggy shoulders, an unlikely happening had we stuck to our army rations.

Alas, it was not until Herself and I were well on our way back to the east that I realised my mistake. But was it really an error of judgement, I begin to ask myself, because today tiddy oggies are mass produced in various sanitised food factories and, unlike those glorious, juicy confections of yesteryear, are akin to sawdust wrapped in cardboard. Ours were hand-crafted in dark farmhouse kitchens by the stout and jolly wives of cunning Cornish farmers.

Any second now someone is about to point out that fifty years back there was still severe food rationing so how could they have made such perfect pasties then. Well, I don't know and I don't care but I do have my suspicions. A real tiddy oggie is made of beef, 'taters, onion and herbs – none of today's diced carrots, thank you kindly – and since beef was in short supply what gave our pasties such sublime savouriness?

The truth about the contents was often before our very eyes. All Cornish farms then had working horses. Working horses only have a certain length of working life......

Furthermore, the woods and valleys were alive with deer and Cornish bobbies were notoriously short-sighted when it came to poaching. And, come to think of it, those Dartmoor ponies weren't too far away either.

No! I don't think we ate much beef in our tiddy oggies but whatever it was I can damn nearly taste it now. 'Pon reflection, therefore, maybe I can unburden my heavy heart and just be grateful for being able to recall the taste of heaven which was to be found in a real, steaming, gravy-spilling tiddy oggie of our soldiering youth.

****

I WAS going on a bit about tiddy oggies – Cornish pasties – and this prompted one of my favourite letter-writers Mrs Madge Taylor of Teversham, Cambridge, to pen me another of her marvellous epistles. She often tells me tales which she remembers from the 26 years she and her husband ran The Blue Lion pub at Fen Ditton just outside Cambridge. They have me laughing fit to bust. This one I pass on to you.

Two Welsh miners were made redundant just before the war. One went north with his wife and they created a fortune making and selling delicious and very popular rabbit pies. The other visited them and asked what their secret was and where all the rabbits came from. His mate swore him to secrecy and said they put extra meat in with the rabbit – horse meat. How much? The proportions, said the pie maker, were fifty-fifty – one horse to one rabbit.

THE SECRET'S OUT – OR IS IT?

TO our military get-together in Chester. Half a century and more since we first met to learn how to speak Russian and perform a spot of assassination should that be deemed necessary. Our training was so secret that there are no military records of our existence. Even in the book "Secret Classrooms of the Cold War", telling the history of the Russian schools which followed us, there is no mention of those two years in which we, the First Intake of the Joint Services School for Linguists, were the guinea pigs. The fact that the whole of Cornwall knew what was happening within our hush-hush compound in Bodmin is by the by. Officially we did not exist. And that is one reason we enjoy getting together. Nothing like meeting up with phantoms.

HOW TO WORK THE SYSTEM

LAST week, we rambled on about local dialects. This week, the army. An ability to recognise the former came in exceedingly handy when I was serving in the latter. Having committed what I considered a trifling military misdemeanour I was condemned to spend several hours each evening for a week scouring out the pots and pans in which our appalling grub had been callously prepared earlier and which had clearly not been cleaned since Agincourt. The Cook Sergeant shouted some nasty words and hurled scabrous-looking cleansing utensils at me. This I did not like. But stay! My uncanny ability to recognise dialects came to the rescue. "Excuse me sarge", said I, "but are you Derbyshire?" He was. "Tideswell?" Bloody 'ell yes, he was. Seems his brother and I were at the same school, we knew the same pubs, you could say we were nearly related. I never scoured another pan. Instead the week became a bit of a blur. Officers' steak every night washed down by endless draughts of the Colonel's claret – "left over from next week's Dining-in-Night in the Officers' Mess", the Cook Sergeant would say. When he was demobbed our Cook Sergeant became a very successful wine merchant. The army's OK if you know how to work it.

A MISUNDERSTANDING

SCENE outside the Senate House in Cambridge recently. Group of Russian tourists being guided by my Russian-speaking friend Michael Copp. It was a graduation day. Did anyone realise what was happening, asked Michael? Yes, replied a Russian in halting English. It was a degradation ceremony.

Such simple linguistic errors are easy to make. In the middle of the last century I was learning Russian as a young soldier. Our tutors were mainly White Russian emigré aristocrats who had fled the revolution. One was a former Cossack colonel. One morning he asked, in Russian, where I had been the evening before. I replied, in Russian, that I had been in a public house. His old eyes lit up. "There is a public house here in Bodmin?" Puzzled, I explained there were several. Would I take him to one that very evening? We went to the Cornish Arms. Full of cider swigging Cornishmen. Where, he whispered – in Russian – were the girls? He wouldn't find any in there, I said. Cornish girls didn't go into public houses. At this we both knew something was amiss. Suddenly he smiled. My translation of "public" and "house" was precise. It was just that in Russian the two words used together meant a brothel.

THE BEST OF BRITISH

MY best and most lamented of friends, the late Doug Gibson of Fulbourn, was British to the very core, which is why he once phoned me from Addenbrooke's A and E asking me to rescue a budgerigar from the boot of his car. The car was wrecked and he was in hospital because he had crashed into a van-load of fox hounds near Barton. Doug never did anything by half. I found the budgie. It was in a gilded cage. It only had one leg and was obliged to lean against the bars of the cage to stop itself falling off the perch. Gibbie fell in love with that budgie because of their close affinity. He, too, had spent much of his life leaning against bars to stop himself from keeling over. Very British.

I may also qualify. Once had a ferret called Ferdinand the Ferocious Fenland Ferret. He walked at my heel along the village street and would shoot up the inside of my trouser leg at the approach of strangers. Never ever trusted another ferret to do that.

HEN SITTER

WHEN Larry McDonnell was asked to look after the hens in the garden next door while his neighbour was on holiday he was, of course, delighted to do so. Larry is like that. Do anybody a good turn if he can, will Larry.

Alas, one of the hens went missing. Larry searched diligently. It was nowhere to be found. Down at The Boot, his local in Dullingham, he told his sad tale and wondered what to do. He felt guilty at losing his mate's hen. Simple, said one of the regulars. Just keep quiet. If there was only one hen missing his neighbour would never notice. Good idea said Larry, that's what he'd do. Keep quiet about it.

Then someone asked how many hens was he looking after? Two, said Larry.

THE GASMAN COMETH

A CAUTIONARY little saga. My friend Eric Eldin, in his time one of the great jockeys and later a highly skilled trainer, and I were enjoying a noggin or two as is our wont, when he told me ruefully of his adventure that very morning. In his Newmarket home is a large cupboard. It had become overful. Eric decided, with a rare sense of domestic duty, to tidy it. His wife said that while he was about this unusual task she would nip down the road and have a quick coffee with their daughter. Eric went into the cupboard and its door closed behind him. It was at this point that Eric realised there was a latch on the outside of the door but not on the inside. He was trapped. Still the missus had only nipped out for a quick coffee. Eric now realises that wives never nip out for quick coffees. Such a phrase is a contradiction in terms. She was away for an hour and a half. Meanwhile Eric had turned off the boiler housed in the cupboard because of the heat. When his wife finally released him he shot off for a resuscitating pint. He forgot to turn the heat back on. His wife, finding a cold house and no hot water, assumed the worst. She called in the gasman. Next day Eric seemed subdued when we met. He told me why. The gasman's visit had set him back ninety quid.

THE 'CRAFT' CLUB

MY widely known inability to remember anything means that I have been invited to join an exclusive association called "The Craft Club" run by two retired senior army officers. The initials stand for "Can't Remember A Flipping Thing" and its members can wear a pretty blue tie with pink elephants upon it. Their tails (the elephants' not the officers') are knotted – if I remember rightly.

Food and Drink

PUB GRUB

TO Lavenham, that Suffolk village of topsy-turvy wooden houses oak-beamed pubs and friendly natives. The scene: wooden tables outside The Angel in the Market Place. The cast: Herself and me basking in warm Spring sunshine, English ale in our mugs, delicious food on our plates. The Angel is gaining a huge reputation for its exciting meals and quite rightly so because it completely eschews "traditional" (ho!ho!) English pub grub – you know the sort I mean, lasagne, chilli con carne and square pieces of totally tasteless chicken tandoori – and concentrates on real food. My "humble pie", a proper pie of moist pork, apple and onion, was simplicity itself but utterly memorable whilst Herself's anchovy and onion tart was, quoth she, "sheer bliss". As the nation's pubs slip further down the culinary slope on the back of the ubiquitous microwaved filth that passes for food these day it is immensely refreshing to find a gem like The Angel. All aspiring publicans and pub chefs should be forced at the point of a bayonet to have a meal there to learn what can be done with a mixture of superb, fresh ingredients and a large dollop of gastronomic imagination. Then we could all live happily ever after.

HOW TESCO MAKE THEIR MONEY

TESCO are making countless millions from their ever-proliferating nosh-flogging emporiums and I have discovered one of the secrets for their success. Or, more correctly, Herself has. It is cunningly simple. They sell tins of pears cut in half. They sell tins of pears cut in quarters. Same weight. They charge 11p more for the pears in quarters.

Now before they mucked about with our perfectly good currency today's 11p was worth approaching two shillings and sixpence, two and a tanner, half a crown, half a dog's collar – call 'em what you like but there were eight to a jimmy-o-goblin and half a dollar would buy you in my younger days a decent pint, a scotch and five Woodbines plus a box of Swan Vestas matches.

So, it's not a bad mark up and if they sell a million tins of quarters in a year then they are close to earning a damn sight more than me. Why the difference? Well, Herself blames the unions. She reckons the

National Union of Pear Slicers and Juice Injectors must charge Tesco a higher rate for their quarterers than for their less skilled halfers. She's probably right. After all it must take a longer apprenticeship to learn how to chop a pear into four pieces than two; exactly twice as long, I suppose. And think of the mess quartering must make of the slicers' sticky little worktops.

THE EGG – GOD BLESS IT

MEANWHILE, when it was announced that hundreds of different types of pre-packed, ready-to-eat meals in our supermarkets were being withdrawn because they were contaminated by a possible cancer-inducing agent, there was a general air of smugness in our domiciliary residence.You see, we just don't eat that sort of rubbish hereabouts. Once, as an experiment, we tried a Waitrose shepherd's pie. Eyes closed it would have been damn near impossible to have decided whether we were eating the contents or the cardboard container in which it was sold. Later we tried a packet of fish fillets. They gave cotton wool a bad name.

Here, for once in our long marriage, we thought as one and agreed that never again would such ghastly gastronomic confections be allowed to sully the sanctity of Herself's kitchen. Hence the smugness.

The fact is, however, that the world's most staple foodstuff has always come perfectly pre-packed and ready for almost instant consumption and, when you think about it, the purposes for which this particular article of food are employed are more numerous and varied than any other.

It is called the egg.

Apart from that ridiculous blip when Edwina Currie (whose real talent lay, so she later told us, in comforting her Prime Minister) frightened the egg-eating section of the population, i.e., all of us, with her talk of salmonella, the egg, perfectly wrapped as it is and available by the billions, has been mankind's dietary mainstay since the hen realised why the cockerel was crowing.

Do not make the mistake of treating the humble egg as a boring part of our daily gustatory menu. That great French chef Escoffier left to posterity some 85 different recipes for cooking eggs, another 46 for various omelettes (or omelets) and 14 for cold egg dishes.

And now that you can just nip down to the big store and fill your wire trolleys with rubbish, kindly allow me to recommend Escoffier's favourite egg dish. "Fry your eggs in plenty of butter, trim the edges. Place on round, thin slices of bread and cover with a foie-gras purée. Arrange in the form of a crown on a dish and pour into the middle a garnish of calf's kidneys cut into dice and sautéed and truffles similarly cut."

Perfect breakfast before a hard day's huntin'.

THE SAD DEMISE OF THE PIKELET

FOR those under a certain age, I should explain that a pikelet is not a juvenile freshwater fish with inward-pointing teeth and nor is it a modified version of a medieval weapon on the end of a stout stick for use by midget warriors. It is, as those over that certain age will recall, a small, round, rather thick type of muffin with a flat, brown bottom and a pale grey top punctured by large holes.

Of all comfort foods this is the most comforting, especially at this time of the year when eaten in a warm room after a day spent out in the cold and wintry wind. All that is required to convert it from an unappetising chunk of apparently flabby rubber into a glistening roundel of gastronomic bliss is a quick toasting (best on an open fire) and the addition of copious lumps of the finest butter. That's what the holes are there for – to hold the melting butter in place until you gladly sink your grateful gnashers into the welcoming pikelet. And this is the point at which I propose to have a moan.

Pikelets, you see, are very much a northern delicacy but even up in that wild, uncivilised territory beyond the bounds of Stamford, the pikelet has fallen upon woeful times what with the national disapproval of fatty foods.We haven't enjoyed any for yonks. But, glory upon glory, Herself found some in our local Tesco and at home of a darkening evening we fell upon them like ravening wolves.

Aaaagh! Our mutual disappointment was like finding the Pearly Gates locked with a "Gone Away" notice attached. Heaven was denied us. Those pikelets were not only thin as half-egg pancakes but they had the palatable allure of over-used cotton wool. But – herein lies Tesco's ultimate sin – the holes in their dreadful pikelets were mere pinpricks. Instead of sucking the butter in they spurned it so it slithered off and coagulated sulkily on the plate. Whichever Tesco executive ordered the bakers to be sparing with their pikelet holes should be drowned in a vat of melting butter.

MUSHROOMING

MAYHAP it all harks back to the frugality of my formative years when wartime food rationing rendered gustatory delights a rarity and any tasty titbit that mother nature had to offer was a bonus and gladly accepted but the fact is that even now I still get an enormous thrill from the first of the autumn hunts.

No, dear bunny-huggers, I am not referring to the tally-ho! variety but rather the gentle and immensely satisfying hunt for the early mushrooms. It beats the charm of blackberrying and sloepicking because the former are easy to find and the latter grow in the same places year after year. But mushrooming is a chancy art with absolutely no guarantee of success but, my word, how the heart pounds when, across a dew-damp meadow, the first gleaming, virginal-white pearls of mushroom caps are spotted.

I have always thought that mushrooming should be a solitary activity unhindered by unnecessary chatter. To walk miles alone on a crisp autumn morning – always in hope – is a simple therapy and the perfect way to start the day.

Part of the pleasure is based on selfishness because you exult in finding the treasure before other hunters who will be in the area at the same time. To be able to show off your basketful of pink-gilled mushrooms to an empty-handed fellow hunter is as satisfying as finishing a game of darts before your opponent has got his first double. There are few things in life better than a decent gloat.

A CURSE ON THE DEEP FREEZE

FAITHFUL readers down the years, all three of 'em, will know that I have a deep dislike of the ethos of the deep freeze. I have never seen the need for them in a civilised and mainly urban society though I readily admit one might come in handy if you were living in a tent with electricity in the middle of the Gobi desert if only to stick your steaming feet in after a long camel trot. But I digress. Today our shops are open dawn til dark and never has there been a bigger choice of fresh and exotic foods. And the belief that fresh food placed in a deep freeze emerges as fresh as when it went in is no more than a modern mirage, a masterpiece of cunning salesmanship.

Old-fashioned I maybe, indeed I most certainly am, but I like to eat seasonal food in the season in which it is grown. Strawberries are for summer not Christmas, peas are best as they pop out of a warm pod and plump little trout should be cooked before they realise they've been hooked.

And so for the first four decades of our marriage we managed very happily without a freezer. But when we moved recently we inherited one in our new house. I looked in ours for the first time t'other day. Couldn't believe it. Herself has gone potty. She need never go shopping again. Enough frozen bread and fish to feed the five thousand, Italian pastas whose names I can't even pronounce and well, I can't bear to go on. But there, at the very top of this ice-bound cornucopia was, wait for it, a packet of frozen Yorkshire puddings. FROZEN YORKSHIRE PUDDINGS!!

Gadzooks and stack me, the woman was born in Yorkshire. I would not say this in public but between you and me the fact is that by this one weird aberration she has not only proved herself a disgrace to her native county but a grave disappointment to her long-suffering husband. Why marry a Yorkshire lass if she won't make fresh puddings? And all because she has allowed her once formidable intellect to be seduced by a flaming deep freeze. The deep freeze is a marriage breaker. I speak with a new-found authority.

AN ELEPHANT IN NEWMARKET?

NEWMARKET, England. Enter, very slowly, a large couple whose joint presence very nearly blocks the wide pavement of the High Street. Each carries the ubiquitous bottle containing a coloured liquid from which they sip with such frequent regularity and fervour that one could be forgiven for assuming they have but recently emerged from a strenuous stroll across the Sahara Desert.

The couple, husband and wife I assume, pause near the Jockey Club. The wife points, wordlessly, to the plastic bag carried by her husband. He pockets his bottle and, also wordlessly, extracts from the bag a large bun which he offers to his wife. I am near enough to notice that the bun is of the variety which oozes thick cream and jam through a layer of sugar.

Now when I talk about the couple being "large" what I really mean is "vast" and of the twain the wife is by far the vaster. Indeed, at the risk of offending the British Society for the Encouragement of Obesity in Marriage, I can tell you that the lady who is (and always will be) centre stage is Sumo-wrestler fat. Little wonder. By the time they have waddled a few yards further on she is pointing once more towards the plastic bag. It is time for another fix. Hubby obliges in the manner of a kindly keeper feeding his favourite elephant.

Here the curtain comes down but mayhap we have seen enough on our little stage to ponder awhile on that frightfully anti-social American import of "grazing" or eating whilst on the hoof. It should be crated and exported back whence it came then we could all replace "meal times" on the family pedestal which that ancient ritual occupied for so long.

WAR TIME FOOD RATIONING

LEFT the recent air show at Duxford thinking, oddly enough, not about those magnificent men in their flying machines, but about food and not the sort of grub which we all think about these days – lashings of this and lashings of that.

What had distracted me from the superb aerial displays were some pamphlets in the museum shop in which the rigours of our wartime diet were starkly and chillingly outlined. To those who were not around at the time, like very nearly everybody, the statistics must be nigh unbelievable and even to those of us who experienced wartime rationing the memories of our spartan lifestyle are dimmed by the passing years.

So in these days of affluent obesity it might help some, nay, many, of us to pause in our headlong dash to the burger joint and similar troughs of iniquity and reflect that there is a life beyond fast food and constant over-indulgence. Well, there was during the war.....

I had forgotten just how fantastically frugally we lived after rationing was introduced in January 1940. This, believe it or not, is the amount of food, which every adult was entitled to, in those dark, perilous days of 1941:

8 oz (226g) of fat (including 2 oz of butter), 2 oz (57g) of tea, 2

slices of cooked meat, 4 oz (114 g) ham, 1 oz (28 g) of cheese, 8 oz (226 g) of sugar, 2 oz (57 g) of jam, 1 shilling (5p) worth of meat, one shell egg. And, no, this was not the daily ration. It had to last the week.

If you were lucky you might be allowed one packet of dried milk a week in addition to two or three pints from the cow. And the Americans sent us dried eggs; again you were lucky to get one packet a month. Of course, amounts varied during the course of the war depending upon circumstances but that's how it was in 1941, our darkest hour.

There were, however, plenty of potatoes, carrots, onions and bread all of which were unrationed but fruit like oranges and bananas vanished until the war's end. To this day I can recall the excitement when mother brought home the first peacetime banana. I was astonished when father peeled it. He cut it into three equal pieces. We stared at this astonishing tropical treasure for ages before we dared to eat it, very slowly.

Food rationing helped not only to stiffen the nation's physical sinews but also its resolve.We were all in it together. Even the King's mother carried a personalised ration card. On it was written: Surname: Queen Mary. Christian Names: Her Majesty.

"BHISTIS" ALL

HAVE you noticed how a strange affliction has gripped much of the nation? I refer to the habit of drinking whilst on the hoof. Everywhere, people are strolling along clutching bottles of water, Coke, milk, sugary fruit mixtures and other disgusting concoctions with which you could not tempt me even if I was trapped under a dead camel in the middle of the Gobi desert on a hot Monday morning. Every few yards these foul drinks are raised automatically to the lips and sipped. Can so many people be so thirsty so much of the time? Are they not aware of the pleasure of storing up a good thirst so that it can be assuaged properly with an almighty slurp in a drinking establishment specially designed for the job – i.e. the pub?

Virtually overnight the natives of this kingdom have become "bhistis" in the true tradition of Empire. And I, for one, do not understand why. Now in case you were not born, as I sometimes feel I was, in the reign of the Great White Empress when the world map was a huge splodge of British Empire red, the meaning of the word "bhisti" may not leap readily to mind. It comes from Kipling's India and means "regimental water carrier". He was the chap who carried goat skins of water to our parched soldiers as they lay sweltering in troop train sidings or as they marched across India's endless arid plains. The most famous of them all was the good, the brave, the faithful "squidgy-nosed old idol" Gunga Din who was, as Kipling made clear, a much better man than the rest of us.

All of which leads us back to the beginning. We are now all water carriers. It is a strange phenomenon which overnight has taken our nation in its thrall. Stand for a moment on any street corner in town or city and count the number of passers-by carrying plastic bottles of water or some sparkling sugary type of potion. Or, to make it easier, count the number who are not carrying a drink. Last week, on King's Parade in Cambridge, I counted just 24 people among a vast throng who were walking bottle-free. On buses, trains, in the shops, cinemas, parks, just about everybody is busy suckling endlessly. Cyclists do it in mid-mad dash, joggers do it without breaking stride and I suspect that when courting couples come up for air the first thing they reach for is a comforting plastic bottle of water.

Why? Why must we be constantly cosseted in this motherly fashion? It is not as though we are camel-born Tuaregs. Is it then an extension of the dreadful American custom which has spread across the Big Pond to these shores of eating whilst walking? Grazing, they call it. Now just about everyone is supping on the hoof. Millions have mastered the art of sipping without pause and without spilling. Whole families drink in unison from granny down to the smallest toddler, bottle to mouth every couple of yards along the pavement.

'Twas never thus. The British, of all people, were adept at building up a good thirst which could best be quenched with a pint in the Dog and Duck. Labourers took a pop bottle of cold tea into the fields – to last 'em all day. Colliers went deep underground with just a tin water can on their leather belts. What has happened?

Can it be a manifestation of global warming? Or is it the ultimate example of one of the more troubling aspects of modern society – the cult of the insatiable need for instant gratification? The ubiquitous water bottle is, of course, a fad, like the mobile phone – what is called these days a "must-have". You have 'em if you must. I prefer the world of Gunga Din.

Sitting on the low wall of King's College counting the passing bhistis I watched a stately lady emerge from the college. "What do you think of King's College Chapel then?" asked her friend. "Quite nice", she replied in the understatement of this and several previous centuries, adding: "Where's the nearest Marks and Sparks?"

FREE FOOD

THERE is a Desperate Dan-sized pan bubbling away on the cooker at this very moment. Within its cavernous depths are the carcasses of a brace of pheasants, left-overs from Sunday lunch, together with a goodly collection of onions and carrots. Apart from the cost of the pan (a wedding present) and the electricity, that wholesome soup is costing us scarcely a farthing or groat. And people complain about the cost of food these days.

I fail to fathom attitudes, especially in the countryside, at this season of the year when game is still plentiful and ludicrously cheap. Pheasants and partridges are available on the feather at give-away prices – indeed, thousands actually are given away by the shoots – and even in the shops a decent butcher will sell you a couple of brace of pheasants, plucked, drawn and ready for the oven at a tenner for the four of 'em. Roasted, casseroled, please yourself and cook them as you prefer. Just make sure you don't chuck the bones away if you want to enjoy rich, free soup for the rest of the week.

But then why, oh why, don't more people take advantage of healthy, cheap, almost free produce from the woods and fields scarcely a barrel's length away from their kitchen hobs? Is it all part of the "I-don't-have-time-to-cook" nonsense or, even worse, the modern social evil of scoffing a frozen fast food take-away surrounded by a silent family sitting entranced by a soap opera on the telly? I dunno. What I do know is this: I made that cauldron of soup. I timed the operation. Chucking the bones in the pan, chopping onions and carrots, adding a dash of pepper and the tap water plus switching on the cooker took precisely two minutes and twenty seconds. And I am a dawdler! I was so exhausted by all this that I had to ask Herself to turn the heat down once the soup had boiled.

I always maintain that one of the greatest of simple pleasures in this ancient kingdom of ours is the Sunday lunchtime stroll home from the pub on a still, frosty January day and to be greeted at home by the tantalising smell of roasting pheasant. It is a peculiarly British, well, actually, English delight because only England has the proper mixture of real pubs and first class local game. The Scots have splendid grouse but rotten pubs, the Irish have smashing pubs and skinny snipe and the Welsh have leeks.

TRICKY CHOICE

PICKED my first mushrooms a fortnight ago. Supply has suddenly dried up. Is some greedy swine getting up earlier than me and plundering my secret patch of the very tastiest of free food that bounteous Nature has on offer? Still, never mind. This year's wild blackberries are big as babies' fists, juicy as ripe melons. I'm not sure where my affections lie these days – cream or custard with blackberry and apple pie or crumble – which is why there will be a choice for Sunday lunch. OK then. Both.

BLETTING YOUR MEDLARS

KINDLY answer the following question and no need to be shy about it: when did you last blet your medlars? I ask the question because when I was with a group of expert gardeners recently most of them couldn't recognise a medlar tree when we saw one and the others who could did not have the faintest idea how to blet them.

Well, the medlar looks a bit like an apple tree and if you have never seen one try to slip into the gardens of Christ's and Emmanuel colleges in Cambridge 'cause they've got 'em in there. Medlar fruit wears a sort of inverted crown and is as hard as a piece of bog oak. Which is why you have to blet them. Bletting is the easiest job in the world because it means, quite simply, that you hide the fruit in a dark drawer until it has rotted inside. Then you scoop out the innards and turn it into the most sublime of jellies with which to accompany a brace of well-hung December pheasants.

It is well worth being aware of the phrase because when unwelcome visitors knock on the door there is no better way of bidding them riddance than by saying: "You must forgive me, I am in the middle of bletting my medlars."

A Sportin' Life

AN EXPENSIVE DAY

I TOOK Herself racing at Newmarket on Sunday and, despite the fact that the meeting was in aid of the NSPCC I was duly savagely punished for gambling on the Sabbath and not just by the bookies. No! It was Herself who actually punctured my wallet and her actions just go to prove that even the most parsimonious amongst us – and parsimony should have been her middle name – are perfectly at ease when squandering other folks' spondulicks.

Thus it came to pass that in a moment of unaccustomed generosity I offered to buy her lunch in that charming balcony restaurant on the July course. We ate a delicious but modest repast but when it came time for the bill just before the first race the cashier had got into a muddle with the till. So I handed Herself three £20 notes, asked her if she would mind settling the account and scuttled off to watch the first race.

Much later in the afternoon with my fortunes distinctly on the wane I inquired how much change there was from the lunch bill. None, she said. It came to almost exactly what I had given her. Thirty pounds. But, I said through rapidly gritting teeth, I had given her sixty quid. I had arrived on the course without any tenners in my pocket. Upon deep reflection she agreed that was indeed the case but she had also been in a rush to catch the first race and, er, had made a slight mistake, a mistake which, alas, it was too late to rectify.

The journey home was strangely quiet. Finally she plucked up sufficient courage to tell me that she had also given the waitress a £5 tip. It was, so far as I was concerned, the tip of the iceberg. My comment should have been recorded for the benefit of posterity except that she didn't hear it and I wouldn't like to repeat it.

GUINEAS WEEKEND

IT'S the Guineas weekend at Newmarket and the punters will pour in by car, coach, train and plane for two days of the finest horse racing in the world – fen farmers clutching their wives' secret egg money, furtive gentlemen awash with cunningly withdrawn loot from distant, off-shore islands, toffs in titfers and the soon-to-be-skint in flat 'ats all united by their perennial optimism.

It has been said that not all villains go racing but that all those who go racing are villains, a scandalous calumny if it were not very nearly true.

Newmarket changes little and the constancy of its attractions is responsible for the continuous in-pouring through the flat season of visitors from the world over. At each race meeting are to be found a profusion of frolicsome fillies, skittish colts, rampant stallions and handsome, soon-to-be-expectant mares. Then, of course, there are the horses.

THE WINNER OF THE DERBY

THE Derby is almost upon us again and I could tell you the winner except I won't. My racing chums all know its name. The only snag is that the name of the winner changes with whichever expert is talking to me and thus far I have a list of certainties for the great race which extends to eight different nags. Now here is the real problem. One of those eight is highly likely to pass the post first. Whoever tipped it to me will come looking for his "present". I won't have backed it but I'll still have to smile bravely, pretend I did, and give him his large bottle of finest malt. I am on a loser before the "off". Even if I backed all eight a dang-blasted outsider would win.

JACK'S NEW SUITS

A DEAR old racing chum of mine has just died suddenly at a goodly age and after a splendidly-spent life. All the regulars at the Newmarket courses – and at Great Yarmouth and half a dozen other tracks – will miss Jack greatly. He loved nothing better than beating the bookies and was always on the look-out for a bargain. But he backed a loser just before the end – in the week before he died he bought three new suits "at a good price". I'll bet Jack is still laughing about it even now!

HOW MUCH?

I WAS beginning to feel slightly bored with the proceedings which had become somewhat mundane when a small, dark and dapper chap slipped into an empty seat a few feet away from mine. The atmosphere changed upon the instant and I suspected we were about to witness something out of the ordinary. I could not have guessed how spectacular the next few minutes were going to be. Nor could the experts who had suddenly deserted the bars and had come tumbling back into the high-domed, tiered building which is Tattersalls sale ring at Newmarket.

Into the ring itself stepped one of the most perfect creatures in the world – aristocratic, proud, seemingly aware of its incredible breeding despite being a one-year-old baby. There was a collective intake of breath as the packed room fell silent and all eyes followed the stately progress of the yearling colt being led round the ring. Well, not all eyes because mine were fixed firmly on the face of my Arab neighbour. By now I knew that history was about to be made for the Arab was Sheikh Mohammed, owner of more racehorses than anyone else in the world. He hadn't turned up at Tattersalls that night for a cup of lemon tea.

The yearling colt whose every move the Sheikh watched with steely eyes was being offered for sale by Lord Andrew Lloyd Webber who had bred it at his Watership Down Stud. A son of Sadler's Wells, the colt's mum was none other than the Top Ville mare Darara. For those of you who may be little versed in the niceties of racehorse breeding take it from me that this magnificent product of the union of that great stallion and beautiful mare was simply the Prince of Yearlings.

Already that evening the Sheikh had paid one million guineas for a chestnut colt named Shami but here was something in a different league. The only question was – who would dare to take on the Sheikh when the bidding began. If he wanted that superb young horse surely nobody could stop him.

The bidding opened at three hundred thousand guineas and with a few almost imperceptible nods of the Sheikh's impassive head the million guinea mark was reached before you could say "Cor Blimey!"

Sheikh Mohammed's eyes never left the coveted yearling. It was as though he was mesmerised. Still the head continued to nod assent and then the auctioneer was calling for three million guineas. If the Sheikh was mesmerised by the animal I was equally mesmerised by him and the atmosphere in that Sale Ring was electric. Nobody spoke, nobody coughed, everyone held their breath. The auctioneer waited quietly and patiently for each new bid and then almost whispered – three million one hundred thousand – three million two hundred thousand – three million three hundred thousand – three million four hundred thousand. But who had made that bid, was it the Sheikh or his persistent opponent on the other side of the ring?

For the first time during that titanic fiscal battle a small smile crossed the Sheikh's face and I thought he had won. But no. Instead of a downward, affirmative nod his head swung just once negatively side-to-side. The duel was over. The Arab had lost.

The successful bidder was John Magnier from the Coolmore Stud in Ireland. At three million four hundred thousand guineas the European record price for a yearling had been smashed before our very eyes. The price was the second highest paid for a yearling anywhere in the world in the last 15 years.

The Sheikh was still smiling as he walked calmly out into the cold Newmarket night with his henchmen. It was as though he had just lost a game of shove ha'penny in the village local.

WHAT ODDS?

PURELY on a personal level I rather wish they had succeeded in forcing the abandonment of the Grand National this week simply because the nag I backed in the race has never been heard of since the "off" and would appear to have disappeared into the timeless mists of the Wirral.

But, of course, the IRA couldn't be allowed to get away with it and they never will; not, at least, if the attitude of one chap I met in Newmarket High Street is a typical one. He said to me: "Trying to blow us all up is one thing. Interfering with racing is an altogether more serious affair."

Talking of which we are on the verge of the glorious Craven Meeting at Newmarket when the flat racing world meets together again for another season after a long winter's lay-off.

Spring is heralded in so many different ways for different people. For many it is the dancing daffodil, or the first croak of the early rooks, prancing lambs in verdant pastures, gangling foals or merely the heart-chilling splutter of a million mowing machines.

For many of us, however, it is the first hauntingly plaintive call of that strange creature, the Newmarket bookmaker. You will recognise him (there are but few females of this particular species) because though 'tis spring he will still be wearing his winter finery to protect himself from the icy blasts of April which roar across the blasted Newmarket heath straight from the heart of the Ural Mountains. Inevitably his coat will be made from the very purest wool garnered from the back of some distant yak or llama. His shoes will be of the softest leather and his tie of such astonishing vivacity that you could spot him standing three hundred yards away in a thick fog. Normally, no matter what the weather, he will be found nestling 'neath a huge umbrella looking for all the world like something from a children's nursery rhyme book – a fairy under a toadstool.

But it is his mating call by which you will the more readily recognise him. It is a mixture of the sergeant major's bawl and the entreating scream of the mullah calling the faithful to prayer. (And prayer is what you will need in abundant portions if you are to avoid the clutches of this ravenous beast).

But the Heath would be bare without him. Spring cannot be sprung at Newmarket in his absence. Happily there is no danger of him becoming extinct. You can't starve when you live off the fat of the land.

WOT CAR?

THE Times has been running some quite charming letters about how to find one's motor vehicle once it is lost in some huge parking lot. Most of us have experienced the problem; upon which floor of the car park did we leave it, at which end of which street did we park the damn thing? You know well what I'm on about.

Times' readers have been providing a number of ingenious, though totally impracticable, remedies like attaching different coloured clothes pegs to your car's aerial (what if everybody did it?). The question, however, brings back to me one of my more embarrassing moments.

Let us remove ourselves to Manchett's Garage in Burwell on the edge of the fens. My own car is not just gasping for professional aid but very nearly coughing itself to death. It reaches Manchetts in extremis. They offer to loan me a car while they try to resuscitate mine. I am anxious to reach Newmarket for the first race which is imminent. Get there with minutes to spare. Park in the middle of thousands of other cars and dash off to the Members' Enclosure. Back the losing favourite in the first. Don't exactly cover myself in financial glory the rest of the afternoon. That's by the by.

After the last race I retire grievously bruised in the wallet. Not a good day. It is, however, to become even worse.

Not only do I not know where I parked my loaned car but I realise with much dismay that in my hurry to get to the flaming races I didn't even note which sort of car I had borrowed. From my short journey 'twixt Burwell and Newmarket I had a vague recollection of its interior but the exterior was totally and utterly beyond my powers of recall since I hadn't looked at it before I jumped in at the garage or after I jumped out at the racecourse. I could well have travelled by camel or dog-sleigh.

I phone the garage. No answer. Despair. But stay! A clue. It being a clement sort of day I had left my raincoat on the back seat of the vehicle. Even a twit like me could recognise his own raincoat.

By now the sun, like my betting ambitions, has sunk and in the increasing gloaming I slip from parked car to parked car in their endless serried ranks peering ever hopeful into back seat after back seat.

Strange lot, some of those racegoers. My totally innocent search for an old raincoat on the back seat of a completely strange motor car led to some of the most remarkable pieces of advice I have ever been offered and it was only as I wandered round that vast car park that I first realised that Newmarket racecourses often have two different forms of sporting activity for the price of one.

HUNTING THE HUNTER

LET us turn then to the fox, the hunting of which (or, rather, the non-hunting) appears to be at the very forefront of our new government's priorities. Quite why this should be so is beyond me since I would have thought there were at least a thousand more important matters which need to be dealt with in order to improve the human lot. But I suppose that envy, spite and malice come high on the political agenda these days which is why the proposed abolition of fox hunting is to be the subject of the first Private Member's Bill of the new parliament.

There really cannot be any other reasons for the Bill because everybody knows in truth that if the hunting of the fox by hounds were to stop this very second not a single fox will benefit. The fox will still have to be controlled, as all abolitionists know, and as they know equally well the most efficient mode of control is the hound – not shooting, not trapping, not gassing – but the hound.

But, of course, it is not the welfare of the fox that the antis have in their sights. It is the discomfiture of the hunter. It is the thrill of the chase in reverse. The hunter is now the hunted and the sound of distant baying is that of the mob in full cry. Today it is politically incorrect for a minority to be allowed to enjoy itself in its own legal and traditional fashion particularly when opposition to that enjoyment is based on social bigotry and ignorance. I have always maintained that if the fox were to be hunted by people wearing flat hats and riding bikes there never would have been any of this crass and histrionic nonsense.

Oh! And by the way – I do not ride to hounds and never have. But I'm beginning very much to wish that I did and had.

BANANA SKINS – WHAT ELSE?

IT is a slightly sad but distinctly true fact of life that the British enjoy nothing more than having a good laugh at someone else's discomfiture which is, of course, why the banana skin was invented.

And I readily confess that I absolutely fell about in a fit of mirth t'other day when I read about some dotty hunt saboteur down in the west country who, much to his surprise, learned a bitter lesson about the cuddly, loveable, bushy-tailed fox.

He was one of a score of anti-hunt protesters who tried to disrupt the legal activities of the East Devon Hunt at Dulford in Devon recently. As is par for the course, so to speak, nine of 'em were arrested after violence broke out but there is nothing mirth-provoking about that.

No – the bit I loved was this: the aforementioned dotty saboteur tried to "rescue" the fox which had thus far quite easily managed of its own volition to evade the hounds. Now I know and you know that

Charlie fox is not the gentle creature of animal aid mythology which is why, when this twerp picked the fox up, it promptly bit his hand and the poor loon was whisked off to hospital, a pained but wiser man.

Yes! I know you shouldn't laugh but, oh deary me, I just couldn't help it.

I wasn't alone because when we are a-natterin' away in The Bushel about the daft antics the antis get up to and the Devon tale is mentioned everybody else falls about. At which point, one chap, through his tears, recounts the fenland fable of the ol' boy who is sitting watching the village cricket match – it was over Ely way somewhere – one sunny afternoon with a hefty lurcher by his side. A newcomer to the village sets himself down on the bench alongside the ancient and in friendly fashion asks: "Does your dog bite by any chance?"

The fenman replies: "Nope." The newcomer pats the lurcher on the head whereupon the dog bites his hand to the bone.

"You damn fool", shouts the wounded newcomer. "You said your dog doesn't bite."

The fenman looks at him and replies: "It don't. This ain't my dorg."

And Herself still cannot understand why I enjoy an occasional foray into a convenient hostelry or why I often come home laughing like a rampant hyena.

PARLIAMENT VOTES ON FOX–HUNTING

SO anyoldhow I'm a-natterin to these two ol' boys over a jar or two in The Champion of the Thames half way down (or up) King Street in Cambridge when one of 'em starts to chuckle.

"Well bor", he says, "I reckon as how they've got they ol' fox 'unters on the run at last." His mate smiles and nods in agreement. We are talking, you understand, a day or two after the House of Commons spent five hours debating the fox-hunting issue before voting for a total ban but his attitude takes me considerably aback for I've known these two blokes for thirty years or more and the only times I've seen 'em outside a pub has been when they are beating on various shoots around the county, ferreting rabbits down the fen, fishing for giant pike or knocking hell out of highflying pigeons with a force nine gale up their tails – the pigeons' tails, that is. Definitely not soppy, daft, bunny-hugging antis this couple I can tell 'ee.

Puzzled, I ask why they are so seemingly pleased at the Commons' vote?

Jack says: "Well, we've been a-thinkin', Fred an' me, and we've decided that this government has finally got suthin' absolutely spot on for a pleasant change. Y'see, we reckon as 'ow all them poxy politicians could 'ave wasted them five hours on debatin' things as 'ave no importance whatso-flaming-ever in this daft world of ours.

"Like for example they could 'ave been talking about why our lads 'ave got to go orf a-riskin' their necks fightin' up in them Afghan 'ills. Or suthin' even dafter like why are our school kids droppin' dead of drugs all over the shop or why ol' ladies 'ave to lie on cold beds in 'ospital corridors for days on end.

"No – they could 'ave been a-wastin' their precious time debatin' about muggers an' burglars an' car thieves an' other such-like socially deprived poor devils. They could even 'ave been gassin' on about making the trains run on time so the illegal immigrants could get to their comfy, free billets quicker."

Jack pauses and Fred and I are laughing fit to bust.

I tell them they had me dead worried for a while. I thought they had flipped their lids.

"Not us", says Fred. "It's those pillocks in Parliament who have done the lid flippin'. Five hours wasted on worrying about pesky hen-slayin', lamb-slaughterin', pheasant-murderin' dangblasted flamin' foxes. Our ol' world a-fallin' apart an' all they can werrit about is fox-huntin'. Total bloody madness."

THE RAT-PACK

DOUBTLESS you read last week the glad tidings that Labour's Hunting Bill is to be amended in order to allow rat catchers to use dogs to hunt and kill rats in sewers and cellars without fear of prosecution. This excellent news means that whatever finally happens to the ludicrous Bill the great British hunting tradition will be permitted to continue albeit underground. I intend therefore to exploit this chink in the armour of that bunch of politically correct poltroons in Westminster by establishing forthwith a new set of kennels which will house Britain's first pack of rathounds.

The kennels will be established at the end of that long drove just to the west of Manea and I shall elect myself as Master. Think of it! The grandeur! Lord Jeacock (as I shall be in due course), Master of the Fenland Pack of Sewer Rathounds, carrying on the glorious traditions of our forebears. And all totally legal!

The hounds will have to be specially-bred beagles with extremely short legs, rather like dachshunds, so that they can harry their prey at speed no matter how narrow the sewer pipe may be.

Hunt servants will wear a livery of vivid yellow so they can be recognised easily when they are in full flight down some of the murkier fenland drains and the Master and Members will be allowed to eschew the wearing of top hats on account of their obvious unsuitability in this type of hunting terrain.

All the normal hunting traditions will be maintained and, as Master, I shall insist that hounds always meet somewhere appropriate, such as the sewerage works at Milton, where stirrup cups will be handed round on silver salvers by smartly turned out dustmen. Glasses of vintage port – maybe Taylor's '47 or Warre's '63 – will be thrown back with many a jolly gurgle before the whipper-in lifts a likely-looking manhole cover so the hounds can move off.

As hounds vanish from view there will be loud cries of "Yoicks" as the field, led by its handsome and dashing Master, follows the pack into the warm, welcoming embrace of the sewers of the Fens. When the first rat is sighted the hounds will begin to sing with excitement and the cries of "View Halloo" and "Gone Away" will echo many a merry mile down the plashy drains while, once again, the stirring notes of the hunting horn will sound thrillingly over Britain's green and pleasant land. Well, under it at least.

AN INGLORIOUS 12TH

HERE I am on this Glorious 12th day of August trapped by urgent business in Norwich and all I can think about are my friends installed in their butts on the moors high above Gunnerside with the grouse curling and hurtling across the heather. I am no city man at the best of times but to be incarcerated in one on the first day of the grouse-shooting season is not only a double tragedy but a piece of appalling self-organisation. I shall write myself a stern letter of disapproval.

One day, no doubt, I shall grow old and sensible and choose the easy life but today those harsh Yorkshire moors are calling and the wet Yorkshire wind is playing mournful tunes on my heart-strings. They will be soaked to the skin up there, my lucky friends, and they will tumble and slither in and out of peat hags the size of moon craters until they approach exhaustion. The pursuit of the red grouse is one of the toughest of field sports and is not for the unfit. But tonight, back in their rented farmhouse my friends will be exhilarated, thirsty as a waterfall and hungry as unlucky lions. I know the scene well – there will be mounds of sausage and mash for supper and beer by the gallon and much laughter. Later there will be malt whisky and more laughter. Wet tweeds will steam in front of the wood fire and, after all the old jokes have been told, a score of guns and beaters will sleep deeply and dream of tomorrow on the stern moors. Alas, I shall dine alone in my hotel but it will not be the talk of fellow guests that I shall hear. It will be the stuttering call of the cock grouse, his "go, go, go, go, go-o back", which I will listen to as I go untired to bed on this, my Inglorious 12th of August.

The only thing which saves me from crying myself to sleep in my overwarm hotel bedroom is the certain knowledge that one of my old chums will drop a brace or two of grouse off at my home when he gets back. And when I return they will be waiting for me, delicious, of course, but not nearly as good as they would have been if they had fallen to my own gun.

HIP FLASKS AT THE READY

I SPEND much of my time taking the Michael out of numerous friends and I suppose I cannot really complain when some of 'em return the compliment. Thus, to my considerable astonishment, I found the following letter published in this country's premier shooting magazine, "The Shooting Times":

"I am considering buying a hip flask to hold sloe gin on shooting days. All my friends seem to have one and pull my leg because, while I accept their drinks, I never have anything to offer in return. What is the best sort to buy?"

The letter is signed "M. Jeacock, Newmarket". Now to my certain knowledge there is only one M. Jeacock in Newmarket and that is moi. And since this particular M. J. owns more flasks than he has hips combined with the fact that I do not recall writing that particular epistle you will understand that upon reading it my suspicions were, to say the least, aroused. As for flasks – I inherited one from a late Manciple of Trinity College in Cambridge which holds a quarter of a pint, I have one with a horse's head engraved upon it, a gift for the 25 years I have served as Chairman of The Swaffhams Cricket Club, which holds a third of a pint and an antique silver, glass and leather job, a gift from the children long ago, which holds a good half a pint. Furthermore I have distributed freely from these friendly vessels more home-made sloe gin to shooting acquaintances in these parts over the past third of a century than the average landlord has sold pints of bitter. Since that letter appeared my phone has been hot with calls from laughing chums whose general message seems to be along the lines of "What's it like to be the biter bit?"

Therefore, it is slowly beginning to dawn on me, as it probably is on you, that the letter to the "Shooting Times" was a hoax. And since "my" letter is answered in the same issue by my "friend" John Humphreys I am starting to develop a certain theory. I am naming no names and making no accusations. But let me tell 'ee this – come the next shooting season one John Humphreys, author, journalist, lecturer and jazzman of Bottisham in the County of Cantab, had better take his own hip flask of sloe gin to the many shooting days we share. 'Cause he ain't gonna get any more out of mine!

WHISKY GALORE

A FEW of us were a'nattering about the coming shooting season over a pint in The Bull at Burrough Green when the subject of boozy beaters came up. Beaters, for those of you newly arrived from the city, are the men – and, increasingly, women – who tap out the coverts and ditches to get the pheasants to fly over the guns and a grand race they are too. Well, there's a bunch of 'em over by Six Mile Bottom who are always rewarded by the landowner with a couple of bottles of scotch at the end of the day's shooting. They are the fastest disappearing bottles of whisky in eastern England. Last year the guvnor filled a gallon whisky bottle with cold tea and carried it into the beaters' hut. There was a stunned and appreciative silence broken only by the sound of lips being licked and throats being cleared. Then, horror! Nay, disaster! The guvnor pretended to trip and dropped that treasure-house of a bottle. As it smashed on the stone floor and the glorious amber liquid gushed around the feet of the beaters they were on their knees in a twink desperately trying to scoop it up.

Here was tragedy on an heroic scale. Old men sobbed with frustration. Then the smell of stale tea began to fill the hut..........

IDIOTS IN THE FREEZING FEN

THEY do declare that the older you get the dafter you become and in the case of one person hereabouts the saying is particularly apposite. I refer, of course, to none other than moi and shortly you will understand why I make the admission. Y'see, there we were, deep down the fen after a few pheasants, when the weather veered from being dreadfully chilly to being impossibly cold. Overnight frost refused to leave the black fen fields and the earth lay hard as iron so that first the feet gave in and became numb and then the legs capitulated in this unequal battle of the senses.

Suddenly, a great wind sprang up from the east, a Russian wind (north east from the fens the first hills to appear on the horizon are the Urals and if you listen hard to the east wind and you've had enough to drink I swear you can hear the troika bells a-tinkling) and what the frost had begun the searing gale finished off. To a man we were, as they say in that part of the world, friz up to our lugholes. There was no cover and no escape and I can safely admit that I have never been so completely cold and miserable in all my long years.

Now any sensible being would have given the cruel elements best and repaired forthwith to the welcoming and warming embrace of the nearest hostelry. But there is a strange and inexplicable tradition in the shooting field which means that nobody dares to give in to the weather. It is a form of inverted cowardice and the first to say "enough is enough" would be ridiculed by his fellows and the subject of much sniggering throughout the eastern counties.

So we stood there icicle-like in the teeth of the storm waiting for the beaters and the pheasants to arrive and the drives went on and on throughout the grey day. The result? I now have as nasty a touch of lumbago as it is possible to imagine and all those of you in the background who are saying "serve the old fool right" would not be wrong.

THE LAST FIRST DAY OF FEBRUARY

THERE are certain well-known phrases in our language which when uttered send immediate shudders of varying emotions through the listener – such as fear, apprehension, fury, disappointment and despair.

Fear, for example, when over the tannoy at the racecourse comes the announcement "Stewards' Inquiry" just as the nag you have backed has come first past the post. At this point you know in your heart that the result is certain to be changed, your winner is about to become a loser and the bookie's mazuma will remain safely ensconced in his wretched satchel.

Apprehension? Well, I speak from long experience here. The phrase is: "'Owzat?" In my case on many hundreds of occasions, I have heard it called as I faced the first ball of the game, felt the leather touch the edge of my bat and heard the dread appeal from the wicket-keeper. My apprehension was inevitably short-lived because the umpire's finger was always high in the air before the appeal was even made. They only used to let me open the batting for the Swaffhams over the years because I was club Chairman and had to be indulged.

Fury? This emotion is produced instantly when, thirsty as a humpless camel, you dash into the local for a quick night-cap only to hear the landlord shout: "Time, ladies and gentlemen please." Hell hath no fury like a drinker scorned.

I believe the deepest despair, the ultimate feeling of disappointment for many of us in this region is reserved for the first day of February each year at the close of which pheasant and partridge shooting is finished for another season. Here the awful phrase is always uttered in a loud voice by the head 'keeper: "And that, ladies and gentlemen, was the last drive on the last day of the season." At this the sportsman's heart sinks because sentence has been passed irrevocably and there can be no remote chance of a reprieve as there is on the racecourse, the cricket field or in the pub. That's it. That's the law. Not only has the game shooting season finished but it's a long time to the next one. Furthermore, believe you me, when you reach a certain age you know damn well that one of these first days of February is going to be your last first day of February. I dislike the day immensely.

MY LAST DAY

AS soon as I said it I knew that I had just pronounced my own shooting epitaph and upon reflection I rather think Herself realised it too although , wisely, she made no comment. It happened at the close of the last pheasant shooting season deep down in Swaffham Prior fen as the watery winter sun slipped quickly below the rim of the distant horizon. The January wind, sharp as a freshly-honed scythe, cut through the stoutest of protective clothing and turned ungloved fingers into icicles. A small gang of us, all regular guns down the fen, had spent the previous four hours tapping out the myriad dykes which criss-cross that rich and fertile plain in order to cull the far-too-numerous cock pheasants which shelter along the drainage banks. It is a necessary end-of-season duty wherever game shooting is taken seriously for a shoot heavily over-populated by old cock birds is an unhealthy shoot.

Herself and granddaughter Lydia had come along for the walk and on the way back to the open fronted barn which has been our headquarters since before it started to fall down, granny and grandchild kept up with the younger sportsmen without difficulty despite the miles we had all trudged during the day. The old man fell further and further behind. Festooned with pheasants, weighed down by gun and cartridges, each stride along the slippery fenland peat more tiring than the last, he knew that by now his chums were opening flasks of hot coffee in the barn and attacking with gusto newly broached bottles of whisky.

Herself came back across the darkening fields and offered to lighten the old man's load. If being stubborn is a virtue then I am close to sainthood. It was then that I uttered my epitaph. I declined the offer forcefully.

"Madame", said I to my wife, "the day I can't walk out of the fen unaided I will stop walking into it." She stared silently at me for a while, in a rather odd way, before leaving me and making her way back to the barn. And with that I marched on slowly, alone. Looking back to that bitter, dank afternoon, I think both of us knew.

You have guessed what I am about to tell you. I am no longer the man I was and if I can't shoot in the old fen fashion where every bird is hard fought for over harsh terrain then I won't shoot at all. I have walked into the fen with my gun for the final time and I am saddened.

But stay! I am cheered by a sudden brilliant thought. Mayhap the ol' boys will give me a lift now and again down to the barn where I can guard their lunchtime victuals – cold partridge legs, pork pies the size of landmines and as potent, bacon butties, cheese sarnies thick as town hall steps, coffee flasks and, er, the bottles. Perhaps I'm not finished with the fen yet.

I have shot game since good King George was on the throne. The sport has taken me to moors, dales, coverts, mountains, valleys, across the golden stubble fields of early autumn, through snowstorms of high winter, into treacherous, boot-sucking marshland and into dense forests dark even at the brightest noon. I have shot with chimney sweeps, lords, farmers, clerks, judges, villains, officers and gentlemen and officers who were not gentlemen, a tiny wisp of a maharajah, jockeys, trainers, farriers, city slickers who couldn't hit a shed if they were inside it, men with guns held together with binder twine and others with matched Purdeys worth a row of houses. I believe I can safely say that I have never shot with a bore; well, certainly not twice. At the end of a day's sport I have found my quarters in lowly taverns, an occasional stately home, once, in Dullingham, under the pub snooker table, in deep armchairs close to dying embers of inn fires and, not just once, in the back of a Land Rover covered by a blanket of tired black Labradors.

But what about the quarry you may well ask? Have you ever regretted all the killing? Well, actually, never. To my gun through the decades have tumbled pheasants, partridges, pigeons, snipe, wildfowl, grouse, geese, woodcock, hares, rabbits and any number of feathered and furred vermin, all apart from the latter, eminently edible. It is the absolute determination of all sportsmen to kill quickly and cleanly so ask yourself this question, please: if you were a healthy, high-flying game bird would you prefer to die instantly in mid-air, unafraid and unaware of any impending threat? Or would you prefer the alternative – a slow, agonising death brought on by infirmity, cold, starvation, thirst and the cruel, prolonged dismemberment by rat, raptor or fox? There are no sheltered homes for birds.

LAST DAY AGAIN

RECENTLY I announced my total retirement from the sport of game shooting. That, I said, was it. No more. After a lifetime with guns, dogs and the finest of loyal companions, it was high time to quit. Well, of course, I could not resist just one more day. Thus, in the New Year I find myself at Six Mile Bottom, down the road from Newmarket, one of the finest shooting estates in the land ruled over by probably the best of keepers, Richard Clark. The weather is gentle, my fellow guns with whom I have shot these many happy years, are in splendid form. After the most perfect of shooting days we retire to the Humphrey family home in Bottisham for game stew and wine. Herself collects me and we go home. This really is my final day. My – our – reminiscences are silent but shared. She knows that I have had the very best of shooting years and that I am grateful for them.

WHAT DOES A DEDICATED SHOOTING MAN MISS?

WHAT does a dedicated shooting man miss most when he is finally forced into dreaded retirement? Well, you can forget the killing. As in hunting and coursing. the kill is but a cog albeit integral – in the whole complex machinery of the sport. There are other, vital elements......skill-at-arms, for example. A sloppy shot is an unwelcome guest anywhere. Guns who cannot kill cleanly should quit the field. Then there is the comradeship of the shoot wherein is to be found old-fashioned courtesies and manners and, frequently, in squelching bogs, on sudden estuary tides and among precipitous fells, the desperate need of a helping hand. Then, of course, the perfect end to the day – the fireside farewell in the pub. Clothes steaming, dogs sprawling, tales growing taller, warm baths and beds calling......

The shooter is basically a true country lover to whom the dying colours of trees in October and the sweet, wild smell of fallen leaves tug gently on the heart strings. The delights of nature hidden from the eyes of suburban beings are made manifestly clear to the shooter out in the wilds and when I am asked what shooting has injected into my life I shall use those lines I learned from another old man like me long ago: "The wonder of the world, the beauty and the power, the shapes of things, their colours, lights and shades; these I saw. Look ye also while life lasts."

NEVER GIVE IN

PLEASE join me for a brief pre-Christmas excursion to the December fen; to be precise, to the Swaffham Prior bank of the lode which runs into the river Cam. There is a squadron of sleek swans swimming sedately behind the two old men who stand on the lode bank, leaning on their long sticks, watching the younger men shooting out in the dank fen. The wind is as sharp as a surgeon's scalpel, overhead the scudding clouds are glowering with menace and lunch is a long way off.

One of the men, ol' George Neal, a proper fenman, his black labrador Sam sitting to heel and quivering with excitement at the prospect of the shooting to come, says: "We've got to be among the luckiest blokes in the world – out here in the wild and the cold and amongst mates. Wouldn't swap it for anything."

His friend says: "One of these years we won't be here, George, me old mate. We shall have to sit down and put our feet up sometime or another."

George gives his companion a look of sheer disbelief. "Feet up! Feet up!" he shouts. "When I can't come out it won't be because I've put my feet up, it'll be because me toes have turned up. Feet up be blowed."

Upon reflection and truth to tell, I have no intention of putting my feet up either – not so long as the pheasant flies and ol' George and I can lean on our long sticks on the bank of the lode the Romans dug two thousand years ago a-listening to the stately swish of swimming swans and the crisp crack of the young men's guns. No, dammit! Feet up be blowed.

George laughed and I laughed and we carried on with the day. There were miles of wet fen to be walked and deep dykes to be crossed and the cold would get colder before the two old friends could go home and, yes, well, honestly, sit down and secretly put their feet up.

The English Pub

THE MIRACLE OF FALLING OFF A BAR STOOL

UNTIL I fell off a stool in the bar of The Boot at Dullingham the other evening (and, no, I wasn't), I never had much time for miracles, according them the same sort of disbelief I normally attach to the concept of kindly bank managers, honest bookmakers and political veracity.

I have changed my mind. Kindly allow me to explain...

A year or two ago, out shooting in Suffolk one wild and wintry day, we found ourselves enveloped in a blinding snowstorm of such severity that we could scarcely see the ends of our shotguns. The blizzard hit me as I was crossing a narrow plank over a deep ditch. I slipped and managed to fall directly upon my right knee. The result was a continuous painful limp which, on bad days, necessitated the assistance of a walking stick.

Since the pain was basically self-inflicted – after all, nobody forced me to wander around deepest Suffolk in the snow – I just got on with it, accepting it as another of life's little problems. Until I fell off the stool, that is.

There I was, minding my own business and listening to another of Malcolm Hall's splendid rural tales ('tis he who runs the Fenland Country Fair at Stow-cum-Quy every year), when, trying to stand up, my heel caught on the stool crossbar and I plunged carpetwards. My right knee took the full weight of the fall and I noticed nothing for a few moments because all thoughts were blotted out by the huge peels of laughter around the bar caused by my discomfiture.

It was only when they pulled me to my feet that I realised something had changed. There was no pain in the knee. I waggled it about. It worked like a well-oiled piston. That was three days ago. I can still trot up and down stairs with the sprightliness of a mountain fawn. A whole new pain-free world opens up before me. I can look forward to entering the grandchildren's egg and spoon races again. I could manage a five-furlong sprint down the Rowley Mile with the best of 'em. I am a different man.

I do not care to listen to any medical explanation. Mine is not to reason why. Just take it from me – miracles do happen.

DIDDLING

MR Larry McDonnell, late of the Irish Guards, lifetime contributor to the Guinness family coffers and father of the landlord of The Boot at Dullingham, recently treated his vast brood of children and grandchildren to a slap-up meal at a hostelry somewhere out in the rolling hills on the Cambridgeshire-Suffolk border – an act, you might think, of simple grandfatherly generosity. Not so. I intend to prove beyond a scintilla of doubt that this seemingly benign old codger was actually using laundered money, the proceeds of a lifetime of cunning crime, to pay for the hooley. The irrefutable evidence will be laid before you ere long.

There is, of course, a national malaise of dishonesty of which McDonnell's example is but an iceberg's tip. Currently another great scandal has been uncovered in the racing game which allegedly involves massive backhanders passing between bloodstock agents, trainers and owners involved in the buying and selling of thoroughbreds. The ungodly burghers of Newmarket are laughing fit to bust at the Jockey Club's sudden interest (they've called the rozzers in) in shady dealings which we all know have been going on ever since they invented the horse's fourth leg. Horse racing is a multi-billion pound industry which encourages villainy to enter into every corner of its huge, murky empire – bent bookies, bribed jockeys, rapacious trainers, crooked owners – so why shouldn't it extend into the great sales rings where yearlings can be sold for millions of guineas? It does. Always, has. Always will. (The Jockey Club should bear in mind that "horse dealer" is perhaps the most pejorative phrase in the English language. For racing folk "pejorative" means "disparaging", by the way).

But all skulduggery has to begin somewhere and I believe it creeps upwards from the lower echelons of our society which brings me back to Mr Larry McDonnell, m'lud. Y'see, despite his air of respectability and despite the row of war medals he so proudly wears on the Armistice Day parade, he has his darker side.

He diddles when he is playing cribbage.

Step into the witness box Mrs Vera Scrutton, wife of "Blind Bob" Scrutton, former landlady and landlord of the now defunct Royal Oak in Swaffham Bulbeck. She and McDonnell spend many a seemingly happy hour playing crib in The Boot. She will tell you that only recently she caught him moving – illicitly – two holes up the cribbage board when he thought she wasn't looking. But she was and she moved his peg two holes back. She will also tell you, m'lud, that she caught him trying to do the same thing two or three years ago and he made the same excuse. He said he had miscounted. I say, m'lud, that it was part of a deliberate conspiracy to defraud Vera Scrutton of her shilling stake in the game.

He can't have been caught every time he tried it on and, though a shilling may not be a fortune, m'lud, it is my contention that a shilling here and a shilling there over a very long lifetime amounts to a half-tidy few bob and I would argue that McDonnell saved up those ill-gotten shillings in order to launder them by treating his unsuspecting brood to a splendid supper. Thus, m'lud, does the rot set in until it spreads to the very highest levels of society.

I might add, m'lud, that at the end of that supper members of McDonnell's family were obliged to render considerable physical assistance in order to get him home and further massive effort was required to get him in to his bed. That's the sort of man he is, m'lud. I rest my case.

MATHS, CRIB AND DARTS

I HAVE had a flash of brilliant inspiration which, although it is too late to help the current crop of A-level students who already know their fate, will undoubtedly be of vast benefit to those who follow on.

It came to me when I read that the Campaign for Real Education claim that many A-level science students are unable to do the following sums: Add 16 to 24 without using a calculator and find two thirds of six.

Now, even I, as near to being innumerate as the average elderly tortoise, could make a decent fist of those two questions and it was while I was pondering what today's maths teachers actually teach that my wizard wheeze was born. The Ministry of Education might care to consider it forthwith.

It is this.Why not sack a few droves of our clearly educationally disadvantaged maths teachers and spend the savings on sending A-level students down to the pub every lunchtime. Therein, if it is a proper pub, they will find the simplest, most cost effective and foolproof instrument ever devised for the teaching of mental arithmetic.

It is called a dartboard. My thick and youthful brain was honed like a razor by the mathematical complexities of "marking" with lightning speed my opponent's score. In a twink I found myself able to glance at the board and work out instantly that if the three arrows were embedded in treble seventeen, single eighteen and double top it came to exactly one hundred and nine. Five hundred and one "up", starting and finishing on a double, is the most popular of dart games and even the thickest of local yokels knows immediately and automatically that if his score has reached, say, four hundred and twenty eight then its easy-peasy to get out with just two darts by whacking 'em into treble eleven and double top. Should he, by mischance, score a single twenty, his third dart must seek out the double ten. Complicated? Only if you have never played darts.

And while Form 4a is waiting its turn for the dartboard, they should ask the landlord to get the cribbage boards out. That splendid game may lack the stern, intellectual requirements of the dartboard but it still has its own numerical niceties and nuances.

Meanwhile, if the savings are sufficient, it might be a good idea to treat the youngsters to just a glass of mild beer while they are wrestling mentally with the complexities of the scoreboard. After all, learning how to drink in moderation is another part of growing up.

OLD AGE

TO be perfectly honest, frank, open and uncluttered by obfuscation I think it reasonable to state that there was not one of us sitting round the table by the fire one freezing night last week who was capable of winning a ten-yard sprint even if we started the day before and were mounted on high-powered motorbikes. I had popped into the White Lion in Newmarket to meet a few old (very old) chums for a natter and it must have been perfectly obvious to even the most casual observer that most of us were cantering slowly down the last furlong towards the finishing post. It was certainly obvious to Jovial Jim, the landlord, who bellowed as he brought the drinks that he very much hoped that none of us old codgers would be so inconsiderate as to pop our clogs whilst we were actually on his premises.

At which point I was smitten with a rare, nay, unique flash of inspiration. "Jim lad", said I, "since you have so little faith in the likely longevity of some of your customers why not turn the likelihood of their early demise to your own financial advantage?" Jovial Jim paused in mid-stride and his eyes lit up like Jubilee beacons as they always do when there is the slightest chance of coin of the realm finding its way into his jangling tills.

"Pray, good sir", he said, or words to that effect, "in what fashion might I turn the unfortunate decrepitude of some of my oldest and most valued customers to my own pecuniary benefit?"

I replied: "Simply affix a notice to the wall behind our table with a clear warning written upon it."

"What, good sir, should the warning say?"

I wrote it out for him there and then.

It said......... "As From Now Any Old Codger Who Dies On These Premises Will Be Charged CROAKAGE".

Jovial Jim laughed so much he damn nearly bought us a drink.

TWO LOVELIEST BAR LADIES IN THE KINGDOM

AS a clanger-dropper I must have been born at the very top of the belfry. With just one sloppy slip of the quill a couple of weeks ago I managed to incur the wrath of a vast swathe of former friends of mine throughout this green and pleasant region. All I did was to refer in this column to the many pleasures which come my way in life including that of having my libations in the Kings in Newmarket poured by THE TWO LOVELIEST BAR LADIES IN THE KINGDOM.

Clang, clang, clang. No sooner had those words appeared in the public print than I began to notice a distinct cooling of welcomes by ladies serving behind other bars in the many different hostelries wherein I am wont to pursue my research into the more esoteric behavioural systems of the villainous varmints I look upon as my friends.

For a short while I was mightily puzzled by the chill factor with which my appearance in many a previously cheery tavern was being greeted by what once were called serving wenches before they were promoted to barmaids and, even later, to bar ladies. It was only when a certain old and friendly potman took me quietly to one side in a busy and somewhat raucous beer-house in Cambridge and kindly pointed out to me the enormity of my latest clanger.

"Look, ol' son", quoth he, "I fear that with a few loose words in that ol' column of yourn you've managed to shoot yourself in both feet. I hear talk that there are landladies and serving girls all over this area threatening to ban you from crossing their thresholds ever agin. This one in 'ere swears she'll never talk to you agin. She reckons you've told her many a time that she's the loveliest serving lady in the land and then she goos and reads that bit in yer ol' paper about them two gels in Newmarket. You won't need no ice in yer gin if she serves yah."

I tried to explain that over the years I had slipped into the unfortunate habit of disseminating terminological inexactitudes and that occasionally I was guilty of, well, a slight degree of exaggeration so that whenever I ordered a drink I found it impossible not to say what a pleasure and privilege it was to be served by the loveliest bar lady in the country. I had been at it for donkeys years and it was meant more as a pleasantry than as a statement sworn on oath in front of a bench of HM's judges. Anyoldhow, says I, they couldn't all believe me because at least two of 'em have got faces like Waffen SS troopers whose parachutes failed to open. I think he said something about leaving that bit out of the paper but being deaf I didn't quite catch his gist.

Well, there we are. Or, rather, there I am and as far as serving ladies are concerned I would appear to be caught between a rock and a hard place. All I can do is to plead guilty to something or other and to assure you one and all what a pleasure and privilege it always is to be served by.........

But then you all know that bit off by heart.

THE DEMISE OF 'THE BOOT'

UPON reflection I suppose we all knew that the end was nigh but when the death sentence was pronounced it was done so in a savage and barbarous fashion.

At lunch time The Boot at Dullingham was its usual jolly self with nary a hint of what was to come the very next morning. The pub's darts and cribbage teams were in the middle of their season, the quiz team was gearing itself up for its next encounter and the lads of the village soccer and cricket teams assumed their favourite watering hole would still be around to welcome them before and after their games.

In mid-afternoon the brewery telephoned and told the temporary manager and manageress, a most amiable couple, that they would be leaving the following morning when the pub would be boarded up and closed. There had been no visit from a brewery representative, no message to the parish council and, worst of all, not so much as a single word of gratitude for the regulars' loyalty over many decades or regret or explanation at the necessity to close down this pub overnight.

There are those, of course, who are not pub-goers, who will be unable to understand the intense sense of loyalty which a pub, especially a village pub, inspires in its regulars. There is more than loyalty – there is a fondness for the place and for the other customers, a sense of delightful anticipation before a visit and a feeling of pleasurable satisfaction afterwards.

It is impossible to be either miserable or lonely in a village pub which has to be the most democratic of institutions wherein no social barrier is permitted to exist. Squire and labourer stand equal before the bar. Pub regulars become members of a family except that in this family there are no petty squabbles, no awkward jealousies and certainly no paltry rivalries – except maybe on cribbage table or dartboard. A proper pub, like The Boot, creates close bonds and deep, life-long friendships.

Thus, inevitably, when a pub closes so also do personal relationships become disentangled. When the meeting place goes so then do the meetings. At The Boot I was an outsider for I do not live in the village but because of The Boot I became a part of the community. Where now shall I meet and drink with ol' George Gentleman who first went to the pub eighty years ago for a haircut and has been going back for the beer just about every day since? Where will I bump into ol' Larry McDonnell, that gentle giant of an Irishman who never harmed a creature in his life except for rather a lot of Germans when he was in the Guards during the war? I could go on. But more importantly where will these friends and all the others who have been enjoying the pub for generations meet now? And – just as importantly – where will the younger generation of the village learn the subtle art of pubmanship?

There is, to be fair, another pub in the village that is noted in the region for its fine meals but it has to be said that this one is no longer a traditional village inn of The Boot variety.

No! The day Greene King murdered that lovely little pub they took the heart out of a community and their unnecessarily brutal way of closing it down left behind a simmering pool of resentment in the village. Their loyal customers deserved better. Much, much better.

Greene King's argument is that the pub was no longer viable though many of us find that extremely difficult to understand and the villagers feel that the old place had been deliberately allowed to decay so that it can now be replaced with a highly profitable building site. But are brewers in the business of selling their products or selling their outlets? Difficult to do both, I would have thought. Trouble is it appears this particular brewery is rather keener on the latter than the former.

Anyoldhow, I was there the night before the boards went up and somehow I wish I hadn't been. It was rather like shaking the hand of a dying chum whose death has been hastened by a disinterested doctor. Farewell, dear ol' Boot. Many of us will not see the likes of you again.

THE RE-BORN 'BOOT'

KINDLY hearken to some good news. You may recall the deep sense of despair and outrage felt by many of us and chronicled by me in these pages when overnight the brewers Greene King closed down that splendid little village pub The Boot at Dullingham. You may also recall the delight and relief we felt when, after a prolonged battle with the brewery, the pub was finally re-opened as a free house by villager Kevin McDonnell and his lovely wife Dianne. The re-opening was not just a victory for that village alone. It showed what can be done when determined locals rebel against arbitrary decisions made by powerful commercial interests to the detriment of seemingly powerless rural communities.

So what is the good news now? Simply this. Some seven months after the pub's rescue and resuscitation Kevin and his missus are doing a roaring trade. The pub's un-boarded windows are again shiny with welcoming cheer. Places in the darts and cribbage teams are eagerly sought after, pub outings – including one to Paris for the great Arc de Triomphe race – are oversubscribed. Herein the villagers meet to plan their celebrations for the Queen's Jubilee, young families gather here for laughter's sake, courting couples tryst shyly here and ancient codgers who thought The Boot and part of their lives had gone for ever – George Gentleman, Larry McDonnell and that outsider Mike Jeacock – just sit and smile at their good fortune at being brought together again by the grit and courage of Kevin and Dianne.

Yes! The good news, the splendid news, is that a village which last year thought its heart had been ripped out is now fully restored to health, thank 'ee kindly. Other similarly threatened villages please note. And that goes for the Chairman and Board of Greene King too.

TIME GENTLEMEN, PLEASE

SO now the government plans to allow pubs to stay open 24 hours a day. Spoilsports, say I. Bang goes another glorious English tradition – that of enjoying an illicit drink at a time of day prohibited by law. What these mini-minded ministers of ours cannot understand is that us peasants only really enjoy ourselves when we are tweaking the nose of authority whenever it pokes itself into our affairs. By far the tastiest pint is that pulled in a darkened cellar by a landlord who has not only called "last orders please" but has locked his regulars into the pub until he decides to let 'em out again .

If there is no battle between "us" and "them" half the fun goes out of life. That's why lads scrump apples from the squire's orchard – the thrill of climbing his wall while he's having an afternoon zizz in the Big House makes the apple taste all the sweeter. That's also why the lads' dads sometimes slip out of the house on a moonless night to filch one of his lordship's pheasants – a poached bird is always gamier than one from the butcher.

And that's why I wish our nanny state had left our pub hours alone because after-hours drinking was just about the very last refuge for your average harmless, fun-seeking scoundrel.

This, you must understand, is a subject upon which I speak with a huge degree of experience for I was introduced to the art of supping ale in a candle-lit bar by my father who spent many long hours practising in the snug of The Crispin Inn in Great Longstone up in Derbyshire where he was then the village bobby. It comforted the village men who drank with him to know that the local upholder of the law was aiding and abetting them to break it. The men always gave him a little cheer when he walked in for a pint after time – especially when he was in uniform.

WHAT WILL HAPPEN NOW?

THE announcement I am about to make will change the lifestyles of many of my friends. And not, alas, for the better. I HAVE BECOME A TEETOTALLER.

I apologise for the shock which this news will bring to those who run pubs, clubs, restaurants and such like hereabouts and to those who believed their savings were safely invested in brewing and distillers shares. I should warn you one and all – once the realisation of the side effects of my decision to abandon the demon drink sinks in, publicans and vintners can forget their dreams of early retirement and shares in the alcohol section of the economy will plummet.

For nigh on sixty years I served the drinks industry to the very best of my not inconsiderable talents. Indeed, some might have argued that my zest in keeping afloat the fortunes of sundry declining Kentish hop farmers, half-skint maltsters and idle Froggie vignerons went far beyond the call of duty.

It all began as a lad when I first discovered the delights of deep draughts of warm ale from bottles with marble stoppers shared with the farmers in the harvest hayfields. Then came mild ales cooled in the limestone cellar of my father's Derbyshire pub. There was bitter beer for us young soldiers at a shilling a pint, twenty pints to the quid. But it was from the pinnacles of Fleet Street where I caught the first sight of all the true glories of the drinking man's world.

There, with the stintless aid of Lord Beaverbrook' s over-generous expenses allowances, we journalists granted ourselves the manifold privileges of discovering the niceties and nuances of the world's most exquisite wines, cognacs, single malts, liqueurs, vintage ports and, always, the very best examples of the brewer's art. It was a spectacular apprenticeship and very soon I became an accepted master of the craft – a delicious craft which was to provide me with daily delights thereafter. Until now.

I have not been converted by a flashing and heavenly light. This cou1d hardly be the case since I have always believed firmly that grape, hop and malt could only have been designed by a profoundly generous and understanding deity. Nope! The fact is that I have been more than somewhat under the weather recently and the goodly denizens of Addenbrooke's Hospital have been busy scanning me and probing my interior from every known direction and by the time you are reading this the medical judges will have handed down their verdict. Now since all quacks insist their patients give up something I thought I would pre-empt 'em. They can't get at me with dire warnings about smoking because I abandoned my sixty-fags-a-day habit over forty years ago. I am not aware that my few remaining pleasures are particularly health-threatening. Book collecting seems fairly lacking in dangerous overtones, decapitating an occasional dead rose is hardly arduous and following the gee-gees is only heart attack territory when you back a winner. I'm on very safe turf there.

I have only two regrets. One is that the soft drinks industry has yet to invent a potion which can be drunk with any degree of pleasure in quantity and over a long period. I still frequent my old watering holes but I defy anyone to enjoy more than a couple of bottles of sweet fruit juices, tomato juice or that foul and dreadful Coke. Secondly, I am saddened by the thought of all those in the drinks industry whose dreams of an early escape to some sun-kissed villa were based on my continuing intemperate extravagances. Go and drown your sorrows my friends.

MONEY I DON'T SPEND ANY MORE

AS a new born teetotaller I find my spending money is not disappearing at the same rate of knots as in former bibulous times. So much so that when I popped into The Boot at Dullingham for a glass of ginger ale and a natter with old still-boozing mates, Kevin, the landlord, inquired morosely what I was doing with all the money I was no longer spending on his many and varied alcoholic offerings?

More to the point, landlord, said I, what are you doing WITHOUT all the money I am no longer spending with you? Kevin muttered something under his breath and whilst I didn't quite catch it I think I sensed its meaning.

Jack the Flaming Cat

OUR NEW KITTEN

THERE are few more divisive creatures than cats. There is no room for esoteric marginal discussions about the little varmints – you are for or agin 'em, besotted or, like me, more than somewhat ambivalent about them. The division of feelings for them extends into this very household and therefore you may be more than somewhat surprised – as, indeed, I was – to learn that we now have a kitten.

The children plotted together and presented it – him – to Herself, a cat-lady if ever there was one. Thus, before I could utter a syllable of protest, the grisly deed was done and where until recently there was a calm, well-ordered home inhabited only by us two ancients and where little happened to disturb the general air of peace and contentment there is now an intruder of such devilish bad manners and impish inclinations that idle relaxation has become impossible.

Brought up as I was in a world of disciplined working dogs I find the unbridled indiscipline of this tiny bundle of hurtling fur difficult to comprehend never mind contain. Therefore, whenever I hear the dread crash of another dislodged ornament I point the finger of accusation not at the offending animal but at Herself because, as I point out with unassailable logic, it is her damned kitten not mine.

Where do they find their energy? The kittens, that is. Not the grannies. Skittering, scampering, climbing, jumping, rolling, clinging and forever scratching. Every curtain is a new mountain to climb, every table a plateau to be explored, cushions are enemies to be attacked with needle-like claws. Herself's dang-blasted kitten is the very Sherpa Tensing of felines with no fear of heights and he prefers to dislodge books from the shelves' summits rather than those down in the foothills.

Already he has scattered my collection of clay pipes so that some lie inaccessible behind our old oak chest. He sent the only photo of my father in his Grenadier's uniform flying as he skidded across the polished surface of my desk.

At which point he pulled himself up somewhat sharpish because he found himself face to face with a prize example of the taxidermist's art. Facing my desk is a stuffed sparrow hawk. I watched the kitten as it surveyed the raptor's fiendish beak and vicious talons. Here, he said to himself, is something to be reckoned with. After a careful – and distant – inspection, the kitten decided that the strange, menacing bird was, after all, innocent enough and tapped it playfully. Then he gave it a good belt around the head at which point I put an end to the game – for two reasons.

Firstly I didn't wish to see my hawk damaged. Secondly, that kitten might get away with bullying a long-dead sparrow hawk but things will be rather different if ever he comes face to face with one on the wing in the wild and the sooner he learns not to mess with them the better for him.

Now here is a strange situation. After spending a lifetime despising cats for their moral inferiority to dogs (did anyone ever see a cat display fearless devotion and sheer unadulterated loyalty towards its mistress / master? I rather think not) I am suddenly beginning to see them in a completely new light. It is all the fault of Herself's kitten. I will tell you something which I wouldn't dream of admitting in public but I am becoming besotted by it. This little creature may never drag me to safety from a raging torrent or keep burglars at bay but I'm sorry to have to admit that he is bringing a new and pleasurable element into my life. Welcome aboard you pesky little devil.

And, no, he hasn't been named. The grandchildren have been asked for their ideas. That in itself was not a good idea. The one with the winning choice will be delighted; the other nine will be disappointed. The law is about to be laid down. It may be Herself's kitten but I will name it, so there!

NAMING THE CAT

AS head of this vast tribe of ours my every wish is a command and every command unquestionably obeyed. Naturally, therefore, I assumed that I would decide upon the name for Herself's new kitten and no ifs and buts about it.

I brushed aside with a firm hand and hard heart (easy after years of practice) all the juvenile suggestions of the grandchildren and the wily urgings of our daughters and announced my decision thus: the beast, I decreed, would be known henceforth as "Spawn of Dracula" on account of its clearly inherited desire to sink its tiny talons into my neck the very moment I fall into a deep kip in my favourite armchair.

My perfectly reasonable order clearly found little favour among the ranks and murmurings of dissent could be detected.

Herself, for example, accepted the logic attached to the name but felt that it was, well, perhaps, a bit on the long side and lacking in Christian charity. After all, the poor little creature could not be responsible for its historical antecedents. And, anyway, when in due course we started to call it in from the garden of an evening, the neighbours would think we really had flipped our lids this time, good and proper. Could I envisage her standing at the door shouting: "Come on in puss. Where are you little Spawn of Dracula? Time for supper."

Well, to be fair for once, I admitted that it was a somewhat difficult scene to envisage and, weakly, I offered to negotiate a compromise. I would, I said, accept the use of its initial letters only.

Her steady gaze bore all the dangerous hallmarks of incipient insurrection. No, quoth Herself. She would not, absolutely not, stand at the door of an evening shouting: "Time for beddy-byes. Come to mummy, you little SO-."

At this very point I was informed that, anyoldhow, the family had already decided to call him Jack and bad luck about the scars on my neck.

(Before the Council for the Promulgation of Political Correctness sends a platoon of stormtroopers over to teach me how to behave towards my family I should explain that all this talk of being in command is a case of the purest wishful thinking. The man has yet to be born who can marry, produce three daughters out of four children, end up with eight granddaughters out of ten grandchildren and still believe for a nano-second that he is anything other than under a permanent female thumb. My lot are cunning with it. They make a decision and somehow convince me I thought of it in the first place. Thus it won't be long before they will say how clever it was of me to name the kitten Jack).

THE TRILBY

I AM trying to hit the computer keyboard correctly without the use of my right forefinger which has been rendered ineffectual on account of the gash inflicted upon it by Herself's dang-blasted new addition to our household, Jack the Kit. These are the very last words I shall write about our vicious little kitten because I suspect that all the publicity I have given him recently has gone to his head and led him to the mistaken impression that he is the leading lad round here and not me, that his wishes are my command instead of t'other way round and that the slightest remonstrance from me will result in a swift scratch.

Not only, therefore, am I obliged to type with a plaster covering the hole in my finger but also, of an evening, I must perforce sit in my favourite armchair wearing a hat.

I should explain. Many years ago I bought a great, tall-backed, winged armchair of Georgian vintage at a posh auction sale in Cambridge. Buried in its cavernous depths I have enjoyed countless evenings down the years protected by its vastness from draughts and the inanities of female chatter. Therein, cocooned in blissful isolation, I read book or journal until drowsiness overcomes me and, unnoticed by others in the room, I slide into that blissful state which passeth all understanding – otherwise known as the armchair kip.

Not any longer. Jack the Kit waits until my eyes close and then climbs up onto the high back of the chair. I have a bald pate. It fascinates The Beast. He extends those sharp things which cats have on the end of their feet and dabs at the barren wastes of my bonce. There are three immediate consequences. I wake up in pain. I shout at the beast. The assembled company falls about helpless with laughter.

Granddaughter Lydia came up with the answer. She kindly fetched my battered old brown racing trilby from the hall stand and bade me wear it for protection. It works perfectly and The Beast has lost interest in my cranial environs. But it makes me feel like an absolute twit.

KITTENS FOR COMPANY

FOUND myself confined to barracks for a day or two last week due to a malady which lingers on. My confinement taught me an important lesson. For much of the time, as Herself whizzed round Cambridge in her capacity as a Tourist Guide, I was alone with only Jack the Kitten for company. To put it bluntly I am far from being besotted by the pesky creature. However, much as I dislike having to admit it, his constant acrobatic clowning, his endless purring concern for my plight and the apparent devotion which he displayed as he followed me whenever I moved to a different room, gave me considerable pause for thought. Mayhap, after all, cats are not the useless varmints I have always thought them to be.

And the lesson I learned? Never before had I realised just how important a part pets must play in the lives of the lonely, the elderly and the housebound. Thank you Jack for teaching me that and stop climbing those damn curtains when I'm talking to you.

VISIT TO THE VET

MANY thanks to those of you who assure us that Jack the Kitten will calm down as he gets older. Actually, he calmed down considerably all of a sudden last week. Maybe it had something to do with a visit to the vet. Jack is no longer the lad he was.

JACK'S FIRST SPOT

FORGIVE me, but I am just a tad tired of being asked by complete strangers how that dang-blasted cat of ours, Jack, is getting on. It seems that if I don't mention him for a couple of weeks half the population round here gets twitchy. Well, he's mature enough to speak for himself so the remainder of this column is his. I'm off to The Boot.

Jack's Spot: Hi there, pussy-huggers! The guv'nor, as he likes to think of himself, is in another of his moods and I put it down to a touch of jealousy because readers worry about me more than they do about him so he's decided that now and again I can have a corner of his column all to myself in which I can say just what I feel like saying and let me tell you he'll live to regret it. He's written some very nasty things about me just because he didn't realise that kittens like to be skittish, swinging from curtains, climbing the furniture and suchlike and anyway I never meant to hurt him when I scratched his bald head while he was having a kip in his armchair.

To begin with he's not the guv'nor hereabouts anyway – Herself is and after half a century of marriage you would think he might have noticed that by now but as She says he's not the brightest star in the firmament. Anyway, thanks for thinking about me and please don't worry because I've found myself a very cushy billet here despite the old man's whingeing and whining which is all gas and gaiters because I know he likes me really. He even slips me some little fishy biscuits as a treat when Herself isn't looking and though I can't stand the damn things I humour him by forcing 'em down.

I've palled up with a mangy-looking local moggy which comes a-visiting and though she's got a face like the back end of an orang-utang I'm in no position to be choosy following my recent trip to the vet. I dread to think what she will do when she learns my little secret. Why not find out in my next ***"Jack's Spot"***?

THE GUV HITS HIS HEAD

Jack's Spot: The "guv'nor" (ho! ho!) was in a bad mood when he went to the races and he was even worse when he came back, miserable old twit. Herself advises me not to push my luck and although everybody knows he is a miserable old twit I shouldn't say it in public. So I won't. I was telling you last week about my budding romance with that frazzle-furred, ill-kempt moggie who started calling on me. Haven't seen her for a few days. Suspect the word has gone round about my operation and the other local moggs say she's definitely not into platonic relationships. Please herself. Never liked the look of her anyway. She's lumbered with a flat, pug-nosed fizzog and is as skinny as a piece of cotton. Looks as though she's just been wrung through a mangle. Good riddance. Mine's the bachelor life from now on, me hearties.

The old man bent down quickly to give me some grub and banged his bonce on a door handle. Now he's got a hole in his forehead he didn't have before. You should have heard him! I couldn't understand his language but I got the general drift. I let out a loud purr which he mistook for one of sympathy. He told me not to worry because it wasn't my fault. Poor fool didn't realise the purr was the feline equivalent of a great big belly laugh. Cor, he did look daft. Blood dripped off his nose, he trod in my food tray, tripped over my water bowl, couldn't find the Elastoplast and still thought I was feeling sorry for him. Talk about purr! Haven't purred so much in all my life.

SACKED

Jack's Spot: I've been sacked! Summarily dismissed! The guv'nor (ho! ho!) ordered me to clear me desk, hop on me bike and skedaddle. And all because last week I called him a miserable old twit. He says that even if he is a MOT – and notice that he takes care not to deny it – there is absolutely no call for me to mention it in the public print. He points out that he holds certain views about the Editor but he doesn't blurt 'em out at every given opportunity. Furthermore, he told me, when he said I could write in my ***"Spot"*** what I liked, I should have realised that he meant what HE liked.

So there we are. Cut off in my prime – for the second time in my short life, come to think of it – just as I was beginning to enjoy the glamour that goes with the job. For two glorious weeks I was the most famous cat within half a mile. Now it's back to the scrap heap with not so much as a last week's fish head for redundancy. But maybe it's not all over yet. Herself has been speaking to him in words of one syllable which even he might understand and "old twit" has passed her lips a number of times. I have a powerful ally. Watch this space.

Cheers for now and here's hoping, ***Jack***

SACKED FOREVER

CAT lovers will look in vain for ***"Jack's Spot"*** at the tail, so to speak, of this column, because when I sacked Jack the Cat as my editorial assistant last week I did so on a permanent basis. He had overstepped the bounds of my paternalistic patience and, anyway, he was rapidly becoming too damn popular not only for his own good but, more importantly, for mine. A modicum of meekly delivered competition was acceptable, even understandable, from one so young but when it was delivered in conjunction with powerful vituperation and a degree of personal malice all aimed unerringly at me I knew it was action time. That is why I yelled "Out damned ***Spot***! Out, I say!" just like Macbeth did when he was enraged by a stubborn haggis stain on his sporran.

Even in his brief career as a feline hack Jack attracted far too many fans for my liking. I didn't get where I am today without recognising a dangerous opponent when I see one and here was I, nurturing a viper to my bosom as he tried to claw me in the back. Another couple of weeks and he'd have taken over the whole flaming column allowing me a slim paragraph at the end under ***"Mike's Corner"***. Anyoldhow, I am a man of iron will and inflexible determination. Jack is out. OUT. End of story. Meanwhile, excuse me please. Herself wishes to discuss something with me. I can hear Jack purring loudly. I don't like the look of this.

SHEPHERD'S PIE

SINCE I sacked Jack the Cat as assistant columnist Herself has not been herself, so to speak. I have few pleasures available to me these days but her Special Shepherd's Pie is top of the list. She hasn't made one since I put the boot in. When I questioned her I swear the damn cat guffawed. There is blackmail a-foot, or, indeed, a-paw.

OUTWITTED

SOME really bad, stomach-churning, horrendous news – I have been outwitted, out-manoeuvred, out-bullied, out-foxed, out-bluffed by the Dreadful Duo – Herself and the flaming cat Jack. I admit humbly and publicly it was a moment of madness when I banned him from this column and although I expected some domestic flak (which, God knows, I got) I had grossly underestimated the strength of his supporting battalions among the readership. Honestly! You'd have thought his name was Man U. Anyoldhow, he's back and you can have him. He can write what he damn-well likes and I hope he slips on a rotting fish-head. I'm off racing.

Jack's Spot: Hi, again, pussy-huggers. Just a brief reappearance to say "thanks" one and all. Herself warned me not to gloat. He hates gloaters. Treat him gently, she said. He's not the man he was. I have me doubts. He dug a hole for a hosta this morning and I swear he was measuring me up. So far he doesn't know I knocked his rotten pot over. Not a word otherwise my name is Hosta. A bigger tail piece next week, huggers, when he's over the shock.

Cheers, thanks and ta-ra for now. ***Jack***

LAND OF HOPE AND GLORY

Jack's Spot: The local cats are seething with envy because I am back in the print again. How they sneered and ignored me when I was given the old heave-ho by "the guv'nor" a few weeks ago. As though I care! What an absolute shower they are; ill-kempt, bog-ignorant, morally bankrupt, low-born alley-cats the lot of 'em. Shameless, they are. Rather stay out all night than curl up at home listening, as I do, to the Old Man playing "Land of Hope and Glory" as he marches up and down in his pyjamas waving a little Union Jack before he goes to bed. I find it very comforting. He tells me I should thank my lucky stars for being a born and bred English moggie. Enough of that, though. Herself says that he is very politically incorrect and warns me not to copy him when he talks about Frogs, Wops, the Hun, Fuzzy-Wuzzies (he reads a lot of Rudyard Kipling!) and the like otherwise the Feline Thought Police will drag me off to Brussels to be "re-indoctrinated" which, she says, somebody should have done to him years ago. Funny ol' house this. Nice to be back.

Cheers all, ***Jack***

SSHHH, IT'S A SECRET

Jack's Spot: I promised last week to tell you something I know the Guv wouldn't like you to hear about. Well, us journalists must be fearless in the pursuit of truth so here goes. Feigning a deep kip in his armchair I earwigged a conversation he had with Herself. You'll never believe it! I distinctly heard him say it really was time for him to learn about E-mails. He would do it, he said, on condition the general public wasn't told otherwise his cover as a throw-back to a useless 18th century dilettante would be blown. Herself laughed and I had to stifle my chortles. "You don't even know how to use your mobile phone", she said. That, he shouted, was because he was deaf and couldn't hear the damn thing when it went off. She said he couldn't hear it because he kept it in a drawer in his desk and anyway he never switched it on. Would she, he asked through gritted teeth (they were either gritted or he had lockjaw), or would she not teach him about flaming E-mails? Now he was not only gritting but grinding and I skedaddled sharpish into the garden. Thunder was rumbling round their dining table. But I definitely heard him use the E-word, mateys. I heard him.

Ho-ho, tara and cheers. ***Jack***

A FAN LETTER!

Jack's Spot: Hi there friendly fans! Hope you don't mind my informal greeting but I feel we are all getting better acquainted. In fact, I know we are because (pause here for deep breath) – I HAVE STARTED GETTING FAN MAIL. I won't go into detail about the kind lady from Ely who says she reads my words of pearly wisdom before the Guv's guff. I wouldn't like him to know that. He is easily hurt. I also had a letter from Mr Jimmy Fielding of Sawtry addressed, would you believe, to Jack the Cat.Yes! Me personally. He says he is really enjoying reading "my spot" each week and urges me to keep up "the good work". Ho! ho! ho! and how about that then? He even sent me a very funny short story he has written about their own cat's mouse-catching adventures. I'm sure it's a grand cat but I don't like sharing the limelight. It can shove off and find its own column. But fan mail! Methinks I need my own headed writing paper.

Cheers and thanks, fans.Yours in seventh heaven, ***Jack the Cat***.

MY BOOK

Jack's Spot: Greetings Fans! I think I'm on the verge of something really big about which I will forthwith acquaint you. The local moggies and I had just finished caterwauling practice (a bit like your choir practice) behind the dustbins the other midnight when the assembled gang – in addition to us peasant pussies we've got aristocats, a Manx, a Siamese, a Russian Blue, an Angora and a Chinchilla with a fine falsetto following his operation – paused to rest the old vocal chords. We are perfecting a new version of "Cats on the Rooftops, Cats on the Tiles" with which to enthral the locals come the autumn but that's by-the-by. The Manx with the inch-long tail spoke for the others and addressed me thus: "Jack we are proud of you. Your incredible rise up the journalistic ladder brings glory upon the whole of our tribe and we salute you. But we want more from you. We want you to write a book." Well fans. I was so shocked, so thrilled I nearly dropped my fish-head. "Your book will be unique", said Molly Manx, "so it must have an eye-catching title, something truly original." I smiled like the true professional writer I am. I was already prepared. Casually I offered: "Success Is But a Cat's Whisker Away" or "Tails From the Dustbin" and "In Life to Paws is to Lose". I left them gawping at my brilliance. The Literary Committee meets behind the bins at number 12 next Friday midnight. Move over Harry Potter.

Yours aye, ***Jack the Cat***.

HE REALLY DOES LIKE ME

Jack's Spot: It is high time to put the record straight especially for those who, I gather, are slightly worried about the relationship between the Guvnor and me. He has made his feelings for me quite plain ever since I arrived here. We got off to a bad start due to my kittenish high spirits. Dammit (I learned that from him) I didn't mean to upset him. Just because I clawed a red line down his bald pate in a playful moment when he was having a kip in his armchair there was no call for a fit of bad temper. Actually, I thought the scar was rather fetching. And when I dug my claws into his shirt the time I jumped on him in the garden how was I to know it was his back I was clinging onto? He pretends to dislike me so much he even refuses to read what I write in "our" column. But Herself was away, grandchild-hopping at the weekend, leaving us alone together. He spent ages playing with me, teasing me with a ball of string at bedtime and never shouted one rude word to me while she was away. So – don't believe a word he says about me. He's just an old fraud, a soppy hypocrite.

So, tara again.Your chum, ***"I'm Alright" Jack***.

BACKING HORSES

THAT flaming Jack the Cat is becoming financially unviable hereabouts. Last week I backed a nag called "The Cat's Whiskers" in his honour.Yes. Quite. Tried to get my money back on "One Cool Cat". You need not ask. Flaming cat.

Jack's Spot: You may not believe this but the Guv'nor is now blaming me for his appalling skill in picking winners on the turf. How the hell (I learned that from him) can I be blamed because two donkeys with vague feline connections in their nomenclatures cost him a few jimmy-o-goblins? Anyway, he's upset for another reason. Herself (my protectress) is a Blue Badge Tourist Guide of great renown. Last week she was conducting some members of Huntingdon WI and their husbands on a punting-ghost tour in Cambridge and they asked her if she was Jack the Cat's mummy? Not, you may note, was she the wife of that Michael Jeacock? All they said about him was that he was very rude to me and should be ashamed of himself. When Herself told him he laughed. But it was a hollow laugh, filled more with envy than mirth. He's jealous.

Cheers All. With a Hey and a Ho and a Hey Nonny Nonny No, your chum, ***Jack the Cat***.

THE CHAIR

Jack's Spot: Greetings friends, fans and, in the Guv'nor's case, foes.

Promised you a domestic secret this week. You will scarcely believe it. I mean, how can a mature (and I mean mature) married couple like Herself and Himself get into such a tiswas over an innocent little creature like me. It's all down to that damn chair in the Ol' Man's study. He finally came round to letting me have a turn in it. Well, he comes home from the races last week clearly bereft of the spondulicks and in a mood I should have recognised. I am in the chair. "Enough", he shouts, "is damn-well enough. Sharing the best kipping chair in the house is one thing. Having it permanently purloined by a flaming cat is another", and forthwith tips me out. Herself, ever defensive, says quietly: "Just buy another chair and you can have one each."

Even I think that's a bit OTT. "There isn't room", he hisses. Now she's trapped him. "At the last count there were over 1,000 books in this room, more pewter beer mugs than in Georgian London, enough stuffed birds in Victorian glass cases to populate a forest and sufficient old assegais on the walls to start a new Zulu war. Get rid of some of that lot and there would be room for another chair, a small billiard table, a chaise longue and a life-size portrait of Bessie Braddock."

Now he is practising hurling those spears at a target in the garden. It's a cardboard box the size of, er, well, a maturing cat. Every time he pins it to the lawn he cackles. I've gone off that chair completely.

Your apprehensive chum, ***Jack the Cat***.

LOST WEDDING RING

Jack's Spot: A touch of title-tattle from the dining table for your delectation, chums and fans. It was Their wedding anniversary the other day and I'm still trying to ferret out how far back their maelstrom of a marriage goes. When I've had a crafty shufty at the wedding certificate I'll let you know. Anyway, a week or two back Herself lost her wedding ring. Very upset, she was, so being an ol' romantic, he gave her a new one for the anniversary. His marital devotion is nothing if not touching. On the card he wrote: "This is your second and final chance." Lovely, I thought.

Cheers and tally-ho! ***Jack the Cat***.

SOLO APPEARANCE

Jack's Spot: I am about to impart the most fabulantastic piece of news. You won't believe it but 'tis true! 'tis true! One day I shall have the whole of this column all to myself. I am awash with excitement and breath-stopping anticipation. Let me explain. The Guv' wasn't feeling too well the other day. (This doesn't mean too much since Herself says that if he coughs once it's pneumonia and twice it's deadly Avian Flu). Anyway he's a stickler for tying up the loose ends. He phoned the editor and I heard him actually say that when he (The Guv, not the editor) slips off to the great racecourse in the sky how about handing over to the cat since all the damned fan mail coming this way was addressed not to him (the Guv), but to me. Fantasmographically the editor agreed!!!! Seems tons of readers have had the same idea. I can hardly wait. His every cough is music to my sharp little ears.

Tally-ho you lucky lot. ***Jack the Cat, Wordsmith***.

HELP WITH OUR CHOIR

Jack's Spot: My shock announcement last week that I shall be the sole author of this column when the Guv' finally kicks the bucket has been greeted with ecstatic approbation by all my moggie mates. One of 'em summed the exciting prospect up precisely. "This", he said, "will show the world the literary excellence what us cats are capable of." I could not have put it better myself. Alas, there is a nasty hiccup in the scheme. The Guv' has taken a distinct turn for the better. He's got an army reunion coming up and he'll hang on for that if it kills him, so to speak. And he's planning to renew his Annual Members' Badge for next year's racing at Newmarket. In fact, the immediate future is looking ominously cheerful. Still, all we can do is keep our paws crossed and pray for the worst. Meanwhile I'm having great trouble with my choir of caterwaulers. I am seeking a perfect rendition of "Cats on the Rooftops, Cats on the Tiles" with which to regale the neighbourhood through the long winter nights ahead. At the last caterwauling practise I realised we hadn't a single deep voice amongst us. Most of us toms are victims of visits to the vet and one or two were clearly never intended by nature for fatherhood. Thus the choir has a distinct tonal imbalance. Bass tomcats required p.d.q. No previous experience needed.

Please help your mate ***Jack the Cat***.

THEY'VE LEFT ME

Jack's Spot: Without so much as by-my-leave they are consigning me to a cat's home for a few days while they toddle off up north for some sort of re-union nonsense. Doubtless Himself and his muckers from the middle of the last century will sit around moaning about the rigours of warm NAAFI beer and cold Cornish pasties – the latter, apparently, being the name they gave to the local talent down in deepest Bodmin where they were a-servin' of 'er Majesty the Queen. I think he's gone a bit doolally because he spends most evenings either shining the toes of his black weddings-and-funerals shoes by spitting on the polish and rubbing it round in little circles or ironing his Intelligence Corps tie. Herself is highly amused and when she says that Military Intelligence must be the original contradiction in terms he just mutters long Russian words under his breath which I suspect are very, very rude.

I do hope the other cats in the home are of a suitable social standing.

Yours in High Dudgeon, ***Jack the Cat***.

BACK FROM THE CATTERY

Jack's Spot: I think they were pleased to see me again when they collected me from the cattery after their weekend away – Herself was all over me, cooing and cuddling but with the Guv' you can never tell. He wears the same grumpy expression whether he's backed a winner or a loser. I was slightly disappointed, however. They didn't bring me a pressie, not so much as a small jar of those renowned Cheshire fish heads would you believe? I'd heard about Cheshire cats and I hoped they might bring me a bit of whatever it is that makes them grin all the time but they didn't so I still don't know what they all find so funny. At least the Ol' Man didn't kick me out of our mutual Kipping Chair in his study when we all got home. Sat at his desk instead and talked to me. He likes this because I've learned not to answer back and tell him what twaddle he talks. I could tell he was thinking about his old comrades because he looked at me and said: "Jack-me-Lad – our fires are crackled out now and will never burn again. But how they blazed, Jack, when we were lads; my word, how they blazed." Then, blow-me-down, he tickled me as he walked into the garden, smiling. Funny bloke. Tough as leather outside, soft as saddle soap within.

Yours, puzzled, ***Jack the Cat***.

ONE THING LESS TO WORRY ABOUT

Jack's Spot: Phew! That's a big worry out of the way. You'd be surprised just how many of us poor cats are stressed out by dreading what happens to us when we are left alone. I don't mean for an evening, or a day or two but when, to put it not too finely, The Providers eventually kick the dustbin? Herself and the Guvnor are no longer in the cradle of youth, unlike me, and though the Ol' Man can be a bit of a pain in the haunch the Ol' Gel manages to prod him into being reasonably understanding of my little foibles so life with 'em isn't too awful. But intimations of mortality lurk in this household so the worry lingers. But no longer. Their Number One daughter Sarah and her two darling little daughters dropped in over the weekend. I earwigged Victoria whispering to Mummy: "If they die before Jack can he come and live with us please?" Oh! What a blissful thought! What relief!... And Victoria and Emily and Jack the Cat lived happily together ever after...Whoopee, fans, that's me sorted out.

Cheers and now I don't care if it snows or freezes. Yours hugely relieved, ***Jack the Cat***.

NEVER GIVE UP LIFE'S PLEASURES

Jack's Spot: Herself went off to a weekend conference leaving me slightly apprehensive – well, you know what he can be like without her restraining and calming presence. Actually he was fine spending all three days racing at Newmarket and from his unusually amicable attitude he obviously backed a few winners. After three days cheering the nags he developed a wheezy chest and complained he had never felt really well since he gave up smoking sixty Senior Service a day over forty years back. "Jack-me-Lad", he said, "never give up any of life's major pleasures. It ain't worth it." Chance would be nice, methought. Life's great pleasures are destined to pass me by. That sad trip to the vet's when I was but a lad put a sudden stop to my ambitions in that direction and when did you last see a moggie with a fag in its fizzog? I'm still trying to find a doorstep saucer topped up with a stiff 'g' and 't' but round here they're mean as muck and only leave a drop of milk out for their own cats. They say you never miss what you've never had. It's what I'm never going to get that worries me.

Yours dejected, ***Jack the Cat***.

RECOVERING AGAIN

Jack's Spot: I'm a bit short of space this week, folks. The ol' twerp can't accept that it's my sagacious input which makes you turn to this column, not his decrepit meanderings. He just doesn't want me to tell you about him and the daffodils but I don't forget anything so come back next week. Meanwhile, though he coughed twice in one day he didn't complain ONCE. And he's ordered THREE new shirts. And he's bought TWO HUNDRED bulbs for next spring. And I thought he was on his LAST LEGS!!

So ta-rah, fans, ***Jack the Cat***.

SQUASHED DAFFODILS

Jack's Spot: Hi again, lovely people. He's chuntering away to himself in the garden dibbing in the last of the new King Alfred daffs. It has started to rain and he's saying rude things about the weather and spring bulbs in general. Y'see, he dropped a right old clanger with last year's daffodils. He carefully lifted all of 'em after they had flowered and died down so he could remake a couple of borders. Laid 'em out in a big, dry box covered in newspaper About two hundred bulbs, I reckon. Somebody (I know who and so does she) put a heavy box of old books on top of his bulbs. Gradually quashed 'em flat. Looked like cold fried onions when he unpacked the box. He daren't say anything because he can't remember who put the books there. But I can and so can she and we're not saying anything either. I'll be sad when he stops gardening for the winter because whilst he's out there I can sit in our joint kipping chair in the study keeping an eye on him. He introduced me to the pleasure of watching other people work. When he comes in he turfs me out so he can sit down and that's another important lesson he's taught me – there is no point in assuming a position of power if you are not prepared to abuse it.

Jack the Cat.

NEW WORDS

Jack's Spot: I've heard rude rumours about my remarkable facility with the English language and suggestions that I might just be getting help with my brilliant column. It is a foul and cowardly calumny and try saying that to my fizzog and see what befalls ye. It is not generally realised that all moggies understand the lingo of their human guardians but it is given to very few of us to be articulate. I am one of the chosen. Always learning new words. Take the other day. 'Twas thus: the Guv bent down to prune a potted rose by the back door and cracked his head on a corner brick. Alerted by his imprecations (another good word that!) Herself appeared, looked at his bleeding bonce and said: "Why on earth did you do that?" He shouted: "Why did I do it? Why? Because I have this irresistible urge to go round smashing my head into brick walls. That's why." Phoning a friend later Herself explained she meant to ask "What?" not "Why" when she saw him. She laughed. "He was incandescent with rage." And that's me lovely new word for the week, folks. Incandescent. Fair rolls off the whiskers.

Cheers from your lexicographic chum, ***Jack the Cat***.

MY FIRST CHRISTMAS PRESENT

Jack's Spot: You know even I recognise that the old Guv's transmogrification (another good word I've just picked up) into the unmapped realm of teetotalism has not been easy. His family and chums were gozboggled by his determination but my theory is that if he can survive 47 years of marriage to Herself there is no hardship known to man that he can't surmount. (Actually it's not my theory it's Himself's but for once I'll take the rap for the ol' boy). HANG BACK FANS. Change of subject. Can you believe it? I've just had my first Christmas present! The card says it's from a "well-wisher" but the Guv won't let me open it until Christmas. It's a big, soft, cuddly parcel and I can't wait. Only snag is if it's really nice he'll nick it before I can get my paws on it.

Roll on the Yule and thanks "well-wisher", Yours, ***Jack the Cat***.

CHRISTMAS CARDS

Jack's Spot: Hi!Hi!Hi! Fans All, The Guv's not best pleased (jealousy?) by all the Christmas cards you lovely people are sending me especially those offering me advice about how to fool the ol' fool if you follow my meaning. This very morn a card reaches me from Bill and Ben who are a pair of short-haired moggies currently residing with the Clarksons of St Martin's Close, Exning. In it the cats congratulate me on having "my staff" (ho-ho!) well-trained and add: "We've got a tip for you. When you've eaten something you thought was placed on the table for you but later realised it wasn't, or you've broken an ornament or suchlike, DON'T DESPAIR. When Janet and

Michael appear just lie down, roll over, lie on your back, put your paws in the air and purr like mad and it will do the trick. They'll think how sweet you look and you'll get away with it – works for us every time." Thanks, Bill and Ben, but you haven't met my Guvnor. He doesn't know how to spell forgiveness never mind its meaning. Any more cards like that, he said, and he wouldn't let me read the damn things. And if he so much as catches me casting an envious glance at his smoked salmon I'll be on jankers until the second Tuesday in Whit Week. So take care, well-wishers. Encode your messages using this new texting language which the ol' fool can't understand. Careless talk costs lives and I've used up two or three of mine already. I like caviar, by the way.

Cheers all, ***Jack the Cat***.

A STAR IS BORN

Jack's Spot: It being the season of good will to all men it's a good time to admit that I'm beginning to pity the poor ol' Guvnor. Not only has he dropped an enormous clanger but he knows it. In his own words he has created a monster – moi! I heard him say the other day that I am getting far too big for my paws but tragically there was nothing he could do about it. 'Tis true that I have become emboldened of late to speak my mind fearlessly but that's what happens when a star is born. I am no longer a fawning moggie but a creature of stature with a public waiting upon my every word. This is what is eating into his soul. He told his chum on the phone: "Ever since I gave that damn cat a chance in life he has gradually taken over. Now he's built up such an adoring following that I daren't even chastise him verbally for his insolence because he will only write about it and I shall be engulfed by public obloquy and opprobrium. If I just chuck him in the garden it'll be in the public print and old ladies will accost me with their umbrellas." Like all cats, I know that "obloquy" and "opprobrium" are both a form of disgrace but I didn't understand one phrase. He said he was now "hoist by his own petard". If it means what it sounds like it brings tears to my eyes. I'll be gentle with the ol' fool over Christmas. Have a Cool Yule, fans, one and all. Cheers, ***Jack the Cat***.

I MISSED THEM!

Jack's Spot: Well, I hope you enjoyed it more than I did – they banged me up in a cat's home while they went off carousing and carolling in black pudden country with daughter Sarah and her brood. Nothing wrong with the home, you understand; good nosh, pleasant people though clearly some of the other moggs came from, well, homes of a less intellectual and socially uplifting background than what ours is. No, what I really missed was not the tinsel and smoked salmon – it was just that the carers in the home were normal people and there was NOBODY TO LAUGH AT!! Y'see, when the Guvnor is about he is a constant fount of amusement. He bumbles through life not quite getting things right but he's so puffed up with his own importance he doesn't realise that as buffoons go, he's the tops. For instance, he gave his mobile phone number to a neighbour in case of emergency over the hols and when Herself said it was a bit pointless since he never ever takes the phone with him when he goes out he shrugged and said it seemed a good idea at the time. So it's great to be back home in Muttonhead Manor where, for my New Year Resolution, I intend to repay the ol' man for all his kindnesses to me over the last twelve months. No, I know. It's a joke!!

Here's a health unto you, one and all, ***Jack the Cat***.

THE LADYBIRD

Jack's Spot: I blame that flaming ladybird. Well, it's not every January morning that you see a ladybird climbing up the curtains in the sitting room. This topsy-turvy weather has brought 'em out a-plenty round here and the one I spotted (ho!ho!) on our curtains led me to investigate further. So I jumped up and tried to catch it. Unfortunately in so doing I managed to temporarily re-locate some of their precious Dutch pottery. In other words I knocked several little figures off a table. From the Guvnor's reaction you might have thought I had vandalised priceless treasures in some bloomin' museum. He wreaked his revenge on poor little me in a cunning but disturbing fashion. He knew I was listening when he told a mate of a wizard scheme for saving a nice few quid. The next time he and Herself went away he wouldn't pay for my bed and board in a cattery (he doesn't, anyway,

Herself does). Instead, he would simply shoot me and get another similar moggie free from a cats' home when they came back. Can you believe it !! Now I know he has a weird sense of humour but this didn't sound very funny to me and, knowing what a tight-fisted ol' skinflint he is, it had a nasty ring of truth about it. Herself could see I was upset. "Don't worry, Jack", she said. "He's only kidding. He wouldn't dream of shooting a cat and, anyway, he daren't shoot you now you are a media star." I was mightily relieved. Then she spoiled it by adding: "But don't push your luck, Jack-me-Lad."

Oh! Woe Is Me. ***Jack the Cat***.

SMASHING A VICE RING!!

Jack's Spot: The ol' buffer gets deafer by the minute and one of these days it'll get him into trouble. Damn nearly did last week. Herself glances at the evening paper and says, quite clearly: "I see they've smashed a vice ring in Cambridge." Ol' know-all grunts. "Rubbish. You've got that wrong. They don't have one in Cambridge and I should know. It used to be one of my favourite sports." There is a sudden nip of frost in the air but he blunders on regardless. "You couldn't keep me away from them when I was younger and if there was one in Cambridge I'd still be using it. Read the story again." She does, slowly and clearly. "Oh", he says. "Vice ring. Not ice rink. I see." It is some time before the air in the sitting room thaws.

Oh! – and by the way, what is a full mental detox? He says I need one. Am I in for a treat?

Yours aye, ***Jack (Sharp Ears) the Cat***.

PS: What's the difference between ice and vice? I've so much to learn.

PAW MARKS ON THE DESK

Jack's Spot: For me that Russian chill has arrived. He woke me up and carried me gently to his desk. I was so surprised I broke into a deep purr. He pointed me at the leather top on the desk. As birdsong fades with the dropping sun so my purring ceased at the sight. There, quite clearly, were muddy marks on the sacred leather. "Those, Jack", he said with immense self control, "are paw-prints.You are our only cat; ergo, you are guilty. Herself forbids me from chastising you verbally.

So I will restrict myself to a gentle rebuke. If you must walk on my desk in future kindly do me the courtesy of WIPING YOUR FLAMING FEET FIRST! Now get out!" I trust he'll welcome me back in if it freezes. More next week pals when he's cooled down or warmed up whichever.

Oh 'eck. ***Jack the Cat***.

JOURNALISTIC DUTY

Jack's Spot: Just had a heart-to-heart lecture on the basic ethics of journalism from the ol' man who reckons he is entitled to dish out a bit of advice after nigh on 60 years in the game. A journalist, he said, must be a fearless and fierce protector of free speech for the hack is the ultimate defensive bulwark 'twixt timid citizen and bullying authority. He said it was our (note the "our" bit!) sacred duty to expose evil and corruption, to defend the defenceless and the ill-used. Nothing, not pressure, threats, bribery, not even personal feeling must stand between us and our duty, the ol' chap said. My fur fair bristled with pride. What a man! What a partner! Then, he added: "But remember Jack. In our game dog does not eat dog and the same goes for cats. So stop snitching on me and reporting my domestic eccentricities to our readers you scurrilous little gossip.You're making me a laughing stock. You'll end up on The Sun, God help you, if you carry on like this."

Mmmm. Now that did give me paws for thought.

Sorry. No more gossip, chums. ***Jack the Cat***.

P.S. To hell with it. Between you and me he put cold goulash on his cornflakes by mistake this morning. Thought it was stewed apple and plums. Language!

TAKING OVER THE COLUMN

Jack's Spot: Dear, faithful chums. My most precious dream almost transmoggified (geddit?geddit?) itself into glorious reality this week when the Guv' took a turn for the rough again and looked like something a less well-bred member of my tribe might have left on the doorstep. Y'see, I know that he and the editor have this arrangement that, should there be a real crisis, then I would step into the breach dear friends, and write the whole column! I've already got it sketched out in my mind and I tell you that when time takes its inexorable toll as it must since I am the only one with nine lives around here, then you are in for a magnificent display of journalistic fireworks. Anyoldrottenhow, as usual, he ruined everything by staggering back into the land of the living and here I am thwarted, frustrated, disappointed and generally not best gruntled. However, I comfort myself with the certain knowledge that my promotion to head columnist around here has about it an air of absolute inevitability.

Yours-still-in-the-wings-but-not-for-ever, ***Jack the Cat***

WET PAINT

Jack's Spot: Now how the hell was I to know the paint was wet? I may have staggeringly high intellectual powers but, dammit, even I am not omnipotent. I mean, the smell of fresh paint is unknown to me because the Guv', the world's worst DIY man, scarcely recognises one end of a brush from the other unless it's on a fox. The paint on the walls of this house is so old you would think it was Protected Grade One. When I popped out for a spot of mousin' all was normal. When I got back home there was this strange pong. I traced it to the wall at the bottom of the stairs covered with the grubby hand prints of ten grandchildren when I went out. Now it was all glistening white – very dabbable. So I dabbed. My paw marks replaced the kids'. Great fun. Dabbed it again. Funny how my paws stuck to the carpet. Plain green carpet. Well, it was. He came in, glanced at wall and carpet. Not a word to me. Just shook his head, turned to Herself. "Your bloody cat", he said. That's all. Hasn't spoken to me since. Don't know what I've done wrong – if anything. It's unnerving.

Will there be a next week? Yours, ***Jack the Cat***

THE PAINT AGAIN

Jack's Spot: He's a funny ol' boy and that's for sure. Not funny ha-ha, heaven knows. Just funny peculiar. Take that business of me and the wet paint on the wall at the bottom of the stairs. Still hasn't berated (good word that!) me for smearing it across the plain green carpet. Just painted over my paw marks on the wall and cleaned the carpet. Not a

single rude word. But all the time he swung his head one side to the other like one of those wind-up mechanical cockatoos as though he was pained at the thought of the fearful reprisal he has in mind for me which sure as hell is hot he has, if you follow me. Herself did nag me about it, however, which upset me since she is normally gentle and kind with me, reserving her vituperation for his endless and mindless misdemeanours. Still, I doubt she'll be nasty to me again. Y'see, she knows that I know precisely how old she was on her birthday last week and love her dearly as I do I know that she knows I might just spill the beans. If only I could blackmail him too. Can't be difficult. He must have more skeletons in his cupboard than Cambridge University School of Clinical Medicine. All snitches, snouts, grasses out there who have any low-down on his low-life write now to.....
Yours hopefully, ***Jack the Cat***.

KIPPING

Jack's Spot: My frequent references to the kipping chair I share with the Guv' are puzzling a number of mates in the Dustbin Club. What exactly, they ask, is a kipping chair? It is quite simply a chair kipping for the purpose of. But what, they wonder, is kipping? I will explain. Kipping is for the lower classes and indolent cats hence the presence of the aforementioned chair in the Guv's study. "Kipping", moreover, is the commoner's equivalent of the upper class "zizzing". It is impossible to imagine a well-trained butler informing her ladyship that his lordship is having a post-prandial kip in the library. No – his lordship is enjoying a zizz. Ships' captains sidle off the bridge for a surreptitious zizz in the wardroom's best chair. Matelots grab a sneaky kip in their 'ammocks down below. A satisfactory kip is not like a well-deserved sleep. Every kip should have a degree of risk or an element of guilt about it. A professional kipper must seize his opportunity and to hell with the consequences. The Guv' reckons he has kipped through lectures, exams, any nag lasting more than half a minute, neighbours' holiday videos and most t.v. films. He has seen the "Alamo" twelve times and still doesn't know who won. These are facts my Guv'nor has taught me, a man who boasts proudly that he could kip for England without any training.

Yours, clapped out, ***Jack the Cat***.

PEACE AT LAST

Jack's Spot: What Ho Mateys! Sound the all-clear siren, let down the drawbridge, splice the mainbrace and scuttle the portholes! The Mad Mob has retreated at last. Yes – we've had all ten of the grandchildren roaring round the domiciliary residence over Easter which is all very exciting but who has had to put up with the brunt of their childish exuberance? Moi, naturellement. Who has had to join in each and every game? Moi, mes amis. They came at us from all quarters: the Bradfords, Tom, Megan, Rosie and Mary from Hong Kong, the Powlsons, Victoria and Emily from deepest Staffordshire, the Jeacocks, Natasha, Abbie and Ben from furthest Burwell and oldest granddaughter Lydia Chambers likewise from Burwell. I love each and every one but I'm exhausted. Me whiskers is limp. At the big get-together I heard Herself say to the Ol' Man: "Aren't we the lucky ones?" That made it all worthwhile.

Cheers All, ***Jack the Cat*** (Honorary Cousin to the Mob).

P.S. They bet me a tin of salmon I couldn't get all their names into my *Spot*.

POLE-DANCING CLUB

Jack's Spot: Now I know a lot of you smile behind his back at some of the antics the ol' man gets up to and the more I get used to his ways the more I do the same. But the fact is that deep down he's a decent sort of codger. Since we are talking about Newmarket I can tell you they are opening a Pole Dancing Club there and the Guv is getting all excited about it. I haven't the faintest what such an establishment is and I don't think he's too sure either. He told Herself that with May coming up it must be connected with the ancient spring rites of the Maypole and a bloke had assured him in "The Bushel" that it was all in aid of the Fire Brigade charity. So he's taking a bunch of racing mates to the Club when it opens. "Got to support Old England's traditions", he told me. "And our firemen do a wonderful job." I tell you – he's all heart. Cheers, chums, ***Jack the Cat***.

MY NEW FRIEND FROM T'NORTH

Jack's Spot: Ay-oop folk. Bit pressed this week. Gorra new chum. Ginger tom. Come down from t'north wi' 'is family. 'Ees a reet good sort, afraid of nowt nor nubdy. And smart? Summed me up on t'spot, like. "Tha's gorra common name but tha' looks a bit posh Jack", he sez to me at choir practise behind t'dustbins. "If tha wants me for a pal tha'll 'ave t'speak my lingo." So ahm tryin' 'ard. Must skedaddle. 'E sez 'e knows summat funny abaht deputy prime minister. Tell thee next week. Tarra, ***Jack the Cat***.

A COMMON CAT

Jack's Spot: Hi-dee-hi again folks. Well, that was very short lived. Last week, you may recall, I chummed up with a ginger tom newly moved down here from Yorkshire. I tried everything to make him welcome including struggling to speak all those thees-and-thous wi' a Pontefract accent. I quickly realised I had made a most frightful mistake, my dear readers. Y'see, he turned out to be common as muck and without the slightest hint of southern sophistication in the length and breadth of his pugnacious, battle-scarred body. An insufferable oaf. And the tales he told us about his fellow Yorkshire tyke, our beloved Deputy Prime Minister, were so lurid as to be almost unbelievable, especially when you think how huge the DPM actually is. Round the back of the dustbins after choir practice we local moggies were aghast at his revelations even though the DPM is a socialist. Anyoldhow, we have decided to ostracise the ginger tom. (Does that mean what I think it means? If so maybe they should try it on the DPM). Must dash dearies. Bridge Club, you know. Byeee. ***Jack the Sophisticated Cat***.

RACIST? MOI?

Jack's Spot: Here we go again – I'm back in the doghouse, cathouse, rathouse, call it what you like but I'm back in it. And it's all the fault of that flaming ginger tom from Yorkshire.You'll recall he came pussy-footing down here with his family recently and at first I thought he was a likely sort of lad. Then I realised that he was, quite frankly, born deep below the salt and last week here, in a few well chosen words, I dismissed him as a worthy companion. Didn't he kick up a fuss! Called a meeting of the Dustbin Glee Club and accused me of gross political incorrectness. Calling him Yorkshire was ethnically out of order, by calling him ginger I was a racist, saying he was a tom was sexist and by accusing him of being common as muck I was guilty of class divisiveness of the highest order. As for saying he was an insufferable oaf – that clearly impugned his human rights to be thick-headed. At this point I lost it. Didn't the stupid twit realise I was a Jeacock cat? "We don't do political correctness in our family", I hissed, "We think it is all a load of retired shoe repairers and if you don't like it here shove off back where you came from." The local mogs applauded but he says he'll come looking for us with some friends. Come you on! We'll fight 'em on the lawns and in the flower beds. We'll never surrender! Tally-ho!! ***Jack the Fearless Cat***.

OH DEAR!

Jack's Spot: I need to clear up one slightly unfortunate matter rather rapidly for I fear I have put all four paws in it good and proper. You know that I have been troubled recently by that odious ginger tom who came here from the north expecting to lord it over us soft southern moggies. Well, among the insults I hurled at the ugly, ill-mannered, Google-eyed misfit was the term "Yorkshire" because that's where he came from and because I have been led to believe that all creatures born within that huge county are common as muck. I've got it terribly wrong. I find to my horror that Herself, my Protectress, the one in whom all hopes reside, is a Yorkshire lass! She might have been born a Chisholm, a descendant of that noble Scottish clan, but it seems she was delivered in Sheffield, of all places! Therefore I have reviewed the situation and I apologise most humbly. To Herself only, a unique example of a proper Yorkshire lady. That ginger tom is still a foul-mouthed, uncouth, swaggering, tight-fisted useless tyke like the rest of 'em from Yorkshire – apart from Her-lovely-self, of course.

Close one that! Cheers, ***Jack***

THE MAD COUPLE I LIVE WITH

Jack's Spot: Hullo again, my little Chickadees,

I wouldn't want what I am about to say to go any further but 'twixt thee and me my two protectors are not just weird – they are batty. There I was, dozing in his chair while the Guv' finished the guff he writes up there at the top so I could get on with my piece (this column must be the only example of a literary sweetmeat where the icing is at the bottom) when I hear him say to Herself: "Have I ever thumped you, my dear?" She replied as though he had asked her the time: "Not yet. Why?" Suddenly I'm wide awake. "Just checking, my ol' dear. Like to get my facts right." Now what the hell was all that about? And was it the conversation of a normal couple, I ask you? Clearly not, which gives me a wizard idea. If I were to jot down all their idiocyn, idyionsincr – all their peculiar conversational exchanges I could have it published. "Jack's Views of a Nutty Couple." It'll sell like hot fish cakes. Or, I could just threaten to publish. I know he would fork out to stop it. Not sure about Herself – she's Yorkshire.

Cheers all, ***Jack ("I'm dreaming of a rich Christmas") the Cat.***

A BIKINI BODY

Jack's Spot: I trust we are happily met, fans one and all! I'm not quite sure whether the Ol' Man has recovered fully from his recent bouts of poorliness or whether he has gone completely doolally. I'll explain.We are in the garden, he in a lounging sort of chair, me stretched out on the grass, when he lets out a whoop of unalloyed pleasure.Y'see he has picked up a glossy magazine for glossy ladies in mistake for his Shooting Times and, idly glancing at its contents, he comes across an advert which clearly states: "Get a Bikini Body in Just 21 Days". I hear him say: "Now there's an offer I can't refuse" and, showing me a picture of a young lady wearing two skimpy bits of clothing he declares he will send for one forthwith. I'm not sure what's going on because, in my state of health, I'm not even interested in female felines. Anyway, I think the advert is for a diet rather than an actual lady but he's too busy writing off for more details. "When the bikini body arrives Jack we'll tell Herself it's all part of my NHS therapy, an aid to reducing my stress." Then he said to himself: "I wonder if I can get one on sale or return?" I think doolally is the answer.

Cheers, ***Jack the Worried Cat***.

VENGEANCE IS MINE

Jack's Spot: Orft us goo agin, mates (as they all say over in Manea),

Last week, you will recall, the Ol' Man had this bright idea of sending for a "bikini body" which he'd seen advertised. I thought he thought it was a real lady's body but I thought it was an advert for a diet. I was much worried because it seemed to me a sure sign he had finally flipped. Nothing of the sort. He was, I discover, taking what is politely known as the mickey out of me. My chums round the back of the dustbins told me I was the one who had flipped for even listening to the Ol' Fool. Then I heard him tell Herself how surprised I looked when he discussed it with me. They both laughed and I have never felt so humiliated. But nobody – not even the Guv' – treats Jack the Cat like a twerp. The dead mouse which lies between his desk and the wall where Herself never sweeps should come into full ripeness any moment now in this weather. And there's another at the back of the cooker in the kitchen. You don't mess with Jack the Cat.

Lovely hot weather, folks! With a tee and a hee and a ho ho ho!
Jack the Cat.

OH DEAR!

Jack's Spot: A muted hello to one and all. Revenge may well be sweet – it can also be dangerous. When I hid those two dead mice in the house last week to get my own back for the Guv' taking the Mickey out of me I hadn't thought it through too closely. Herself found the mouse behind the cooker in the kitchen fairly sharpish but it took him that bit longer to trace the other down the side of his desk. The pong still lingers and serve him right. What I had not considered in all this was that, despite my views to the contrary, the Ol' Man is not as daft as he looks and, after weighing up all the evidence, he came rapidly to the conclusion that there could only be one guilty member of his household. Only I could catch and kill two mice and only I was so wacky as to think of depositing them in remote corners of the

homestead. He reminded me how, ultimately, he was in charge of my nine lives, glancing at his gun cabinet the while. For this episode he would fine me one life. Per mouse. All Hail The Guv!
Ta-ra, ***Jack the Cat***

THE WRONG BUTTON

Jack's Spot: Hi again, Fans. Quiet sort of week during which I have mended my ways, watched my 'ps' and 'qs', kept my head down, minded my business, turned a new leaf, rounded the corner, reformed, gone straight. In brief, I have mellowed. I am walking on eggs ever since the Guv' warned me that I am down to seven lives after hiding those dead mice in the house. Still, some things you should be told and blow the consequences. Like when Herself was backing out of the drive on Saturday. Was she too close to the big pot with the little tree in it? He put his head out of the passenger's open window. She pressed the wrong button. The window shot up and thwacked him under the nose. Herself feigned a lady-like deafness until his tirade ended.

Yours, ***Jack the goody-goody Cat***.

DEFENDING THE GUV

Jack's Spot: I reckon that what with the number of vocal bashings the Ol' Guv' gives me, I am entitled to dish out a fair whack of flak in return. But that does not mean to say that I will not defend him to the last whale tail from those who pour scorn and insult upon him. Thus did the following sorry situation arise at the quarterly meeting of the Cats' Save and Divide Club at the dustbins round the back when that scurrilous Yorkshire lout of a moggy pipes up and declares to one and all: "How many of you think Jack's Guv' is a miserable, humourless ol' twit like wot I do?" Well, the others are frightened of the Yorkshire tyke so half a dozen paws shoot up agreeing with him. This narks me considerably and then I remind them that I'm not only chairman of the Club but treasurer also and I control all the finances. Those who insult my Guv' had best bear that in mind. Immediately half a dozen paws shot down and I set three of the largest members onto the guttersnipe. He scuttles off hissing with fury. The fact that I might secretly agree with him is not the point at all. I can say it. That loon of a pale faced foreign immigrant is not allowed to denigrate (good word that) my Guv'. Cheers for now fans, ***Jack the Loyal Cat***.

THE CAT MAG

Jack's Spot: I get a sticky feeling that my long, idle and unprecedented apprenticeship is slithering towards its close. How that long-suffering editor of ours stands it I know not – here we are one week and then we're missing the next. Must be because of his deep personal charm, immense professional skill and vast experience which are only equalled by his inane sense of old-fashioned Christian charity. Or whatever?! My Guv' never knows which hospital, never mind which ward, he's likely to find himself waking up in from day to day and here am I lurking in the background all frustrated-like with me quill-filled paw. But it's the Guv' with those endless hints of his about my ***'Spot'***. Time for fresh dustbins, he cries! Put some sophistication into your pearly lines, Jack-me-Lad, says he. He suggests I write some pieces for this posh new mag that's just come out called "VAGUE, The Journal by Cats for Cats"; filled with feline fashion and fripperies and fiddle-de-daddle. I've tried. I sent them 800 words on "How to Straighten Out Your Drooping Whiskers" and another 1000 words on "Marriage Prospects for Neutered Toms". But I'm still waiting. And I sent 'em the story going around hereabouts (true) of the mouse who liked to dress up as a comical clown in our local mouserie. Two of my chums bowled the pompous twit over and were sharing him for supper when one cat said to the other: "I don't like the taste of this mouse. There's something funny about it." Clown – funny! Geddit?

Still waiting for my first editorial cheque from "V, The J. by Cs for Cs" nonetheless and for once I have me doubts.
Yours in a tizzy, ***Jack the Cat***.

Nearest and Dearest

YOUNG BENJAMIN JEACOCK

THERE are cascades of honeysuckle in the garden, the fen is fast filling up with plump, grey partridges, I backed a winner at Newmarket on Saturday and, oh yes, we've had another grandson. He is to be named Benjamin Michael Jeacock but I think we'll stick to Ben so that he won't be tarnished with his grandfather's name and reputation when he's playing cricket and rugby for England as he most assuredly will. I've already bought his first cricket bat, the rugger ball is ordered and his name is down to join our fenland shoot as soon as he starts to shave. So, all is well and I do not care a tuppenny fig for any of the woes the world has to offer. Cheers! little Ben. And may you walk the paths of peace and plenty in the long years ahead.

HIDING THE WHEELIE BINS

MY bride of several decades is not as daft as I have occasionally suggested. For a long time I have tried to work out how to hide the three wheelie bins which desecrate the otherwise scrumptiously-potted patio outside my study windows. I have drawn designs for exotic wicker-work, planned an evergreen fence, even called in a garden designer and all to no avail. Last night during supper in the garden Herself said: "Why don't you just move them round to the side of the house where we can't see them?"

I have. We can't.

VICTORIA PLUM

I MANAGED to cut through the wire of our electric lawn mower recently and because I haven't the faintest idea how to mend it the daisies on the front lawn are now tall enough to hide a middling herd of Friesians. Late frosts have turned my prized Buddleia into black, wizened stumps, the roses are firmly refusing to bloom and the little black bitch has dug up three nicely maturing clumps of Norfolk lavender. I can't back a winner in a one-horse race and the white shirt I wear for weddings and funerals has developed a frayed collar.

But I do not give a tuppenny tosh for misfortune's chill advances because last Thursday was my birthday and for the first time in six decades I was given the perfect birthday present; quite definitely, absolutely certainly, the most deliciously perfect of all possible birthday presents.

At exactly five minutes to midnight on my 64th birthday our eldest daughter Sarah gave birth to her first baby, a beautiful daughter, Victoria, our eighth grandchild. How about that for timing? So you see why nothing matters. Blow, blow, thou wintry winds. Dig away thou mangy hound. I careth not. Our Little Plum, Victoria, is the most beautiful birthday gift anyone ever received, and I am grateful beyond belief.

DESIGNING A BOOK PLATE

I AM designing my own bookplate. This is the posh ownership label normally only found on the inside cover of fine volumes in the great libraries of some of our ancient families and in the name of bibliophilist equality I have decided to join the club. Usually the plate shows off a family escutcheon, much quartered with armorial bearings and invariably bearing the legend "Ex-libris" followed by the name of the book's owner. The plates are always serious and are more a means of swanking about family dynasty than proving ownership. Alas, escutcheons in this family are a bit thin on the ground so I have invented one. It is based on a charming drawing by an old chum of mine, a keen medieval scholar, of a knight preparing for the joust watched by his lovely lady. I have re-drawn the picture slightly so that the knight is now taking his armour off rather than putting it on and looking at his lady in a fashion which suggests that he is anxious to found a dynasty of his own there and then. It is clear that any jousting in the offing is more likely to take place in my lady's chamber than on the Field of Mars. Under the picture I shall have engraved: "Ex-libris Michael Jeacock" followed by my new family motto: "A Knight to Remember".

FUTURE PERFECT

THAT granddaughter of ours, little Megan Bradford, has been at it again. The other afternoon, as all four-year-olds do now and again, she went into what we call in this family a bit of a strop – strop being a noun connected to the adjective stroppy. Her mum Rachel shook her head and said: "Megan, what on earth are you going to be like when you are a teenager?"

Whereupon Megan, eyes glinting, stamped her foot and said quietly and firmly: "Mummy, when I grow up I'm not going to be a teenager. I'm going to be a vet."

SEVEN DOWN ONE TO GO

THE best news of the week is that we are a grandfather again, as Mrs Thatcher might have put it. Number two daughter Rachel has produced a beautiful, bonny, bouncing sister for Tom and Megan who have decided, for reasons that remain unclear to me, that her name is "Radish". A perfect name for a little, round cherubic girl who, like the radish, is full of wind.

On a freezing day before she was born Rachel was sorting out clothes for the new baby. Grandson Tom, age three, was quite horrified. "Hasn't she got any clothes on, Mummy? Oh she will be cold."

Now that's seven grandchildren so far and another one due in the merry month of May. I'm not sure that I am physically strong enough to cope. T'other day after a family lunch Lydia and Natasha decided to sit on me, one on each shoulder, whereupon tiny Abbie forthwith joined in by climbing up the chair and sitting on my head. I tell 'ee, it takes a real man to be a granddad.

KEEPING THE BIGGEST SECRET OF ALL

TO tell or not to tell? That is the down-the-ages question which bedevils all grown-ups at this time of the year – well, all grown-ups who have young children, grandchildren, nieces, nephews, God-children or even a couple of friendly kids next door. It is a question which dare not breathe its name in public lest some bright-eyed, excited child overhears us talking or is clever enough to read about it in the public print and whose Christmases thereafter will be for ever sullied by disappointment.

So let us be maturely circumspect in our approach to this problem in order not to sadden those little ones who still believe in you-know-who and who would be devastated to learn at the last moment that he is actually un homme qui n'existe pas. (I use my awful French to further baffle any inquisitive tots who may have an ear to the keyhole or an elder sister all too ready to interpret what I am so carefully trying to discuss at the moment).

Y'see, I believe that of all the shocks that a growing-up child can experience one of the most distressing is the discovery that the once-a-year visitor with his sherry-soaked fizzog and strangely soot-free beard is actually a con-trick. It is far worse than other juvenile horrors like the first lecture from an embarrassed parent about the birds and the bees (though why they ever chose that particular form of expression I shall never know because when I first vaguely heard about it all I put a bird and a bee together in a cardboard box. Nothing ever came of the liaison).

I can recall precisely the Christmas when an elderly uncle, filled to the brim with my old man's only bottle of scotch, laughed at me when I hung up my stocking on the Eve and threw my carefully penned letter into the fire so that it could be swiftly and efficiently delivered by the elves to you-know-who.

"You don't still believe in all that rubbish, lad", he chortled. Well, actually, I didn't because I had heard nasty rumours at school. But the point was – I wanted to go on believing it. It was the most exciting part of Christmas, lying abed with eyes tight closed, listening, endlessly listening for the slightest hint of the scrape of a hoof on the roof. OK, so I never did hear the reindeer but until that Christmas Eve I knew they were out there. I hoped they were out there. I prayed they were out there.

That night when I knew for a fact that they were not out there, I went to bed with a sob and a heavy heart and my Christmas was never the same again.

VICTORIA, FATHER C. AND A KITTEN

GRANDDAUGHTER Victoria – our "Little Plum" – went with mum to visit the local Santa Claus in his grotto and told him what she really would like for Christmas. On the way home, like millions of other four-year-olds are about to do, she changed her mind. What she really, really wanted, she said, was a kitten. Mum, not overkeen on the prospect of a Yuletide kitten, explained gently that she had already given Father Christmas her list and he had gone home to get the toys ready for all the children everywhere so she couldn't tell him about the kitten.

There was a long pause. Then Victoria looked at mum and said firmly: "Well, I'll tell God 'cause He listens to everyone and He can tell Father Christmas."

I have a strange feeling that very shortly there will be a feline addition to Victoria's household and, since it absolutely must arrive via the chimney, will its name be Sooty?

SOCKS AGAIN??

IF I was a centipede with corns I couldn't make use of all the socks which Santa brought me – not if I wore a different pair every day for a fortnight. I've even got a scarlet pair with little pads on the ankles which light up and play "Rudolph the Red-Nosed Reindeer" when pressed. I shall reserve those for the next time I have lunch in the Jockey Club.

Naturally I was much moved by the kind thoughts behind the purchase of the mountain of wool which cascaded into my lap on Christmas morn but I am somewhat worried that if this trend continues – and it has been happening to me every December 25 as far back as I can recall – sheep may well become an endangered species.

Every Christmas has its highlights and one of ours was when granddaughter Megan Bradford down in Brighton (she's five and was Mary in her school nativity play) was asked by mummy Rachel if she knew why Jesus was born in Bethlehem. "Because", said Megan, "Mary and Joseph had to go there so that Joseph could pay for the taxis."

THROUGH THE EYES OF A CHILD

BEFORE we consign another Christmas to the archive of memories would you mind terribly if we were to slip back to a few days before the festival itself because there is a magical image which I wish to share with you.

Come with me, please, in your mind's eye, to one of the most beautiful buildings in Christendom – the Lady Chapel at Ely Cathedral. It is lit by a sullen December sun. It is empty. An elderly woman and her granddaughter walk in. The child's eyes are filled with wonder at the splendour of her surroundings. "Is this a castle, Granny?" she asks. "Who lives here?"

Granny says: "This is one of the places where Jesus lives. It isn't a castle. It is a wonderful church."

The child says suddenly: "Can we sing something, Granny?"

The lady of many Christmases looks down at the child, smiling. "What would you like to sing?" she asks.

"Can we sing 'Away in a Manger' please ?" says the child. "It's my favourite."

In the cold, grey, Christmassy stillness of that marvellous chamber, they sing the old carol together, my wife and our six year-old granddaughter Lydia

There is, thanks be to God, more to Christmas than tinsel and toys.

ANOTHER DISASTROUS WEEK

I'VE had one of those weeks. First, another birthday. Why on earth do we celebrate them? OK if you are just starting out. Not so good this end, let me tell you. I'm running very short on birthdays. A strong wind blew my favourite garden pot over one night and smashed it. Drove into Cambridge for the Book Fair. Fancied a nice copy of a hunting book. At thirty-five quid decided I couldn't afford it. Back at my car, a thirty-quid parking fine is stuck on the window.

HEADING OFF THE INVASION

SON Simon is away soaring above the moors and dales of Derbyshire hang-gliding and all I can say is that if he is as cack-handed in the air as he is on the ground he must have posed a threat to all passing birds, low-flying airliners and any barrage balloons left over from the war.

Talking of which – no doubt Simon would have flown over Monsal Dale which was part of his grandfather's beat as the local bobby thereabouts during the war. Then the London-Manchester railway line ran through the Dale, carried over the river by the lovely viaduct. Imagine, please, the very beginning of the war, invasion imminent, nerves jangling. One moonlit midnight our police phone rang. Father's sergeant in Tideswell. A farmer's wife was certain she had seen parachutists dropping into the Dale. The Germans had arrived. The Sergeant's orders were simple. Go there with all speed, Jeacock, and don't forget your handcuffs. And, said the Sergeant, whatever excuse they make nick 'em for trespassing. That's the Duke of Devonshire's land.

Mother was in tears and I was shivering with excitement as Dad armed himself with handcuffs and truncheon and mounted his police issue sit-up-and-beg bike to do battle with the Hun trespassers. To me, as he pedalled off in his tall helmet, he wasn't the village bobby any longer. His bike was a lily-white charger and his truncheon was his knightly lance.

When help, in the form of the Tideswell sergeant, found my old man hours later he was asleep under one of the viaduct's arches, enveloped in the powerful perfume of the half-empty whisky bottle which his friend, the landlord of the pub on Monsal Head, had provided "to put him in a fighting mood". The Sergeant threatened to report Simon's grandfather for being drunk in charge of a pair of handcuffs but, after finishing the other half of the bottle, decided that, on this occasion, Jeacock's valour had overruled his discretion and he left him to sleep it off.

CALLING UP MERMAIDS

'PON reflection I am not at all sure that I did the right thing over Christmas. Y'see, Herself and I spent the Yule with our number two daughter Rachel, her husband Richard and their four little terrors down at their lovely home in Brighton and a right merry Yule it was. I bought the little ones some small candy walking sticks to hang on the Christmas tree and for a reason which still escapes me I told them that a mermaid had cooked them and asked me to give them to the four Bradford children for being so well behaved. A mermaid? Certainly, I said. And I told them I knew how to call mermaids up from the sea floor. All it needed, I said, getting in deeper so to speak, was to stand on the shore and shout: "Hellooooooooo. Where are you?" Shout the words twice, I said, and if she doesn't appear then you bellow at the top of your voices: "Where the hell are you????"

I know I shouldn't have done it but I did. Next day on the sea front at Hove they stood in a line and we all tried it. This episode elicited some very strange glances from a number of staid Hove burghers out for a breath of refreshing sea air. I am not sure they altogether approved.

SPOOKY...OR WHAT?

BEFORE this season of ghoulies and ghosties is over, allow me to tell you a true tale which, when I heard it, chilled the very blood in my veins. Well, if it didn't actually do that it certainly confirmed a ghastly suspicion which has lingered ominously at the back of my mind for close on the half century of our marriage.

Please try to imagine the scene. As many of you know Herself is a Cambridge Blue Badge Guide and, as such, she was conducting a group of the paying public around the city on a "ghost tour" on Hallowe'en itself, pausing here and there to describe the weird goings-on which happened in different buildings and narrow alleys of the older parts of the city of Cambridge.

For authenticity's sake, Herself wore one of those tall, black witch's hats with a wide brim and a pointed top, a six-inch-long hooked nose complete with large carbuncle, a straggly grey wig, four-inch coloured fingernails, terrifying black and white make-up, purple lipstick and a black gown. Not a pretty sight.

Herself and the by-now-fascinated group paused in one of Cambridge's lanes outside an elegant shop in which a strange apparition sometimes appears going up the stairs. When one of the staff follows him upstairs, he just isn't there.

The shop's proprietor, whom we know slightly, kindly popped out to verify Herself's hair-raising yarn. And, without so much as a second glance at the hideous harpy in charge of the group he nodded a casual greeting: "Evening, Mrs Jeacock. I didn't know you did ghost tours as well."

There is one inescapable fact involved here and it is this – anyone who manages to look like a witch whether she is wearing witch's make-up or not is highly likely to be...well...a witch. (And if further proof is needed why did she acquire a new kitten just before Hallowe'en, eh? And how come she is so familiar, so to speak, with the creature? And why does it scratch me and not her? Go on, tell me!). What is more, when I mentioned this to one of the girls she looked incredulous and said: "Dad! You've been married to her all these years and you never noticed before?"

GARDEN GNOMES

THE moment I set eyes on the two little beauties I knew that my life was about to change for the better and so it has. As they emerged from their wrappings each smiled shyly and I was smitten.

They are two of Snow White's Seven Dwarfs, Dopey and Grumpy, and they are magnificent garden gnomes, pot-bellied, florid of countenance and clearly excited by their new home. They came to me a couple of weekends ago as gifts from the Bradford grandchildren who nipped up from their home in Brighton with mum and dad on a delightful surprise visit for my birthday. Our daughter, Rachel, and husband Richard were deeply apprehensive about their children's choice of presents for the old man but they need not have worried. I love 'em – grandchildren and gnomes alike.

Now, in our over-sophisticated modern world, I suppose the gaily caparisoned garden gnome is the epitome of naffness. They do not adorn the tailored lawns of the Cambridge colleges nor do they enliven the immaculate parterres of our stately homes. They are banished from the neat gardens of our suburban social climbers and are viewed by the sherry-sipping classes with the same degree of distaste as would be the appearance of a lager bottle at a Sunday lunchtime drinkies party.

In other words they are socially beyond the pale and utterly unacceptable in smug society. Well, now that I am a gnomic granddad, I disagree. They are, for example, a huge fun addition to the garden. Take Dopey, for instance. For a reason I can't quite explain, he and I found a mutual affinity the moment we met and now I swear his soppy, plastic grin widens whenever I bid him 'good-day' at his home among the white geraniums. I haven't quite got close enough to Grumpy as yet to understand why he still scowls at me when I pass by him amongst his irises.

Why, I wonder, has it taken me so long to recognise the innocent pleasure which the gnome has to offer to the gardener? They need no feeding, watering, mowing or hoeing. They listen to your every word without murmur of dissent, content to be harangued on the most obtuse subjects which, in other quarters – like the kitchen – would elicit counter-arguments and cries of "rubbish".

They have to be the friendliest creatures on earth; more faithful than the dog, less demanding than the cat and considerably less expensive than any nag. Which is why I was greatly cheered by little Mary Bradford, aged four and youngest of the Brighton Mob, who whispered to me as they left for home that soon I might be given the other five dwarfs – and Snow White as well!

So the Jeacock Home for Stray Garden Dwarfs is now declared open. Welcome, one and all. Hey Ho! Hey Ho!.........

I leave you with a rough translation of Chekhov's little-known poem on the subject:

"The garden gnomes of England
Are cast with one intent.
They are made for gardeners
Whose forks are slightly bent.

"They lurk not in beds of nettle
But in borders sweet with scent
For they're the pride of gardeners
Whose forks are slightly bent"...

EVERY CLOUD ......

OUR Powlson grandchildren over in Staffordshire have a cat. Last week it caught a shrew which duly expired. An official funeral in the garden was arranged complete with little grave and a farewell note. Victoria, aged seven, said to younger sister Emily: "I'm glad it died. I like digging."

TEXTING MADE EASY

BACK home, Herself decides to be bold and send her first "text" message – one of love and best wishes to number three daughter Naomi who is that day marrying her Ian in Florida. Two hours later granddaughter Natasha phones from her home up the road in Burwell. She is twelve with, to my certain knowledge, no immediate plans for matrimony. "Thanks, Granny, for the text message", she says, "But wasn't it meant for Auntie Naomi?"

LOOKING BACK

I'M not much of a tellyman but I did force myself to watch "The Wizard of Oz" with a large lump of the family over the Yule and much enchanted I was too. They refused to believe I had never watched it before and worked out that since the film was made when I was six (in 1939) I must have seen it sometime 'twixt then and now. Well, I hadn't.

Why had I not seen it when I was little, asked one granddaughter? Because, said I, the Picture House was a long way from my home, a four-mile walk there and four miles back, so we didn't go very often. It also cost a tanner.

Why not go in a car? Because we didn't have one. There were only two in the village – one each for the squire and his brother. The only bus left early in the morning and came back in the evening.

Then why didn't we watch it on the television? Because the village didn't have any electricity or gas in those days and we'd never heard of tellies.

They all guffawed at my silly fib. What happened when it was dark? How did my mummy do the cooking? Well, said I, after dark we lit oil lamps and candles and our homes were filled with a warm, flickering light, not the cold glare of electricity. And cooking? Well, mummy always had a fire burning in the grate to boil water and soup on and a hot oven at the side to bake our bread and cakes and roast our pheasants and partridges and to cook, very slowly, delicious rabbit pies, beef puddings and stews rich with field mushrooms

But without t.v. what did the children do after school? We stayed out as long as we could, replied granddad, playing in the fields and on the moors, bird-nesting in the woods and fishing in the river. Then we trudged home hungry and tired to those lovely, twinkling lights.

But didn't you miss the exciting programmes on the telly? You do not miss what you have never known, my little ones, said I. And excitement? Adventure? Plenty of that, my dears. We had books. In bed we dreamt of heroes in the distant lands of our Empire, of derring-do on the high seas, of dead-shot cowboys and of the men and women who made our country great. We were happy without television, my dears, and, frankly, your old granddad still is. I just hope they didn't see how damp my eyes were at the end of the film.

BEN'S FIRST PHEASANT

GRANDSON Ben, still nobbut a lad, shot his first pheasant just before the end of the season. He was out with his father, Simon, and me down the fen, three generations of Jeacocks, shooting men all. Ben was proud as a cock pheasant with two tails but he'll never know how much prouder his dad and granddad were. And, no, we don't care what the antis think.

NAOMI'S DATE WITH ROYALTY

IT is with no small degree of pride that I tell that among the distinguished guests invited to that glorious and moving service in St Paul's Cathedral last week for the Queen's 80th birthday was our youngest daughter, Naomi. It wasn't just the fact of her being there but the reason for her invitation. Naomi is a Principal Prison Officer and she was chosen, to her immense surprise, to represent the Prison Service on this historic occasion. I will not tell you why she was picked out from so many of her colleagues because I do not wish her cranium to expand further. Suffice it to say she was deeply honoured and so she should have been. She and her husband, Ian, came home much moved and, I sense, with a deeper understanding of that mystic bond between monarch and subject.

MICHAEL'S 70TH, RACHEL'S 40TH

WE are currently recovering from a mighty gathering of the clan Jeacock, our four children, their better halves and all ten of our grandchildren. As part of the joyful festivities (we were celebrating my latest birthday and that of number two daughter Rachel) we had a bouncy castle in number three daughter Naomi's garden. One jolly game was to jump backwards over the castle's upturned front as in a high jump or pole vault.

Inevitably it came to our turn. Easy-peasy, said I, hurling myself SAS-sty1e at the cast1e. I didn't quite make it. I bounced off, got stuck on the top and it took the united strength of all ten grandchildren to push me over the wretched front.

Herself sailed across in one swoop, dang, blast and drat it.

VICTORIA AND CATHOLICS

OVER in France number one daughter Sarah, husband Nigel and their two little ones, Victoria (6) and Emily (4) were driving to their holiday destination when Victoria asked why there were so many statues by the side of the road. Because, said Daddy, it's what Catholics do and there are a lot of Catholics in France. Did Victoria know what a Catholic was, asked Mummy? Living in the country back home of course she knew. A Catholic, said Victoria, was one of those things that they have in a field to stop cows from getting on to the road.

DEFROST COOKER!

FOR more than forty years I've had my doubts and of late they have become more or less confirmed. I refer to Herself who has demonstrated down the decades of our marriage that so far as eccentricities are concerned I have by no means cornered the market.

For example, there is scarcely a flat surface anywhere in our house which is not covered by pieces of scrap paper upon which she has written reminders to herself about important tasks which she fears she might forget to perform should they not be emblazoned in large letters, on the back of Tesco receipts or some such.

In the very early days I once found a note on the dining table saying: "Go shopping" and when I ventured to suggest that since the larder was so clearly bereft of comestibles that even she could hardly forget to replenish the shelves she replied tartly that she couldn't really be expected to remember everything. And so it has continued throughout our aeonian marriage.

Unhappily – and I apologise to posterity for the omission – I never kept any of her self reminders because, upon reflection, they could have been turned into a splendidly massive, albeit somewhat unbelievable, social document and international best seller.

Howsomever I have saved one example which I found on that self same dining table only the other morning. The message, in huge letters, consisted of just two words and an exclamation mark. It said......DEFROST COOKER!

Now even by Herself's ingenious standards this was a corker and I intend to have it framed. During breakfast and at an appropriate moment I inquired casually as to the cause of the strange domestic accident which had caused our cooker to become ice-bound. I pointed to the reminder. Had she perhaps meant the fridge?

Her look would have withered plump grapes on a sunny vine. "I know exactly what I meant", she said, or, rather, hissed, "and so do you."

LADYBUG ON A BUS

HERSELF and I took seats next to each other on a double decker bus into Cambridge. I was busy trying to analyse the runners and riders in a particularly difficult handicap at Brighton on the "Telegraph's" racing page when I felt the dreaded wifely nudge in the ribs. This is always a dangerous signal because inevitably it means that my attention is required. I abandoned my search for a long-priced winner.

"Look", quoth she and held out her left hand upon which a tiny, very young ladybird was clambering over her wedding ring. "Poor little thing", she said.

I assumed for a moment that she felt sorry for the creature because it was in such close proximity to that simple gold band which had chained her to me over so many weird years of matrimony and that she hoped the insect would not fall under its malign spell.

But no. She explained that she could not bear the thought of that innocent little beetle living and dying on a double decker bus. "Fancy having to spend your life on one of these machines when beyond these grimy windows there is the whole fresh world of nature waiting to be explored."

I mumbled something about bus drivers having little choice in the matter and that anyway perhaps this was an urban ladybug with a strong predilection for the safe environs of an omnibus albeit a mucky one.

The white-haired lady in the seat in front of us was quite clearly listening intently for her head was tilting backwards and I can't say that I blame her.

As we pulled into the bus station Herself walked the length of the bus with her left hand held high, eyes fixed firmly on the ladybird she was so determined to save from a dreary death aboard the X11. She released it into the murderous fumes of that horrendous bus station and I have grave doubts that it managed to make its way into the friendly embrace of the Fellows' Garden of nearby Emmanuel College.

The white-haired lady from the bus looked at us from a distance and I noticed she was shaking her head.

TOM THE COLLECTOR

OUR grandson Tom Bradford is heavily into collecting beer mats, I'm very happy to say, mainly because it gives me the perfect excuse as a devoted granddad, to, er, well, to wander hither and thither in pleasing pursuit of different examples of the brewing artist's art. I have been obliged to explain to Herself, who is a novice in these matters, that it is churlish and unmannerly to call into a hostelry and ask the landlord to bung you one of his beer mats without doing him the courtesy of purchasing a glass or two of his very best.

How pleasant it is, therefore, to be able to combine grandfatherly duty with pleasure knowing that Herself can hardly complain, let alone nag. But there is even better to come. Tom phoned from his Brighton home the other evening. He and his tribe are coming up to stay soon. "Can we go on a pub crawl, please?" he begged me. "I need some more beer mats."

That's what I call a grandson. Tom is eight.

MAJ THE BLESSED

SINCE Easter has become almost as firm a family festival as Christmas let us begin with a short and jarring tale about the most important member of our vast and increasing tribe. Our little black bitch Maj is the icon, the very jewel in the crown of our family, so far as our grandchildren are concerned, and when they arrive at our house in their hordes they stream past Herself and me oblivious to our outstretched hearts and arms screaming: "Majimix. Where's Majimix?" Compared with that dangblasted dog we two are but specks of sand in the desert, gravel on the driveway. But even the greatest amongst us makes the odd, grievous mistake. The Blessed Maj is no exception. As far as food is concerned she is the canine equivalent of a salivating hoover. T'other day she tried to eat a piece of cheese in the garage. The cheese was in a fully sprung mousetrap. I can guarantee absolutely and without the slightest tinge of doubt that Maj will never try to eat a piece of cheese in a loaded mousetrap ever again. No. Not ever again. (Note to all dog lovers – happily she wasn't physically hurt. Her yowl of protest when the trap sprang was more inspired by angered pride and astonishment.)

HERSELF'S NEW COMPUTER

HERSELF is now the owner of a new computer. Why she needs it I know not because to my certain knowledge the fountain pen I bought her for her wedding present is still in perfect working order. Does she know something I do not? Is the world supply of fountain pen ink about to run out? Is there a sudden and unexplained international dearth of blotting paper? Has our Great Leader issued a new Presidential Decree banning the ownership of fountain pens because they are the artefacts normally used by the pro-hunting brigade to sign their letters to the Daily Telegraph?

Her most recent acquisition astounds me and I am bemused by her decision to leap into the hitherto unplumbed depths of futuristic technology since I've always had the vague impression that she still doesn't quite understand the complexities of the inner workings of her fountain pen. But, come to think of it, after four decades of marriage, I have never quite come to understand the complexities of Herself's weird and wondrous mind so I suppose that makes us both about par for the course.

I should have realised that dangerous waters lay ahead when she started attending computer lessons at Bottisham Village College because, 'pon reflection, there is little point in learning how to compute if you don't have a proper computer upon which to apply your computing skills.

What worries me, though, is where will it lead us? Into which uncharted seas are we about to sail? Y'see I have this burgeoning and frightening premonition that Herself is determined to set her course towards the internet or e-mailing or whatever. These are matters of which I wot not and which, quite frankly, I have not the slightest desire to wot of. There are stormy clouds ahead and I feel an urge to scuttle the portholes before all is lost.

(But belay there, me hearties! A sudden and pleasing thought emerges from all this. If Herself is determined to set sail towards those shores where endless surfing is all the rage this will require her to spend long hours in front of the flickering screen. This in turn, shipmates, will lead inevitably to equally long hours of unaccustomed silence within the creaking galleon of our marriage. So splice the mainbrace, lads. Unscuttle the portholes. Get stuck into the grog, me hearties, we are sailing into calmer waters aboard the Good Ship Computer. Yo-ho-ho and a bottle of claret.)

THE BIRTHDAY BOY

THE birthday began in earnest with coffee and brandy at a table under that giant sun umbrella at Don Pasquale's in the Market Square in Cambridge which tasted better than usual because an old mate paid for it. Then the birthday boy found a first edition of the New Naturalist Monograph on "The Badger" in a bookshop which should have known better but didn't and charged him half the price he would normally have expected to pay. This, he murmured quietly to himself, is a proper birthday. Can it possibly improve?

It could. Another old chum treated him to a pint of cool cider as they sat and nattered under a cloudless blue sky in the ancient courtyard of The Eagle where all around was laughter and good will. He spent some of his birthday money on sturdy garden plants, nascent and anxious to burst into life. Back home a tribe of grandchildren arrived whooping and shouting and offering sticky kisses before scoffing the birthday cake they had brought with them – for him. The first rose of summer had chosen this very day to bloom and, just above it in the high honeysuckle, young blackbirds twittered in their nest.

In the pub that evening the birthday boy won three games of darts on the trot and later, in the garden, supped with Herself on creamy-fresh Cromer crabs and local asparagus spears thick as broom handles. I might have rounded my birthday supper off with some of that cake if my grandchildren had left me even the merest sliver which, of course, the greedy grabbers had not. Howsomever, it would have been churlish in the extreme even to have harboured a greedy thought at the end of a day like that.

OUR VEGETARIAN

AS a schoolgirl our number two daughter Rachel went through a phase of being intensely vegetarian and, naturally, we tried to cope helpfully with her fodder requirements. All went swimmingly for a long time – until one summer Sunday morning when Rachel walked into the kitchen filled as it was with the glorious aroma of young lamb roasting on a bed of garlicky new potatoes. Herself was busy preparing Rachel's tomato and basil spaghetti when our daughter sat at the kitchen table, head sunk in her hands. "I can't stand this any longer", she cried. "I can't stand the smell of that roast lamb!"

I tried to explain gently that while we accepted and understood perfectly her right to be vegetarian she must accept that we carnivores in the family had our rights also and they included roasting meat in the oven even if it meant that the kitchen was invaded by what, to her, was an unwelcome and repugnant odour but which, to the rest of us, was the very essence of Elysian fragrance. We had to learn to be mutually tolerant, quoth I.

Rachel looked up, clearly distressed, and for the first and only time she shouted at me. "You don't understand", she wailed. "I don't find the smell of roasting lamb nasty or repugnant. I find it irresistible."

Thus ended our family's one foray into vegetarianism. Rachel threw the spaghetti away herself.

Not, you should understand, that this vast and burgeoning brood of ours is in any way averse to vegetarian dishes – to the contrary and though I would not wish this to come to the ears of our excellent butcher in Newmarket, Mr Eric Tennant, we frequently sit down as a family to a vege meal. (Actually, Eric, and calm down, by frequently I really mean occasionally. Very occasionally). But it's always good to get back to the lamb. You ask our Rachel.

Some of you may be wondering why I am harping on about the pleasures of roasted meat at this perilous period in the life of the countryside. I do it deliberately because I believe utterly that one way in which we can help our stricken farmers is that we insist from henceforth on buying British lamb, British beef, British pork – and, just as importantly, enjoying it.

FAREWELL TO MY LITTLE BLACK BEAUTY, MAJ

THROUGHOUT her long and inglorious life she rarely behaved with even a scintilla of propriety, her greed was gargantuan and even though she was bred to the gun in the finest kennels in the kingdom the only time I took her shooting she retrieved a pheasant perfectly – and then she ate it.

At an early age and without the benefit of any training whatsoever she mastered the art of canine slothfulness and for many a full summer her most enervating activity was moving round the garden in time with the sun so she could lie where the grass was warmest. Although fanatically loyal to her adoptive family that loyalty evaporated upon the instant when it came to their food. No epicurean treasure was sacred if she could reach it. I can picture her now, in her first year with us, dashing from the kitchen, a piece of fillet steak between her teeth with Herself shouting in the background: "Your dog has just stolen your piece of steak."

By now you will probably have reached the melancholy conclusion that I am writing, in the past tense, about our little black bitch Maj. Alas, I am and it saddens me more than I can say to have to tell you that she is no more.

Little Maj, the doyenne of daft dogs, died exactly thirteen years from the day she was born in a royal keeper's cottage on the Queen's Sandringham estate. Herself bought her for me as a birthday present when Maj was just a snub-nosed pup. My wife was not to know, could not have guessed, that she had found for me up there in the middle of that vast regal estate a creature which was to become not just my best friend but the adored icon of an entire, far-reaching family.

Maj – we named her Majestic Lass because of her royal parentage – came to us before our four children had provided us with a single grandchild. She was to live to be loved by all ten of them. It was Maj who introduced those little ones (the oldest is but eight) to that strange and inexplicable link which seems to form automatically between children and animals.

It is not an exaggeration to say that she became a vital and important part of their young lives even though some lived long miles away.

Squeaky voices on the phone demanded not to know how granny and grandad were but always: "How's Maj?" When Herself and I and the little bitch drove off from visits the farewell cries from the grandchildren were always "Bye Maj. Love you Maj. Come back soon Maj."

The little black bitch countenanced with delighted good humour all of their unintended buffetings and pokings and never even curled a lip in gentle warning to them to calm down. I very much doubt there can be a better tutor than a family dog to teach young children to understand the ways of loyalty, gentleness and endless, devoted, undemanding friendship. Our Maj was, in that respect, a star.

Despite her enviable idleness and her insatiable appetite she never once nagged me or complained in all the years of our closeness and, you know, there is neither being nor beast closer than the family dog. Unlike children they do not go off to school, they do not get packed off on holidays, they don't go off to work on their own when they get older. They do not and cannot fly the nest. They are with you and part of you from the beginning to the end.

Well, now it's over. Or is it? Perhaps not.

Not while memories linger of an imp-faced, irresistible little black bitch whose presence and antics brought joy, delight and a uniting affection to our entire family.

Suddenly, I realise I have an apology to make. Maj was not just a part of my family. I have written about her and her strange ways for close on thirteen years. Whenever I am recognised by friend or stranger throughout the region invariably their first question has always been: "And how's that little black bitch of yours?"

She became, unknowingly and unwittingly, a much-loved member of a far larger family than my own. I like to think that for many of you, too, she will be terribly missed.

REMEMBERING MAJ

IT is more of a trickle than a torrent, I suppose, and it takes a little time to realise that it is happening. It begins, naturally, by missing the familiar and ever-friendly face; then, slowly, you realise just how much has disappeared. The set routines of more than twenty five years are suddenly abandoned. The bracing walk before breakfast is no longer the pleasurable necessity it once was during the lifetimes of the two dogs – first Sam, the World's Worst Gundog who was followed by Maj, the lately and much lamented Little Black Bitch. But the habit is strong and you still rise early – mustn't keep the dog waiting.

All dogs become creatures of routine and so do their owners. The animals know to the minute when it's "grub up" time and so does the provender which is why, even when the dog has died there is still at the back of the mind the constant thought that you should be heading home for feeding time.

Apart from walking and feeding requirements a bereaved dog owner also begins to realise just how undemanding their pet always was. Willing to lie in the kennel or – in summer – on sunny patches of the lawn for long hours without complaint, upon his or her return the owner is welcomed not with a murmured nag about "where on earth have you been?" (as might well be the case with other members of the household!) but with a welcoming yelp and wildly wagging tail..

But of all the many pleasures which master and dog share over the years the greatest must be that of gently and peacefully nodding off in each other's company. To settle into the warming embrace of a deep armchair with your well-walked, well-fed and blissfully contented pooch curled at your feet is the very pinnacle, the summation, of that strange, invisible bond which links humans to dogs. Even now I cannot settle my head for a short winter's nap without automatically looking round the room.

The more I have thought about the relationship 'twixt owners and dogs since Little Maj left us the more I am convinced that we humans are the ones who have got it all wrong. We don't look after dogs. They look after us. The realisation that this is so trickles rather than pours over you.

A complete stranger stopped me in the street the other day and said how sorry he was to read of Maj's death and told me he knew exactly what it meant because he had lost his own dog recently. Then he told me that he spent much time working abroad. "Whenever I got home the kids would shout: 'Hi Dad – hang on a minute, we're just watching Coronation Street' – or whatever.

"But", he said with a happy laugh, "it was my dog which never failed to rush over to greet me."

CHRISTMAS NEARLY DIDN'T COME

LURKING at the back of my mind is the vague suspicion that an E-mail (E-mole? E-mule? or whatever) is some sort of modern missive and if I had the faintest idea how to work one I would have it winging its way to Santa Claus as of this very moment. My advice contained therein would be of the utmost importance and urgency – it being that time of the year. It would read as follows:

"Dear Santa,

I realise it is a stressful part of the year for you and your helpers but if you wish to preserve your hitherto unrivalled and untarnished reputation for delivering the goodies bang on time I urge you most seriously to read on.

Y'see, I have just been subjected to a most disconcerting Yuletide experience and I am worried lest the same misfortune should befall your good self. If you could please put the wrapping paper down for a jiffy and pay attention I am certain you will find my tale – and my warning – of considerable interest.

Herewith the yarn. – Herself, that is, my wife of these past four decades, is a granny which, upon reflection, is hardly surprising since I am a grandad. T'other day she decided to up and leave me for a few days while she delivered a huge suitcase filled with presents from ourselves and other members of our large family to four of our ten grandchildren – this mob being the four miscreants who are ensconced with mum and dad Bradford down in Brighton. There were presents for the parents as well. Herself boarded one of those express coaches accompanied by the aforesaid vast and loaded suitcase (no insult intended to your good self) and duly delivered the gifts ready for the Christmas festivities of which you wot.

A few days later Herself then returned on a homeward-bound coach. This time the suitcase was crammed to the gunwales with the Bradford family presents for the rest of our ever-spreading tribe, dozens of 'em. Presents, that is not, tribal members.

The kindly driver jumped from the coach in Newmarket, and, after she had pointed to her case, he hauled it from the bowels of the vehicle and she set off dragging it on its little wheels towards a taxi in the High Street. The coach sped off towards Norwich. A young man had also got off the coach. As she reached the taxi a voice behind her said, "Thanks for helping me with my suitcase but I can manage it now." The voice turned out to belong to a small chap who works for that aristocratic doyen of Newmarket trainers, Sir Mark Prescott. His case was exactly similar to hers. The lad had a couple of other bags and presumably thought the kind and elderly granny was giving him a helping hand. Herself had pointed out the wrong piece of luggage to the driver. It was his all right and ours was hurtling away into the Norfolk night complete with more Christmas presents than you can normally fit on a decent sized sleigh.

Herself arrived home and announced: "I've left the suitcase with all the presents on the coach." I realise, dear Santa, that you are a man of deep sensitivity so I do not propose to upset you by repeating my comments. Suffice it to say that the silence prompted by my utter and initial disbelief turned rapidly to a voluble and colourful outpouring of distinctly un-Yuletideish phrases.

Now, Santa old lad, herein lies a moral. Should perchance you have any granny elves amongst your gift wrappers and sleigh packers sack the lot of 'em forthwith and to hell with the season of good will. Beware of grannies bearing gifts. Sure as chimneys are sooty they'll make a cock-up of it.

PS. There should always be a Happy Ending to all Christmas stories and there is to this one. The very helpful, though slightly incredulous, Jetlink coach company staff went to endless lengths to trace Herself's vanished case stuffed with children's treasures. They found it and it was delivered safely back to Newmarket High Street early the following morning. She duly collected it from a smiling and understanding coach driver and now all is well.

But Christmas grannies, Santa? Daft as brushes all of 'em. Daft as brushes.

I remain Sir, your obedient and expectant servant and Herself's constantly bemused husband.

NEVER AGAIN!!

WE are in the throes of house moving and if there is a more painful condition known to mankind it can only be incurable gout or seven weeks of incessant toothache. We swore we would never do it again and now, by George, we're swearing again.

Well, I mean to say, it's enough to make the saint himself swear. Where on earth does all the rubbish come from? And why did we bring it with us when we last moved? And, more to the point, why are we taking it with us again this time?

I tell' ee, if there were a national museum of the world's most useless objects we could stock it overnight without noticing the difference. Why, for example, have I got a pair of sheep shears from around the turn of the century? Why do I keep a set of rusty corn scales? Into the miscellaneous box has gone a hundred 20-bore shot-gun cartridges (my gun is a 12-bore) and a portable typewriter I last used when I reported the election of Archbishop Makarios as the first President of Cyprus, an event now lost in the mists of antiquity. We have enough inherited curtains stashed away in never-opened boxes to keep the daylight out of the whole of Chatsworth House. My collection of tattered "gardening" sweaters must be uniquely useless because none fits me. But they're all going with us. I could go on but I am beginning to embarrass myself. I am also beginning to realise that among the most insidious words ever strung together in the Eng1ish language are: "Well, you never know. It might come in handy one day."

Oh but the books! Sometimes they frighten me because there is about them a strange and unnerving air of fecundity. In other words, I am convinced mine are the only books in the world which breed. This must be the answer to their ever-increasing numbers. Aeons ago I promised myself that I would forswear my life-long vice of buying them and I am nought if not a man of my word. So that, as I explained to Herself as we packed box after box of books, had to be the answer. Unreasonably, in my view, she totally rejected the hypothesis. But packing much-loved books is one of the slowest processes known to mankind for the simple reason that it is impossible to pick up a long-neglected friend without dipping into it. Here I find the memoirs of an old Fleet Street chum and his tales throw back the curtains of memory which have been half-closed these full forty years, so much so that I cannot put the book down; there I pick up "Biggles Breaks the Silence" by Captain W.E. Johns, a smashing tome first read on the snowy Christmas day it was given to me nearly sixty years ago. Again, strangely, the tales of brave Biggles ("and in another reckless bound he reached the level ice") seem as familiar as if I read them only last week.

Anyoldhow I've got to stop it because we move next week and at this rate I'll still be reading when Chris Bonar and his merry removal men arrive. Now shall I pack those green wellies with the rip in the ankle? Suppose I could always put a patch on.

A DAY IN THE LIFE OF........

OUTSIDE, the sweet gentle sounds of a traditional English autumn herald the birth of another lovely day – the lulling notes of pounding pneumatic drills bringing us the unwanted boon of underground cable wires, the soothing clatter of wheelie-bins being bashed into the dustmen's lorry and, as lilting background music, the subtle tones of screaming electric strimmers clearing the verges. With a hey and a ho, hey-nonny-no. Hurrah for Merrie England.

Yes, well, I know it's all part of progress but it's the sort of cacophony I can well do without especially as it greeted me on my return empty-handed from a pre-breakfast trawl around fields soppy with overnight rain. Perfect mushrooming weather – wet and warm. So perfect, in fact, that some bright wally beat me to my favourite picking grounds this very morn. I could see his footprints and, here and there, the white remnants of carelessly plucked mushrooms. Not a single one did he leave for me so I'm faced with a dreary breakfast, there's a nasty letter from Her Majesty's tax collector and that damned racket outside is making me wish I hadn't insisted on having another glass of wine with dinner last night.

There is only one good thing about the whole situation and that is – the day can only get better. Indeed, I'm determined that it will. Perchance a stroll through the dripping woods above Warren Hill at Newmarket whilst the horses are a-training. Mayhap a trip into dear old Cantab. Then who knows? A beautifully-bound bargain in David's Bookshop, maybe. (They had a magnificent "Gulliver's Travels" in there the other day for a mere £3,800 – yes! three thousand eight hundred smackeroos. Cor, I wasn't half tempted.) Followed, certainly, by a reviving glass of Greene King's finest in The Eagle in Bene't Street with my old chums Bob Wass and Chalkie White. There we will whittle away the passing minutes by discussing the important matters of the moment like what's going to win the 3.30 at Sandown. Thus, refreshed intellectually and physically, maybe a slow amble across the market place pausing only to take on board a pound or two of the very last samphire of the season from one of the excellent fish stalls there with, oh well, yes, a lobster for supper paid for by the forthcoming winner in the 3.30 at Sandown.

Round the corner to King Street for one of those devilishly spicy spaghettis in The Bun Shop accompanied by a soothing glass of Chardonnay. Yes! The day is certainly going to get better. Cheers, one and all and tally-ho. . . . .

****

And a very good day it turned out to be. All went according to plan except that Chalkie's certainty in the 3.30 at Sandown is still on the missing list. That man couldn't tip bricks out of a barrow. Still, the lobster was delicious albeit somewhat more expensive than I had hoped. Win some, lose some.

Meanwhile the cable lads have moved on, the dustmen won't be back for a week and the strimmers are silent. And you know what I'm about to say now – yes, I was up so early this morning the mushrooms were still growing when I found 'em. They are in the pan now, plump pink flesh turning silkily black as they simmer in the bacon fat. Perhaps you will excuse me. Herself calls from the kitchen and her breakfast is about to make an old man happy. Sadly, today can only get worse .

COMFORT STOP?

AS a result of having spent a long, varied and, on occasions, fairly exciting life, I am not easily unnerved. But unnerved I most certainly was the other morning. The unnerving came about in this manner: there I was, not bothering anybody but sitting quietly and serenely in a cubicle in the public conveniences abaft the Lion Yard car park in Cambridge, at peace with the world and contemplating a coffee and brandy at Kim Benedetto's place, Don Pasquale's, in the Market Square, when first the snout followed by the eyes of an Alsatian appeared through the gap beneath the partition wall. When I say Alsatian I do not mean one of the Franco-German wine-making variety but the large dog sort. The beast seemed somewhat astonished by my presence. The feeling was mutual. We gazed at each other in silence. Was it alone? If so, er, why? What should I do? Ought I to say something? What, I asked myself, had become of privacy? When I reached Don Pasquale's I ordered a double brandy with my coffee.

A GOOD DEED REWARDED

I HAVE a slender parable to present unto you. It proceedeth thus; a couple of Saturdays ago I was privileged to be asked to open the Church Fete at our old village of Swaffham Bulbeck where the Jeacock tribe lived in huge happiness for a couple of decades or so. I accepted the invitation gladly despite the opening ceremony clashing with racing at Newmarket. I knew that I would be among friendly and familiar faces and, anyway, the English summer fete is one of the most civilised happenings yet invented by mankind. (Or, if you insist, personkind).

Nevertheless I must admit that I felt to miss an entire afternoon's racing was a sacrifice too far and I made cunning plans to combine the two pleasures by slipping off from God's acre – for the fete was held in the churchyard – at the first opportunity to join villainous friends upon the blasted heath of Newmarket. I had, you see, selected half a dozen absolute certainties from the list of runners in the morning paper.

But as always happens with me my best-laid plans went awry. Firstly I was asked to perform the most difficult task in the world, namely, to judge the village children's art exhibition and, of course I was desperately anxious to give first prizes to each and everyone of them so my final decision was a long time a-coming. Then I kept bumping into folk I hadn't seen for ages and I wanted to know about their grandchildren and they wanted to know about ours and so the time drifted happily by. Naturally it is impossible to avoid fete teas especially when there is a gentle warmth in the summer breeze and children whose granddads and I played cricket together on The Denny were serenading us with their tuneful recorders.

So I sat myself down on a lichened tombstone and made a slight pig of myself on moist, fruity cake and rich strawberry thingamajigs. And time slipped happily by as, indeed, did the racing down the road at Newmarket.

By now I began to see a grand design in all this. Someone Up There was deliberately delaying me, preventing me from reaching the louche racecourse by plying me with the irresistible pleasures of an English church fete. So, suffused with pleasure I abandoned my racing plans and when, later, I checked the racing results I found that not one of my selections was in the first three. A benign influence had saved me from a nasty fiscal hiccup.

But where, you ask, is the nub of this little parable. I'll tell 'ee. A couple of days later I received a charming letter of thanks for my meagre fete-opening efforts. Enclosed was a cheque for one hundred pounds. I had scooped the first prize in the raffle.Yea, verily, He works in mysterious ways his wonders to perform.

CELEBRATING AN ANNIVERSARY

WE have been enjoying some spectacular sunrises recently and one of stunning beauty illumined the eastern horizons on the morning of my first anniversary. Later that morning there was a scattering of rain but by then I was sheltering in a Cambridge bookshop. Lunchtime found me playing cribbage in The Boot at Dullingham amid much laughter and friendly ribaldry. At dusk I was deep down the fen watching old shooting chums hang up their bag of pheasants and partridges on the wall of a crumbling, open-fronted barn close by the lode which the Romans dug just four centuries after the birth of Christ. Deep dusk and sudden frost shrouded the party in a twink and it was time for the Red Lion. There, with another shooting party, was my son Simon and little grandson Ben, the last – in my time – of the sporting Jeacocks. It was a lovely scene, there in the tweed-crowded pub, scarcely changed since the crossbow gave way to the flintlock. I was glad to be alive.

And that was how I celebrated the first anniversary of my new life as a teetotaller. Exactly a year had passed since I last touched alcohol. Not so much as a rum baba has tempted me since and probably never will. I still do the social round and as I stand there, glass of ginger beer in hand, I am frequently asked two questions by the un-reformed: has it been difficult and has it been worthwhile?

To the first the answer is – yes, it damn-well has. To the second the answer lies in being able to watch the daily rising of the sun.

The Way Things Were

BEEF ABOUT BEEF

I WRITE this on the eve of the day which, as all Scots, Irish and Welsh know, is dedicated to St George. We English still can't get ourselves too worked up about it though I have long celebrated the day with platters of beef and flagons of ale and so I shall tomorrow – hopefully. I am to be a guest of the Gog Magog branch of the Royal Society of St George whose members are under the vastly mistaken impression that I am the world's greatest living expert on the history of our patron saint. It would be somewhat surprising if I was since he never actually existed. But then, as a life-long journalist, I have never allowed the facts to interfere with a good story. I pause here somewhat shaken having read some of the past menus of the Gog Magog mob's St George's Day dinners. Here is roast haunch of wild boar accompanied by a sliced fillet of venison, there Dover sole followed by roasted leg of English lamb, another time fillet of sole before plump roast goose, turbot and lamb.....but no sign of any roast beef! Gadzooks! Can these be Englishmen? We didn't once more into the breach, dear friends, on fish and lamb. 'Twas beef, me lads, beef. And bread dunked deep in beef dripping. Lamb is for the French, mes garcons. Lamb is for the others.

MY BELOVED DESK

JUST about every word I have written for nigh on forty years has been hammered out on my lovely old desk designed and crafted for a long-gone Senior Tutor at Magdalene College in Cambridge around the time the old Queen's reign was drawing to its close. It came to me in a roundabout sort of way and with its twelve drawers, its patina of countless polishings and its glistening black leather top it positively exudes elegance.

Alas, in recent times I have grossly abused its hospitality by imposing upon it an ugly, vulgar computer and printer both totally out of keeping with this lovely creature from a gentler, less raucous age. The presence of that baleful electronic intruder distressed me for ages and I am quite certain that the desk sulked and agreed with me.

This week I decided enough is enough. Both machines were showing signs of intransigence anyway and were refusing to accept even the simplest of my commands. Here was our excuse and my desk and I bade a relieved farewell to our two cumbersome and unwelcome guests. They now repose, unmourned, in some Stygian graveyard where all wretched computers should end up.

Now, a sheen of pleasure lights up the face of the old desk which is burdened merely by a silver inkwell, a contemporary friend. I have bought a "dipping pen" to go with it and some black ink and the two of us, desk and hack, will saunter backwards together into a calmer, quieter age.

(Don't worry. I haven't gone totally potty. I am borrowing Herself's new, sophisticated computer for writing longer pieces but that rests on a plebeian desk of vastly inferior social quality elsewhere in the house. It will never sully my aristocratic workhorse).

Now to the hidden costs of the pen and ink world. Is there something about modern ink of which I wot not? Is there a world shortage? Is it suddenly a finite, endangered commodity? I ask because of its price. I bought a small bottle of perfectly ordinary, everyday ink for my silver inkpot. The bottle contained 57 ml. It cost £3.28. Now Einstein I am not. Indeed I am close to being innumerate. But even I can work out that at £3.28 for 57 ml, this ink would cost £57.40 a litre – with VAT £67.37.

And you can't even drink it!

SWEETIE LADY

THE day it was announced that Tesco's tills ring up £64,000 every minute, an old, crippled lady hobbled from the dim recesses of my memory to remind me of a vanished world. I don't quite know why or how she emerged from my sub-consciousness when I read that Tesco headline – the supermarket's pre-tax profit for the year had increased yet again to £1.71 billion – a sum which would have been totally beyond the comprehension of that wrinkled and kindly spinster of my childhood.

Y'see, she too, like Tesco's, was a shopkeeper. Her shop was in the front room of her tiny, limestone cottage half way up (or down) a steep street in my Derbyshire village of long ago. I'm not even sure about her name because we all knew her as "the sweetie lady" but I rather think she was a Miss Nuttall.

She sold us her meagre stock of tough toffees, gob-stoppers on sticks, gaily coloured balls of chewing gum from big glass jars and occasionally, just very occasionally because this was still the time of sweet rationing, a precious Mars bar. She lived huddled in a wooden armchair by her small, black-leaded fireplace in the kitchen, emerging creakily when the brass bell on her sitting room door announced the arrival of a customer. She must have made some sort of a living, though God knows how, but then her needs were few.

Her father had left her the cottage and, like the rest of us, she had few bills, certainly not for fuel, for the simple reason that the village had no electricity, gas or oil. Our fires burned wood from hedgerow and copse and our water came to us free from the wells. Those who grew their own vegetables made sure there were enough for the likes of the "sweetie lady" whose digging days were over and often she would find a freshly-gutted rabbit hanging on the nail outside her shop door.

Miss Nuttall sold only sweets. And that brings me to the point of this little parable from the past. Then, you see, it was unthinkable to enter into competition with other tradesfolk in such tightly-knit communities. My old man ran the pub where he sold only beer and spirits. The village baker baked and the grocer stuck to groceries. The butcher would have laughed if you'd asked him for a tin of mustard or a jar of pickles. "You'll get them down the grocer's." And every week from the market town there came round a man and a boy with a horse-drawn van selling paraffin, nails, needles and suchlike. No overlapping. That would have been called greed. They had no need of greed.

Which is one reason, I suppose, why gentle Miss Nuttall, the "sweetie lady", suddenly came to mind when I read those almost obscene profit figures issued last week by that vast supermarket chain spreading octopus-like over the face of our once green and pleasant kingdom.

It is not just the huge profits which are so disturbing. It is the thought of how much damage the growth of the supermarket has inflicted upon the social fabric of our society. Contented village shopkeepers – gone for ever. Market town high streets stripped by chain store greed of their traditional and friendly shops – grocer, baker, butcher, fish merchant, greengrocer – gone for ever, all of their wares for sale out of town in one huge, impersonal emporium housing the altar of Mammon.

Well, some will say, this is progress and it is inevitable in a rapidly changing world and so it might be. It won't stop some of us remembering. And don't anyone try to tell me that a motorised trip to Tesco's with a troop of chocolate-hungry grandchildren contains the same element of magic as walking 'em, hand in hand, up the village street, to find out what treat "the sweetie lady" has for us in those old glass jars in her cosy sitting room.

WALLOPED BY MY OLD MAN

THE first time my daddy gave his little boy a smack for being a very naughty little boy was when he caught me and some of our gang nicking paper packets of five Woodbines from the village shop. Actually, in the interests of historical accuracy, I should say that I didn't call him daddy and he didn't call me his little boy. I addressed him as "Sir" and he called me "lad". Furthermore, it wasn't a slap he gave me but a full-blooded clouting. He was the village bobby at the time and he reckoned I got away with it lightly because I only suffered the one belting since he was both bobby and father. The other lads got a good hiding from him and another one from their own fathers when they got home.

The old man larruped us in public on the village green watched by the other lads' parents, grim and silent in their approbation. Today his action would be viewed as barbaric, medieval and my father, the bobby, would have ended up in the very courtroom out of which he was so determined to keep us.

That was the beginning and the end of my career of crime other than an occasional nocturnal foray among the Duke's well-stocked pheasant coverts down the dale and his numerous grouse coveys up on the moors. But that wasn't thieving. That just sort of came natural-like to us youngsters, a part of growing up in the Derbyshire countryside.

Now whether that public drubbing had the desired effect is difficult to say. Certainly us ten-year-olds learned a swift and unforgettable lesson up there on that freezing village green dusted with the first snow of winter. Maybe we didn't realise it at the time but with the thwack of his police cape he instilled into us a recognition that crime most certainly does not pay and can lead to retribution and public humiliation. It also carries with it the loss of pride both personal and parental. The gang decided there and then to pack it in. We had brought shame upon ourselves and our families and that is a terrible cross to have to bear even at that age.

And so, just occasionally, I can't help wondering if we are doing the right thing by our young folk when we refrain from using chastisement as a tool to point them in the right direction. O.K! Maybe my old man's recipe might have been somewhat over the top but it sure as hell didn't do me and the gang any harm.

ME OL' SHUT-KNIFE

SINCE we are talking about the pottiness of modernity let us turn our attention to the penknife, that once ubiquitous and innocent artefact which is now on the endangered species list. Not so long ago a lad's penknife was the first definite step up the long ladder towards manhood and these lovely little implements graced the trouser pockets of just about every male from boyhood to senility. They were objects which elicited both pride and envy among schoolboys everywhere and were never discarded. Some lasted a lifetime. If "Made in Sheffield" appeared on the blade then the bearer of the knife was comforted by the thought that, no matter how cheap, it was unquestionably of the very highest quality because, of course, it was the work of a British craftsman.

Well, lads, youths and gentlemen, the time has arrived when perforce we must hide our friendly penknives from the prying eyes of misguided authority. Should you be caught carrying one with which to innocently sharpen a pencil, cut a thumb stick from the squire's hedge, open an otherwise impenetrable plastic container, peel an apple, whittle a safety match, cut a rose for your sweetheart, scratch a lottery card or just cut a piece of string, you are likely to find yourself taken in charge for carrying an offensive weapon.

No? Well, how about a former neighbour of ours who was arrested recently in a random police check in London for carrying a Swiss Army knife – there are millions of 'em in pockets all over the country and they're about as dangerous as a wet vest. I can't comment on this case because he has yet to come up before the beak but knowing the young man as I do I suspect the court is in for a rare treat since he is not one to be cowed by over-zealous authority.

I admit to carrying a knife – always have, always will. It's a pity Nicky hadn't borrowed mine for his London visit. It is rather a special one. It was given to me in 1995 by the then Supreme Allied Commander Europe, General James L. Jamerson, as a thank-you for some minor service I did for him. His signature is engraved on the knife with the magic logos SACEUR (Supreme Allied Commander, Europe) and SHAPE (Supreme Headquarters Allied Personnel, Europe). If Nicky had been carrying that instead of his common-or-garden Swiss job I reckon the rozzers would have saluted him and waved him on his way.

PENKNIVES AGAIN

WHY can't the authorities recognise the difference between the humble, innocent, innocuous and short-bladed penknife and the large, pernicious and hugely dangerous long-bladed weapons beloved of the thug classes and carried with evil intent?

People are blaming "the modern knife culture" for the continuous terrible spate of murders and stabbings by knife-wielding evil thugs. But there is nothing new about the British knife culture. We've always had one. Goes back centuries. Knight and knave wore them at their belts. In my youth a boy's most prized possession was his knife – be it a small, apple-slicing, wood-whittling, pencil-sharpening, prising-stones-from-horses'-hooves pocket variety, a sharp clasp knife for skinning rabbits, gutting trout and cutting a staff from the squire's hedge or the much prized sheath knife beloved of boy scouts. You couldn't play Cowboys and Indians without one – how else could you scalp a captured Cowboy?

Knives were tools of our every day life. Now they are tools of everyday death. What has changed? Sadly the truth is excruciatingly obvious. The knife hasn't changed. What has changed is the sort of lad who carries one today.

So what is the answer? Abolish all knives? Will such a ban include all kitchen knives? All scissors? All tradesmen's tools? The list is endless. It is yet another example of a knee-jerk reaction to a problem whose solution lies elsewhere – in this case with the police and the courts

WHAT HAPPENED TO.....?
WHAT DID WE DO BEFORE.....?

LONG after the close of day and shortly before ambling off into the land of Nod I stood in the garden gazing heavenwards and marvelling at the diamond-bright constellations of the night sky. Or, to put it another way, doing nothing of the sort since in these parts it is impossible any longer to see the heavenly bodies because of the hellish glow from a million electric lights. Goodbye lovely, magical stars.

Back in our (brightly lit) home I sat for a while a-thinking of our changing world whereupon I was suddenly seized with an idea for a brand-new game. It costs nowt, it is totally environmentally friendly and, once having adjusted your memory cells, it is dead easy to play. I'll start you off and all you have to do is to add your own ideas to mine. We'll call the game "WHAT?"

It is in two parts. Part one: "WHAT Happened to.......?"

Good manners, bobbies on foot, proper pubs, God, loyalty, sportsmanship, the dawn chorus, hopscotch, whip and top, decent black puddens, orderly queues, marriage, honesty, pride, patriotism, hoop bowling, barmaids with big smiles and ditto chests, teachers wearing gowns, respect, meadows, corncrakes, fair play, decency, bank managers, tolerance, contentment, tranquillity......the stars???

Part two: "WHAT On Earth Did We Do Before.......?"

The tele, plastic money/bags/PLASTIC(!), microwaves, dirty hospitals, E-mails, mass obesity, garden centres, cash machines, flat-pack furniture, fridges and freezers, wirelesses plugged into ears, on-line banking/shopping/buying and selling, sleeping pills, stress counsellors, central heating, credit cards, old folks' homes???

Those of you over the age of 50 will believe me when I say that in my youth all the items in the first section of the game were part and parcel of our everyday lives. You will also agree with me that none of the items in section two existed – nay, did not even play a part in our worst nightmares. Therefore, it is pointless to try to play the game with members of the younger generation because they are unlikely to have the faintest concept of the world encompassed in part one and they most certainly will not be able to imagine that a world could possibly exist without the aids mentioned in part two.

Warning: playing this game can seriously damage any lingering belief you may have harboured that progress is a good thing.

"ANTIQUE" PLATES

BOUGHT some second-hand pudding plates last week purely because they are decorated with fox-hunting scenes. Since it won't be long before the fanatics make it illegal for us to eat from such obscene platters I thought I should get in quick. Were they of any antiquity I wondered? Maybe late 19th century ventured the shop lady. I forbore through kindness from pointing out that printed under each plate was the legend: "Dishwasher and microwave safe".

TROOPING THE COLOUR

POPPED up to London Town to watch the Trooping as a guest of my good friend Douglas Cloughly, late of the Coldstream Guards and quartered frequently these days in the White Lion near his home in Newmarket. You can always tell a man from the Brigade of Guards no matter how long he has been softened by Civvy Street. He carries with him not just the eradicable outward signs – shoulders back, chest out, chin in – but an indefinable air of soldiery superiority which comes from knowing that without the slightest scintilla of doubt the Guards are, well, the best.

I should know. My father was a Grenadier and deep into his eighties he never walked anywhere. He marched. Like Doug there was ne'er a bristle of his moustache out of place and to be seen in public without a tie was for him an act of sloppiness contrary to good order and military discipline. I don't think he ever forgave me for being born too small to follow him into the Brigade but as I pointed out to him that was more his fault than mine. When they bunged me in the Intelligence Corps he was mortified. To a Guardsman that wasn't proper soldiering.

Anyoldhow it was the turn of the Irish Guards to Troop their Colours this year and a magnificent job the Micks made of it as even an old Coldstreamer and a Grenadier's son were obliged to admit. I doubt there is a finer example of military ceremonial anywhere in the world and it was my privilege to watch the incomparable spectacle in the company of a man who, like my old chap before him, had paraded there on Horseguards in the presence of his monarch. I often wish I had been just a couple of inches taller.

As for London, Doug and I fled the terrifying noise and bustle of that madhouse without pause and hastened back to the calm and (comparative) sanity of the White Lion.

DERBYSHIRE IN THE SNOW

SOME of the best fibs are those which are made up on the very spur of the moment. Which brings me to the seasonal gift I have bought for our house this Christmas. It is a large oil painting of a snow-covered Derbyshire hillside dotted with sheep, a charming landscape after which I have lusted since I saw it in the gallery window. The cost was met by my winnings from a slight investment in a horse named Longstone Lass which I had backed on the scientific racing principle that Longstone was the Peakland village where I spent an idyllic childhood. Herself complained about my extravagance. There was little point in explaining that the bookies had actually paid for it since I tell her my horses never win otherwise she will want a share in the spoils. The fib came to me in a twink. "My dear", said I silkily, "I have been saving hard to pay for the picture because I know it will be a great financial boon to you at some time in the future."

She looked exceedingly sceptical but I pressed on. "As you know, my dear, I was born in the Derbyshire hills – conceived there as well, shouldn't wonder – and I have always wanted to die there. Thus, when my time is nigh, instead of having to transport me all the way up there, all you will have to do is to stand the picture at the foot of my bed and I will depart in peace. It'll save you a small fortune."

I was, she said, a kind and thoughtful husband and she was much moved by my financial sacrifice, the very essence of Christmas. During dinner that night she asked me, as though in passing, the name of the horse which had paid for the painting. Some marriages are founded on trust; some, apparently, are not.

SHAKESPEARE'S 'BLEEDING' MAN

RECENTLY there has been much ado about the propriety for several silly reasons of teenage Romeos and Juliets kissing each other on stage in Shakespeare's play. Busybodies should realise that mucking about with the Bard can be dangerous. At school we did

"Macbeth" and put it on in the town hall. The lad playing Duncan, the Scottish king, was the son of a Free Church minister. Unfortunately, Duncan's first line in Scene 2, Act I, is: "What bloody man is that?" – referring to a wounded sergeant. The Minister absolutely banned his son from using that particular adjective. At a meeting between Minister and Headmaster the latter, a wily old boy, proposed a compromise. What if "bloody" was replaced by "bleeding"? Fine, said the naive Minister. Word got round, Bakewell Town Hall was packed for the first night and only the Minister wondered why the audience collapsed with laughter as his son spoke the censored line, for ever engraved on my funny bone – "What bleeding man is that?" For the remainder of his unblemished life Duncan's dad was known in the district as "that bleeding Minister".

HALYCON DAYS

IMAGINE, please, the following scene.......

A group of lads, none of 'em older than seven or eight, meet on the village green soon after an early breakfast. Some are dressed as red indians and carry bows made from yew boughs and arrows tipped with grey goose feathers. The others wear cowboy outfits made by mum and have toy pistols strapped to their sides. Nearly every day of the long summer holiday starts like this and the two "sides" set off up cow-mucky Church Lane and head for the distant moors. They will whoop and holler all morning in the open wilderness disturbing only the curlews, herons and grouse. By lunch-time (no, in Derbyshire it is dinner-time) they are miles from the village and, hot and thirsty, they tumble hurriedly down dizzyingly steep slopes into the dale. The river water is clear and pure. They drink from it and they swim in the shallower stretches alongside the Duke's dappled trout. Cowboy and indian alike catch crayfish. In late summer they gorge on blackberries, wild raspberries and hazel nuts. Then it's the long, uphill trudge back to the village for tea – mounds of jam sandwiches and cups of cow-warm milk. Mum and dad are totally unconcerned about the day-long absence of the cowboys and indians. There is nothing to worry about. They've only been up on the moors and down the dale. They've only been playing.

I paint this picture for you because research shows that today's children are being denied the opportunities for play enjoyed by previous generations due to their parents' exaggerated anxieties about their children being harmed by strangers. The result is that a whole generation is being mollycoddled out of all proportion to the actual risks involved. It is terribly, terribly sad.

You see, I was one of those lads who grew up wandering over miles of heather and splashing the afternoon away in the cool waters of the River Wye down in Monsal Dale. We never looked over our shoulders in apprehension. Parents never bade us beware of strangers for the simple reason that in our tightly-knit communities there weren't any. The men we met on moor and in dale were farmers, drovers, shepherds and keepers and they were our dads, brothers and uncles. Childhood to us, poor though we were, was quite simply idyllic. Today when I think of all the children who are being denied the simple but blissful joys of my own halcyon childhood I could weep for each and every one of them.

A thought comes to me. We had to take it in turn to be cowboys and indians because in those jolly days of total political incorrectness red indians were always the baddies and cowboys the goodies and the cowboys always had to win. Can you imagine what today's long haired, bearded and be-sandalled teachers would have to say about that?

GOD BY ANY OTHER NAME.....

THERE is some current argument about the rights and wrongs of modernising the language of The Lord's Prayer. Whatever they do won't worry many of us wrinklies because we shall just carry on using the traditional version. But I must confess to an early misunderstanding of the prayer and for years as a lad I thought God's name was Harold. "Our Father, which art in heaven, Harold be thy name......"

A GOTCH

WE have been nattering recently about East Anglian dialects and I rediscovered a lovely word recently. The word is: Gotch. Around here it means a large earthenware jug or pitcher. ("Fetch the gotch, bor' – bring the jug, lad"). I came across possibly the granddaddy of them all in Clare parish church the other day. Now in a glass case their gotch was given to the bell-ringers by the vicar in 1729 and holds 32 pints of beer. In my present state of total sobriety I gazed upon the wondrous vessel with deep envy for the bell-ringers of old Clare. Then I wondered. Did they empty the gotch before they started or when they finished? If it was before then Clare's peals must have been the merriest in the whole of Suffolk. Ding dong.....oops.

Modern Living

A LIFE OF POVERTY

I AM led to understand that Herself and I are teetering on the verge of poverty and have been for a very long time. Y'see, I read somewhere that one of the poverty indicators used by the social services is the lack of a second telly in the household, preferably one in the bedroom. And on top of that the poverty line is also crossed when families rely on second-hand gear in their homes. Well, that's us for sure.

Take our furniture for example. There is scarcely a modern piece in the house and, what is worse, we have to make do with stuff which in some cases is one, two or even three hundred years old. We've never complained – we just got on with it. Same with the plates, knives and forks, glasses, candlesticks and such like; most of it was old when Herself's father inherited it. Now it has filtered its way down through the years to us and whilst other people may eat from the very latest gaily-caparisoned plastic platters we feel it would be needlessly expensive and overly ostentatious to replace our ancient tableware with something more in touch with the times simply to try and keep up with the Joneses.

No, I can assure you that bringing up a family with only one telly was absolute hell and I truly believe that Herself and I deserve a hefty retrospective government grant for living such a rough, poverty-stricken existence for so long without so much as a chirrup of complaint. Did our children ever compare their sad lot with other more fortunate friends whose parents had ready access to the edible treasures from the deep freezers of the big stores in the High Street? No they damn well did not. In winter I was forced to venture out into the storm-tossed fens and the wilderness of Norfolk with dog and gun in order to keep family starvation at bay by bringing home an occasional pheasant, partridge, mallard, goose and hare. The children managed to survive with these offerings of a bountiful nature and cauldrons of thick soups, home-baked bread, main crop taters from the garden, great, steaming treacle puddings, tarts bursting with our own apples. Now the jams and jellies of autumn came into their own as we all sat around our meagre log fire at tea-times, making do with hot toast and muffins oozing sugary compotes of raspberries, goose-gogs, red and black currants. My God it was tough being poor.

Summer was slightly better because I made sure we were self-sufficient in vegetables and fruit from the garden, though even my long-suffering mob objected now and then about the amount of asparagus they were obliged to eat with their home-made mayonnaise during the season. As a poor man, I did my best for them and sought to vary their diet. So much so I often sacrificed what little leisure time was available to me by journeying northwards in order to return with a catch of salmon and trout from Scottish rivers and lochs. My, how their pinched little faces shone with hungry anticipation as I emptied a silvery haul from the boot of my car (second-hand, please note, albeit a 3-litre Rover).

Anyoldhow, with a pinch here and a scrape there and a visit to the Oxfam second-hand clothes shop we seem to have managed – despite qualifying in this nutty world of ours as being officially poor. But we still haven't got two tellies. We have to make do with books but even they are all old and second-hand. Some even have previous owners' names in them. Oh dear, how much further down the social ladder can we slide?

BRING BACK THE DOLLY

NEW washing machine arrived this week. Frightens me half to death. Switch it on and it lights up like Blackpool Illuminations. Why, to make life easier do they make it more complicated? I grew up with the clothes boiler heated by a little fire, the three-legged wooden dolly for swishing the clothes round, the scrubbing board and the cast iron mangle with wooden rollers. Heavy ol' work but healthier than three expensive hours in the gym. Bring back dolly days, says I, and get over-plump mums off their backsides every Monday.

Yes, I know so don't bother to write. That last bit was pure sexism and I don't terribly care. I'm also into ageism, political correctnessism, beards and open-toed sandalsism, tie-less politiciansism, schismism and any other ism which borders on the farcical. But I find nothing remotely funny about racism.

****

AH! The excitements of our electronic age! I think I have mastered the intricacies of our new washing machine – the one that lights up like Los Angeles on Christmas Eve when you start it – but perhaps not. Herself told me to press the button on the right when it had stopped so I could take the washing out. I pressed the button on the right – the machine started washing again. You should have pressed the button on the left of the one on the right, she said.

OOPS! SORRY!

AND talking of problems, how on earth can we stop all those sales people from interrupting our daily lives with their endless phone calls offering us cheap double glazing, free kitchens and 99 per cent off a new conservatory? Finding the right sort of put-down without being totally offensive is difficult. But it is possible. Fran, one of the lissom young ladies who cater for our thirst-quenching requirements over at that elegant watering hole in Newmarket, the Marlborough Club, was phoned by a particularly pressing salesman who assured her that his firm had the perfect conservatory for her home. They had checked her address and would be very happy to pop round and measure up – all for free of course. Would she mind if they made an appointment?

"Delighted", said Fran, all friendly like. "But you might find it a bit difficult when it comes to measuring the site. I live in a third-floor flat." Which she does. End of pressurised phone call.

ST GEORGE'S DAY DUMPLINGS

WELL, now it is official. The Day of St George, the English patron saint, is not "a special occasion" according to magistrates and police over Norfolk way. They have just jointly opposed an application by landlord Tony Bennett for an extra one hour's drinking at his pub, The Otter, at Thorpe Marriott near Norwich, to celebrate St George's Day on April 23.

Norfolk police told Norwich magistrates that there was no mention of St George's Day in any of their procedural guides. "It is the view of the constabulary that St George's Day is not a special occasion." To be fair, magistrate Roy Church did grant the drinking application but only for a "charitable function". Which isn't the same thing at all to a full-blooded Norfolk Englishman.

Now, oddly enough, Norfolk is famed in our part of the world for its dumplings which, as you know, are at home in a rich ol' stew and that is precisely what those rozzers and beaks have got themselves into in Norwich – a right rich ol' stew. On Norfolk kitchen tables dumplings fall into two categories, heavy ones are called "sinkers" and lighter ones are known as "floaters". But the word dumpling has a third meaning. It is used to describe a plodding sort of person, one who is literally as thick as a gastronomic dumpling.

I very much doubt that I am alone in believing that, so far as our patron saint is concerned, the Norfolk police and magistrates are "sinker" dumplings who have fallen into a stew of their own confection.

The big snag about getting all of a tiswas about St George is that he never existed and he only emerged into the English lexicon when he became the talisman of Richard the Lionheart. But non-existence is no reason for ignoring his continuing influence in our national psyche because, dammit, we all believe in Father Christmas, kindly bank managers and honest bookies but, take it from one who knows, they simply do not exist (though I still wonder about F.C.).

We really took dear ol' dragon-bashing George to our national hearts after the battle of Agincourt in 1415 when St George replaced Edward the Confessor as England's patron saint. Way back then they didn't muck about – they just declared April 23 a national feast day and got stuck in to the ale and victuals.

It was, of course, just before Agincourt when Henry V delivered himself, via Shakespeare, of the most stirring of all battle cries:

"I see you stand like greyhounds in the slips,
Straining upon the start. The game's afoot:
Follow your spirit; and, upon this charge
Cry 'God for Harry! England and St George!'"

Or, as some of 'em over Norwich way might prefer it:

"Cry 'God for Harry! England and a certain person of a vague, charitable status.'"

****

THIS April 23rd will be my first St George's Day as a teetotaller and I am beginning to wonder how I shall replace the foaming flagons of yore – the flagons of England's finest cider and beer of yesteryear which washed down my platters of roast ribs of beef, pies plump with our own orchard apples and wedges of prime Stilton. Roast beef of Olde England and a flagon of chilled lemonade somehow lacks a certain Shakespearian grandeur about it. Alas and flaming alack.

OPENING THE CASINO FLOODGATES

THIS government is causing a great brouhaha by insisting that gambling is good for us and the more of it the better. It intends to wave another of its magic wands which will make planning restrictions covering gambling casinos vanish overnight.

Why any government should wish to convert our pleasant little kingdom into one vast Las Vegas is totally beyond me, although there is a lingering suspicion at the back of my mind that the whole ghastly wheeze may have something – just something – to do with another stealth tax. Y'see, I cannot rid myself of the tantalising image of the Chancellor of the Exchequer wearing a croupier's eye-shield, sitting round a green baize table with his cigar-chomping, casino-owning cronies sharing out very large lumps of coin of the realm extracted from you and me on the roulette wheels and one-armed bandits. "Fifty million for you – fifty million for me – fifty million for you – fifty mill......"

Mmm. I fear it will not be a pretty picture when our government ministers are seen snuffling their snouts in the same deep trough as the bunch of Godfathers who will, sure as hell is hot, move into the casino scene. Roulette wheels and the Mafia are inextricably intertwined and where there are Mafiosi there are drugs and where there are drugs there are guns. Well done, President Blair.

Friends might well accuse me of hypocrisy since I have been a well-known fixture at race tracks over the years. True. I gamble on the nags and always have done. I hide behind the defence that horse racing is an intellectual pursuit involving deep study of form and breeding, a knowledge of the idiosyncratic habits of horses, owners, trainers and jockeys and the varying nuances in the undulations of the different racecourses around the kingdom. The horse itself, God wot, is one of the most magnificent creatures on earth, especially when it wins carrying your money. The thoroughbred equine world, crooked though it undoubtedly is (and always was) has a sort of soul of its very own which is more than can be said of a million faceless machine bandits and small black balls for ever cascading around pre-set roulette wheels. Hypocrite I may be but I still oppose vehemently the opening of the casino floodgates and the social sickness this will bring to our already debt-ridden society.

IT'S NOT THEIR FAULT

THERE is a small farm just beyond the edge of a quiet fenland village. Living there is a newly-widowed lady, alone now, apart from her dog. I have known her, as I knew her late husband, these many years. Whilst not wildly remote, their farmhouse is sufficiently far from the madding crowd to be idyllically quiet and peaceful. Alas the idyll is now a facade.

For a long time, even before her husband died, the farm has been under virtual siege. If the place is left unoccupied for even the briefest period, in move the thieves. Machinery and farm implements disappear. Recently the villains took with them all of the widow's washing from her line in the garden.

She is not alone in her dilemma. Farmers all over the broad acres of the fens have similar stories. The police seem to be singularly incapable of sorting this growing menace out. The talk, therefore, turns more and more, to that of self-protection. My friend the widow is now prepared to defend her property with her dog and, if necessary, with other means of force. And who can blame her?

You have merely to glance at a copy – any copy – of a local paper any day of the week to read of muggings, stabbings, car thefts, burglaries, criminal damage, offensive and threatening behaviour ... the list is endless ... in communities across this once tranquil region.

But worry not, because an explanation for this exploding phenomenon is at hand. I was much moved by the pronouncement recently of a leading sociologist that, no ifs or buts about it, villainy in our youthful population is caused entirely by bad parental example so that, in effect, we should forgive the young their trespasses for they know not what they do.

I was so touched by the certainty of the validity of this assertion that the muse stirred within me. Here is the versified tale of a couple of lads whose excesses were clearly all down to mum but for whom it went badly wrong:

"She had the voice of an egg-bound corncrake
And the face of a well-rung bell.
She had the heart of a hungry bloodhound
That was spawned in the depths of hell.

But to us she was our mummy
Who daddy was she ne'er would tell.
She taught us the skills of the gutter,
My brother and me, did old Nell.
Which is why, on a moonlit night
We must watch the stars from our cell."

Kindly reflect on that the next time you are mugged by a gang of vicious young thugs as you walk quietly on your way home or your farm is besieged or your shop is plundered. Forgive them for they know not what they do.

OL' JEACOCK'S ALMANAC

BY an odd coincidence, New Year starts in January again which means that it is time for Jolly Jack Jeacock to glance into his crystal sphere and to present you with his annual Almanac. 'Yer 'tis:

January. Once more we will be able to doff our caps in admiration for the lorry drivers, particularly those from foreign parts, who will refuse to be bullied by the elements into driving safely along the A14 in this neck of the fens. These motorised maniacs will ignore snow, ice, sleet and fog and continue to drive like bats out of hell, bumper to bumper, nose to tail, along one of the most dangerous stretches of death-dealing roadways in the country. Petrified locals would be well-advised to make the Huntingdon to Cambridge journey via the alternative route through Totnes and Budleigh Salterton.

February. Pheasant shooting finishes on the 1st and with no cricket or decent flat racing, this dreary month is best ignored.

March. A junior government minister will murmur condolences at the increasing number of deaths and serious injuries on the Cambridgeshire section of the A14. We will be told: "The government will no longer tolerate this intrusion into the right of our 70-year-olds to get to work on time."

April. The demand for sick notes will multiply as the flat racing season starts. As usual, the sick and stressed will recuperate en masse in the bars and bookmakers' enclosure over in Newmarket.

May. The loons who rule us from Brussels will issue a 40,000-word directive assuring the travelling community of its inalienable human right to doss down wherever it fancies. This pronouncement will cause much hilarity among the citizenry of fenland towns and villages who have long suspected that human rights are never extended to honest, hard-working, tax-paying and law-abiding folk.

June. This will be a blazing month of long, hot days enriched by startling blue skies and balmy evenings suffused by the myriad scents of early blossoms. The heat-wave will bring back the female fashion of ever shorter mini skirts and skimpy floral dresses. (This, you understand, is not so much a professional forecast as an old man's self-indulgent dream. It'll probably chuck it down every day and the girls will be covered up in long macs and wellies).

July. Funny time of the year because of the rapidly changing seasons and these days July can easily be mistaken for August what with early hedgerow berries and the harvest being safely gathered in a month too soon. My best-planned runes and incantations are all of a muddle so to hell with it. Those who wish to make sure of a proper mixture of summer sun and a plenitude of pulchritude will take my advice and book a cruise round the Med.

August. The languorous torpor which normally settles on fenland this month will be rudely disturbed by a government announcement that another new town is to be built on all "those useless, empty fields lying fallow" between Cambridge and Manea. When told by the experts that the fields flood in winter, a government spokesperson will say: "Maybe, but they say the summers out there are lovely."

September: Addenbrooke's Hospital will cut admissions for all new patients to two days a week to allow the medical staff sufficient time to fill in administrators' forms. A senior proforma designer will explain that it is simply a question of priorities.

October. A new generation of Cambridge University students will arrive, anxious to begin their three-year boozeathon. They will be awarded automatic degrees if, during the three years, they can claim to have a) spoken to their tutor more than twice; b) written an essay which they haven't nicked from the internet; and c) spotted a uniformed rozzer on the streets of Cambridge.

November. Another public inquiry will be told by an incomer to Smithy Fen that he and his family wish to settle down there. Why else would they call themselves "travellers?"

December. Christmas will fall around the 25th this year. Start saving now. Meanwhile, I feel a hibernation coming on.

WONDERFUL PRIZES

WHAT have we done in this household to deserve the immense largesse which kindly strangers are heaping upon us at the beginning of this grey and chilly new year? Very shortly Herself and I will be so rich that even Croesus will squirm with envy in his golden grave.

It started with the Reader's Digest. Their glad tidings reached us in the first post after Christmas. We are, you will be delighted to hear, potential winners of £250,000 in the third and final stage of their 98th grand prize draw. And all we have to do is to order some of their books! What a doddle! What an incredible piece of luck! They say we are "potential" winners but in my heart I know this is the real McCoy and on the strength of our windfall Herself has already ordered a giant-size packet of Camomile teabags and some ginger biscuits in a tin with a picture of Windsor Castle on the lid.

Then, blow me down, if the phone didn't ring and a charming lady with an Indian accent informed me that the Jeacocks had been specially chosen to receive, absolutely free, double glazing for the whole house. All I had to do was to phone the following number...

I tried to point out to this generous soul phoning from the other side of the world that there were perhaps rather more deserving cases since we were already fully double-glazed but she carried on talking. Perhaps she was lonely.

And before you could cry "Bingo", a letter from Spain arrived with the incredible news that we have won – outright – the Bilbao Lottery. I couldn't for the life of me recall entering this particular competition but the ol' memory is not what it was. Our prize runs into hundreds of thousands of Euros, a coinage which I cannot quite comprehend, and this time all we have to do is to send these nice Spaniards some of our money so that our winnings can be released from their bank. It sounds complicated but their letter is on printed notepaper so it must be official and above board. Anyway, we are selling the car to scrape enough cash together so we can claim our Spanish fortune.

And all in the first week of 2005! If it goes on like this, they'll end up shovelling doubloons through the letter box. We are rich! rich! rich! Or, er ... are we?

WOOLWORTHS EMPORIUM

A NICE lady behind the till in Woolworths made me an offer the other day which I had to refuse because I had no idea what she was talking about. As I paid for a light bulb, she kindly asked me if I was interested in ... and there followed a string of incomprehensible letters. My deafness didn't help but it sounded to me as though she was asking me if I would care to take advantage of a special offer of something called CDSANDVDS. My first thought was that Woolies had overstocked on a cure for a nasty sort of disease. If so, no thanks. Another bloke in the queue, about as old, deaf and daft as me, thought it was something to do with being a blood donor, you know, the letters were different blood groups. Whichsoever, I still can't fathom why the till lady laughed so much when the two antediluvians tottered off arguing about other possibilities.

COMMUNICATION BREAKDOWN

THE disclosure last week that, in a moment of stark madness, I had considered trying to learn how to do an e-mail sent family, friends and the slimy inmates of the world of journalism into paroxysms of chortles. I had not realised just how all-encompassing was the circle of acquaintances who are aware of my total inability to cope with anything remotely contemporary, complicated or technical. They view my increasing insularity from the real world as a weakness. I look upon it as a blessing.

I have developed a monk-like belief in the sanctity of simplicity. I cannot conceive of a life-style which requires me to spend hours every week watching films on videos. Somewhere along this route is the point of insanity. If I miss a film on the telly I have to miss another film while I am watching the first one I missed. Very shortly I shall have to record all the films I am missing while I am watching all the films I have already missed. Enter the gentlemen in white coats. You will find me curled up in the corner of the room, whimpering.

For more years than our allotted biblical span I have managed to travel hither and thither without phoning all and sundry to let them know which bridge I am passing over/under at that precise moment or that the bus driver's name is Fred and that he looks like that bloke in the video we might just fit in during the third Friday in Whit Week.

Now, apparently, you can take photographs with telephones. Why? I can't recall ever phoning auntie Nellie from my old Box Brownie but we seemed to get by.

So why did I suddenly decide to learn about e-mails? I blame my innate sense of adventure. I was overcome by this sudden urge to take a great leap into the unknown. When I asked Herself to teach me how to make one – an e-mail, that is – for one exhilarating nano-moment I felt as though I was the first man on the moon. At last I was entering the vast world of science. Where would it all end?

Well, it ended the minute she showed me a book about the internet. Instantly I am in a different world where a new and incomprehensible language is universally spoken. I am too old to learn another language. Do I really need, at my age, to connect a Zip drive to my computer's parallel port? Must I log on to a window? I don't much like being told where to plug my audio input jack and I flatly refuse to create a new bitmap image. I was so moved by the idiocy of it all that I filled my fountain pen and wrote the following...

"I can hold a conversation
In Russian and Romanian
And my French is very "oo-la-la".
My Hindi is rather rusty
And my German upper crusty
But my French is ever so-la-la.
Though my Finnish never started
From Sanskrit I am rarely parted
And in Chile my Spanish rings loud and clear.
But can I speak computer?
No! I can't speak bloody computer.
It is completely foreign to my ear."

Come with me, Jack. We'll sit in the garden with a book and have a zizz.

EXACT FIGURES

AND talking of experts, from which bran-tub do they drag their figures? Here is the Chief Medical Officer of Health telling us that when – not if, but when – Asian bird flu comes flopping into our islands then 50,000 of us will die. Note that 50,000. Not 48,371 or 51,102. Then our local head health wallah joins in. In Cambridgeshire, 800 people are for the last big cough. Note again – 800 precisely. If they can be so accurate, why can't they give us a list of names? If I'm on it I want to know. Do I order my member's badge at Newmarket races for next year or not?

A TERRIBLE – WONDERFUL WORLD

THE following episodes happened in the past fortnight ...

Act 1: A quiet market town, late afternoon. An elderly bloke (me) saunters along, happy as Larry. Close by a woman screams. People rush from nearby shops. Round the corner the screaming woman lies on the pavement clutching her stomach. Blood seeps down her left leg through a jagged hole in her trousers. She shouts: "I've been stabbed. It hurts. It hurts." Nearby a burly young man clutches his shoulder. He, too, is bleeding heavily. Bewildered, he says: "I only tried to stop him and he stabbed me." Their attacker has fled. Ambulance and police arrive, lights flashing. The injured are taken to hospital. This is the heart of Newmarket on a quiet October afternoon. I think – what a terrible world we live in.

Act 2: Five days later, the same elderly bloke walks into a bookie's shop 100 yards from where the attack took place. A deep voice says: "Well, if it isn't that old so-and-so Jeacock." It is a friend of many years. We shake hands, back the same horse – a certainty – it loses and we both laugh. My old chum can well afford to laugh at life's little disasters for he is Colin Everett, retired policeman, of Little Wilbraham, near Cambridge. Exactly twelve and a half years ago Colin Everett phones me, his voice little more than a whisper. His heart is finished and he is dying. Would I say a few words at his funeral? Then the miracle-workers of Papworth give him a heart transplant. Twelve and a half years ago! As we part I think – what a wonderful world we live in.

A VERY BUSY BRIDGE

DESIST from your labours, gentle reader, because with a hey! and a ho! and a hey-nonny-no! it is chuckle time again.

Let me not complicate the joke. You may recall with a wry smile earlier stories about the plan to erect a towering Bridge of Reeds spanning the A14 to the east of Cambridge near Stow-cum-Quy. It will, they say, become one of the most striking landmarks in England. It is the brainchild of an outfit called the East of England Development Agency (EEDA) and, no, I don't know who appoints its officials but I've a damn good idea who pays for 'em.

Now hear this: someone, God knows who, has estimated that our Bridge will be crossed by 60,000 (yes, sixty thousand) walkers and cyclists EACH DAY (my capitals). I'm no Einstein but I reckon that's close on 22 million hearty hikers and bikers a year. Still, as the EEDA says: "The bridge breaks new ground and will be a true landmark we can be proud of. The fact that it will provide access on foot or cycle to thousands of acres of rich natural habitat should bring invaluable benefits and great enjoyment to future generations." Hmmm!

Next on the agenda? A project manager will be appointed (I know, I know) and "bids will be developed for funding the Bridge itself." The begging bowl goes first to the National Lottery. The cost, at present rates? Just nine million quid. It should start in 2008. And if the Lottery won't cough up, who will? I don't know but I've a damn good idea.

****

LAST week we discussed the bafflingly weird concept of the proposed £9,000,000, 177-foot-high bridge of steel "reeds" which, when/if it finally spans the A14 east of Cambridge, will become an "iconic landmark" for our region, or so the East of England Development Agency assures us. One particularly baffling aspect of this Alice-in-Wonderland scheme is the forecast that 60,000 walkers and cyclists will use the bridge EACH DAY to venture out into the fens. Herself has done some more sums. Not only does that mean that nigh on 22 million hikers and bikers will cross the little bridge EVERY YEAR but that 2,500 AN HOUR or 41 EACH MINUTE of EVERY DAY will be hurtling in and out of the fens to fulfil that forecast. Brace yourselves, fenfolk.

RE-INTRODUCING A GREAT TRADITION

MEANWHILE, seasonal greetings and thanks to the Post Office for bringing back to vibrant life that ancient national tradition which was in danger of dying out – the Great British Queue. The remedy was so simple. Close as many small post offices as possible and the idiot population will be forced into the few remaining in the High Streets. Then – hey presto! – they've suddenly created vast crocodiles of wheezing, coughing, sneezing, ill-tempered citizens shuffling towards a counter where the staff are certain to nip off for a comfort break as soon as you reach it. Christmas crackers.

THINGS YOU WON'T MEET IN THE COMING YEAR

HERE is my list of the things you are least likely to come across in the coming year. Let me know your score next January ...

A happy jogger, a perambulating constable, a smiling bank manager (any sort of bank manager), a genuine asylum seeker, a gentleman footballer, a politically-correct fenman, a redundant civil servant, a mobile phone-free child, an animal-loving animal libber, a miserable beekeeper, a dead donkey, a Cambridge biker with a bell, a blushing bride, a travelling "traveller", a gay rabbit, a bucolic property developer, a literate teacher, a family bakery. And I bet you didn't see many, if any, last year.

GOOD WEEK FOR THE NUTCASE BRIGADE

A GREAT week for the onward march of the Nutcase Brigade. One after another the wierdos have come crashing out of the trees and, if you are wondering how it is possible to march and climb trees at the same time, just take it from me that this lot are capable of performing the most dexterous of tasks just so long as the right mixture of total battiness is involved. Yea, verily, they can't even wait for April 1.

Loony Lot 1: Some toddlers' teachers have decided that Baa Baa Black Sheep is disgustingly and politically incorrect. From now on, kiddywinks, it's Baa Baa Rainbow Sheep if you please. Readers from outer space may find this difficult to comprehend. Me too.

Loony Lot 2: Similar mad mob won't allow Humpty Dumpty to break after his great fall from the wall. That would make him disadvantaged. Whoever heard of broken eggs?

Loony Lot 3: The faceless geniuses of Brussels say the shells fired by our Royal Horse Artillery on ceremonial occasions make too much noise. Only hope they won't object to the noise our guns make when we pop over the Channel again to dig 'em all out of the mire after they've surrendered to the next Fuhrer to pass that way.

Loony Lot 4: Closer to home, retired teacher Betty Wilbraham was told to remove her titfer when she sat down for a bite and a drink in an Ely pub. Seems her rain hat was a security risk – it restricted the pub's CCTV coverage. Well, maybe the pub was right. She may have been a member of the WI for 40 years, she may wear glasses, she may have led a blameless life *so far* but from the newspaper picture of her it is plain that 82-year-old Betty Wilbraham is potentially as rough a tearaway as you will ever see on a CCTV punch-up.

SO WHO'S IN CONTROL?

WITH Herself away for the weekend, I'm lolling the evening away chat-free on my ownsome, Beethoven's Fifth crashing and banging away in the background as I renew my friendship with Housman's "Shropshire Lad", happily cocooned in my own simple pleasures. Then the flaming phone rings.

It's an old mate with whom I am always delighted to share a natter except when I'm being privately entertained by a master composer and a half decent poet. However, I hide my irritation and ask the purpose of his telephonic communication at this late hour? Sorry and all that, says he, but could I give him my e-mail address as he wishes to send me an invitation? To what, I ask? A luncheon party with some long-standing Cambridge mates in a pub over St Ives way, says he. Where precisely, which day and what time? He tells me. I accept. There is a pause. But, he says, I haven't given him my e-mail address. How can he send me an invite? I explain he has just invited me and I have just accepted. Why send an e-mail?

If it is possible to hear a man shrug his shoulders with frustration on the phone, that's what he is doing right now. It is as though I am spoiling a game. But the others, he says in a steely voice, will get an e-mail. He would like to send me one as well. Why? Because that's how everybody communicates these days, he says.

Why, I ask? He says he will see me at the lunch and rings off, distinctly huffed. Beethoven, too, is silent and Housman's ghost, I suspect, is gazing out from the top of Bredon Hill aghast at the madness of the modern world.

I mention this because a recent survey showed that children are way ahead of us oldies in their abilities to understand and operate the most complex of modern gadgets. This surprised me not a jot since we have in our family a clutch of bright young clickers, faxers, e-mailers, texters and specialist operatives in the distant and baffling world of the internet. We call them grandchildren. The survey shows that youngsters are able to control incredibly sophisticated gew-gaws with little or no difficulty. What terrifies me is not the way the children control their electronic toys. It is more the manner in which the toys are now beginning to control them – and us!

Take the case of that self-same chap who was playing Beethoven when his phone rang. Being fairly deaf, he was sitting close to the gramophone or whatever they call them today. But he still got up and walked across the room to pick up the machine's remote control to turn the music down. I was glad nobody saw me do it. They might have thought that the toys were getting their malign grip on me as well.

WHO AM I? ASK BARCLAYS

THEY don't know much about ageism at Barclays Bank and that's for sure. They have issued an edict which demands that if its customers wish to draw cash from their accounts they must produce TWO of the following.....

Passport (haven't got one), European National ID Card (certainly not), UK Armed Forces ID Card (marched away when I was a lad), UK Driving Licence (yes), Student ID Card (ho-ho), Company ID Card (ho-ho-ho) Debit or credit card (no), Building Society Pass Book (sorry, no), Pension Book (pension goes straight into the bank), Disability and Living Allowance Book (not just yet, thanks).

Now I cannot be the only elderly gentleman who no longer goes abroad, who has never heard of a European ID card and wouldn't want one if I had, who gave up soldiering half a century ago, who never had a student ID card, or a Company ID card, who doesn't want one of their debit or credit cards, who doesn't care for Building Societies, who doesn't have a Pension Book and who is not yet disabled.

So, where does that leave me? One out of two means no cash. I suspect the same goes for millions of the grey-brigade. I know it is designed as a security measure but it is still potty, totally potty.

Which reminds me of the old lady who was asked by her bank if she had any proof of identity. Carefully she removed a small mirror from her handbag, looked into it and told the bank cleric "Oh yes! That's definitely me."

MUSICAL CONTRAPTIONS

I OFTEN wonder how many of my generation have allowed modernity to overtake and confuse them. I certainly have. I am fond of classical music and for most of my life I have been able to enjoy the works of great composers, orchestras and singers in the comfort of my own home. All that was needed to bring this miracle of pleasure about was one of those cabinets inside which was a sort of circular platform with a short steel thing sticking up in the middle.

You then took a round record with a hole in it and placed it onto the sticking up thing. When the record began to go round you simply lifted a kind of arm with a pin on the end and lowered it gently on to the record. Then the room began to be filled with sweet music and all you needed to do was to sit back, glass of wine in hand, and relax.

Not so any longer. We have acquired, for reasons entirely beyond my ken, a plastic monster of a music-playing machine, the operating complexities of which are clearly designed to prevent, rather than encourage, the glorious dissemination of recorded music.

Herself understands how to operate this ridiculous machine and hitherto I have allowed her the privilege of dealing with it. Alas, she retired early t'other evening and, anxious for a touch of Mozart, I found myself alone and sorely puzzled. Kneeling before what looked like a spaceship control panel I counted 41 knobs, dials, twiddly bits and buttons some of which lit up when pressed. But where to place that little disc thingamajig I could not discover.

Being disturbed from her repose by my frustrated rantings Herself reappeared, haughty with contempt at my inability to come to terms with so simple a device, and produced the required music in a series of apparently easy manipulations which I'm damned if could follow.

Take it from me that The Magic Flute loses much of its magic when accompanied by a late-night lecture on the desirability, nay, the necessity, of coming to terms with the twentieth – never mind the twenty-first – century.

ERIC AND HIS E-MAIL

THE phone rang. I answered it. Please bear in mind that I am fairly deaf and have little or no understanding of the electronic complexities of the 20th century, never mind this one. Our answering machine (no I don't know how it works) happened to come on when Eric's call came through. Thus I am able to repeat our conversation verbatim.

Voice: "Hullo. It's Eric."

Me: "Yes."

Voice: "What is your E-mail address? Only I've got a quiz here that Sid wanted and I was going to send it to you to give to Sid. What is your E-mail address?"

Me: "God only knows."

Voice: "If I give you my E-mail address can you send it to me?"

Me: "What am I going to send to you? I thought you wanted to send something to me."

Voice: "You've got an E-mail haven't you?"

Me: "My wife has but she isn't in and I don't know what the hell it is."

Voice: "Oh. Can you write the address down? It's a very easy one."

Me: "What? Write down my address?"

Voice: "No. My E-mail address."

Me: "Hang on I'll get a pencil. I don't know what I'm bloody doing here."

The conversation continues along similar lines. I am baffled and worried that I am mishearing. Who is this Eric? Who is this Sid? Eventually when Eric says my wife Kathy will know what to do I point out gently that I think my missus is called Janet. "Oh" says Eric. He has dialled the wrong number. Our friendly farewells are muffled in laughter and we disappear from each other's lives as quickly as we entered them, strangers still. Funny ol' thing these modern gadgets.

LANGUAGE OF YOOF

I HAVE decided that despite my rapid advance into the realm of wrinkledom I must try to get to grips with the language of 'yoof'. Apparently there is a new trend in their strange sub-culture especially among girls, of dismissing the advances of would-be suitors with subtle yet clear messages. I overheard two examples last week. Pretty girl to callow youth: "Save yer flannel to polish yer shoes." And later equally pretty girl to even callower youth in the pub: "I hope yer rabbit dies and you can't sell the hutch."

GOD REST YE MERRY......

IT is late evening. There is a loud knocking at the door. I open it to discover four youths singing, if that is the right word, "We wish you a merry Christmas, we wish you a merry Christmas" and a grubby hand is held out for coin of the realm in recompense for this invasion of my November privacy. I try to point out that Christmas is over a month away. The biggest lad says: "No it ain't. It's closer to three weeks." I do not wish him the compliments of the season.

JUST RING THE BANK

WHAT follows you may think is a fable of our times. It is not. It concerns an Old Man who shrinks with apprehension from the fiendish appurtenances of modernity. Thus it came to pass recently that he tried to telephone his local bank to cancel an appointment there. His bank no longer accepts calls and he was transferred elsewhere to a centralised answering station though where he knew not. Patagonia? The lower foothills of the M'Boko peaks? His call was answered by a Disembodied Voice.

OM (plaintively): "I cannot get through to my branch of your bank. Please let them know I cannot make my appointment this morning. My name is.......the branch is......."

DV: "A few security questions first. Date of birth, please."

OM (puzzled): "What has my age to do with you phoning my branch?"

DV: "Part of the procedure. Your mother's maiden name please."

OM (firmly): "Please just cancel my appointment."

DV: "How much did you last pay into your account and when?"

OM (trembling slightly – with rage): "Just get in touch with my flaming branch and one more ridiculous bloody question and I will seek you out whoever and wherever you are and, and......."

DV: "How many standing orders do you have?"

OM: "Aaaaargh."

I know this to be the truth and not a fable because I was the Old Man who finally put the phone down.

FAIT ACCOMPLI

IT has been a very bad week. I should never have done it in the first place and, having done it, I should certainly not have admitted it. Well, not in public anyway. The whole business was a ghastly mistake and I apologise hugely and profoundly. I just don't know what got in to me although, to be fair to myself, it wasn't actually my fault. As with all the other great moral crises which have afflicted me during my long and somewhat lurid life the blame can be placed fairly and quite squarely upon Herself. I would never have dreamed of doing it and, as a matter of fact, I would not even have known how to go about acquiring it. Herself performed the dirty deed by means of cunning and stealth so that before I knew whether I was arriving or departing I found myself presented with a completed fate, as the Froggies would say.

As a result I have found myself being approached by friends and acquaintances nodding their heads in disbelief and muttering to themselves: "You of all people!" and "I still can't believe it", or, simply "Why?"

Well the reason is that Herself went out one day all innocent-looking and bought the damn thing without telling me, before I could so much as raise a howl of protest. When I arrived home that fateful day there it was in the middle of my desk gleaming with a derisory glee. Modern technology had triumphed. Herself had triumphed.

Then I made the ultimate error. I admitted in this very column that I was now the owner of – I can scarce find the strength to repeat the revelation – a – oh dear, well, yes – a mobile phone.

For how long have I raved and ranted and railed against the impertinent intrusions of technological demons? For as long as you and I can remember, that's how long. Then I am trapped by Herself much to my public embarrassment and humiliation.

Reader Luke Morris of William Smith Close, Cambridge, is not alone in admonishing me but his letter is typical and I quote it in a mood of humble contrition. He writes: "I sat in the garden, poured myself a large Scotch, and cast my eyes over your column. I was rendered speechless to see that 'they' have got you signed up with a so-called mobile phone. How can you, a figure of such common sense, decorate yourself with the very emblem of cool Britannia? You'll be on-line, posting e-mails and providing us with a "Cyber View from the Fen" before you know it. God forbid! Tell me this is not so!"

Well Mr Morris and all the others saddened by my sudden transmogrification from cloth-eared and innocent backwoodsman to seeming technological sophisticate there is good news. I haven't the faintest idea and have not the slightest intention of finding out how to use the dang-blasted thing. Ever! Honestly!

FEATHER PLUCKING COCKATOOS

URGENT warning: take immediate flight should you ever find yourself in the company of a feather-plucking cockatoo or parrot for you are in danger of a nasty assault and I'm not thinking of their beaks.

Until last week I was blissfully unaware of the threat lurking within your average, innocent-looking parrot cage and so, I imagine, were you. However, read on for the unpalatable truth....

In a bizarre court case before Cambridge Magistrates last week an unfortunate couple from Mepal in the fens were accused by the RSPCA of causing unnecessary suffering to two birds, Sally, a lesser sulphur crested cockatoo and Sydney, an African grey parrot. The birds, alas, had plucked out their own feathers.

Enter the witness box to give evidence for the RSPCA one Neil Forbes, described to the court as a leading avian expert. Mr Forbes informed their Worships – quite seriously – that the most likely reason the birds plucked their own feathers was because they were sexually frustrated which, for a magistrate, has to be a change from hearing excuses for riding a bike without a bell.

The avian expert went on to say that a hand-reared bird grows up thinking it is human and when it reaches sexual maturity it becomes attracted to humans. At which point even the most bored Justice of the Peace might sit up and begin to take notice.

There is more. Mr Forbes, the bird expert, said, slightly ungrammatically: "When this bird reaches breeding age they are in biological terms 'breeding machines' and will naturally want to breed with a human. This is without a shadow of doubt in my mind, obsessive compulsive disorder and this is because their sexual frustration has gone on for so long."

You might wish to read that previous paragraph again. I did and I'm still laughing.

Sally, the featherless cockatoo, had suffered over the years, he said. Of that there was "no doubt". Sydney, the grey African parrot, had lost his feathers more recently although quite why was not explained to the court.

The magistrates threw the case out and, once again, the RSPCA was left with feathers on its face so to speak. But disturbing questions remain.

After this avian expert's revelations how can anyone ever again admit to being a cockatoo fancier? How can a kindly parrot owner smile indulgently upon the pet in the cage in the corner of the sitting room lest the bird mistakes the signal, bursts into a sexual frenzy and starts ripping its feathers out?

SAVING THE MASTERS OF CAMBRIDGE

I'M getting slower on the uptake. Standing on Magdalene Bridge in Cambridge t'other day with an old chum when a car passes us. The car is packed to the roof with plants. Looks as though the driver has cleared the banks on the upper reaches of the river Limpopo should there be such a stretch of water.

"Wow", says my friend – or words to the effect. "He's got a helluva cheek. That car was full of cannabis plants. Fresh ones, too. And it's not as though it's midnight. It's broad daylight." We split up and went our innocent ways. Innocent? It was only when I reached home that I suddenly realised that my unworldly friend was clearly not as innocent as I had assumed. How on earth did he know what fresh cannabis plants look like? I'm damned if I do. Wouldn't recognise one if it was growing in my garden. Honestly, officer. Honestly.

All of which prompts me to recall that many years ago when Cambridge University and cannabis were at daggers drawn and in my own little way I was able to prevent a large number of very distinguished college Masters and Fellows from spending time in less salubrious establishments. I had written a report for The Times whom I represented in Cambridge then. It concerned the landlord of a Cambridge boarding house whose guests, unknown to him, had smoked the evil weed in his house. Off to jail he went. The Masters read my piece in horror. They had not realised. They, too, were landlords of huge boarding houses. They, too, faced the full wrath of the law. Could I help? I wrote a large piece that day which duly appeared in The Times. What with that and the influence of ex-Cambridge men in Westminster the law was changed upon the instant and our dons slept happily in their palaces.

FREEDOM FOR TIBET

THE President of China dropped into Cambridge last week to be feted by the authorities. Naturally there were those who objected to his presence in this epicentre of civilised tolerance. The police, in considerable strength, sought to minimise the visual impact of the protestations which centred on the plight of poor little Tibet crushed by the might of modem China, and in the main the police succeeded.

The rights and wrongs of welcoming a harsh dictator to Cambridge are for others to comment upon. But let me tell you that when I walked down King's Parade on the day of Mr Jiang's visit the sight of the Free Tibet flag fluttering from the flagpole atop the tower of the University Church of Great St Mary, a glorious symbol of pride and hope for the world to see, made my heart leap up.

Here was the spirit of the real, the true Cambridge.

Michael's Illness

HELPING THE DOCTORS

THE phone message from my G.P., God bless her seemed slightly odd. Would I be so kind as to pop down to the surgery next week and help her with some medical students? Knowing how hard-pressed the NHS is these days I said I would do what I could but I wasn't much good at medicine and, anyway, what had the students got? Patiently, so to speak, she explained they hadn't "got" anything. It was what I had "got" which would interest them. Would I mind if they practised on me?

At which point I felt more than somewhat relieved. Thus, in due course, five keen, young students proceeded to prod, poke and pummel me discussing meanwhile bits and pieces of my interior the existence of which was news to me. I hope the experience will help them in their future careers though I suspect they may not come across the like again. When they reminisce about a life-time of doctoring at their reunion fifty years hence I can hear one of them say with a laugh: "Ah yes! But there was never anything like that Newmarket stomach in the summer of "'04".

BENDING THE TRUTH FOR A GOOD CAUSE

I AM fast becoming an expert on our local hospitals – I've "done" Addenbrooke's, Newmarket and West Suffolk in the last three weeks and, no, I'm not going to give 'em points out of ten because I may be back in one or t'other shortly and the last thing I need is to disgruntle the staff.

I am not an inspector of hospitals, you understand. I visit them so they can inspect me. I had thought once of donating my body (not just yet) for scientific research but I reckon that I have been so thoroughly researched whilst alive that it would be pointless. I must have the best documented interior since they opened Tutankhamen's tomb.

Anyoldhow, there I was having a quiet coffee in the caff in West Suffolk in between the X-ray and the consultation, when I notice the yob at the next table talking into his mobile. The hospital is smothered in large notices saying staff, patients and visitors MUST turn off their phones whilst in the building. Clearly there is a very good technical reason for this requirement and the thought that this mindless twit might be interfering with a delicate operation in a theatre nearby infuriated not only me but the big chap sitting opposite me.

In words of one syllable he told the telephonic twerp to turn off his machine forthwith. And who the 'ell did 'e think 'e was, came the inevitable reply? My table companion rose, leaned over the miscreant and said very slowly: "I am the senior consultant in this hospital in the department of cardiac resuscitation and if you use that machine in here once more you may well be in urgent need of my professional skills."

The yob left his coffee and vanished. I congratulated the consultant on his decisive action. "Comes with the job, mate", he replied. "I'm really a taxi driver waiting to take my fare home. In our game we soon learn how to deal with rubbish like him."

JACK TAKES OVER

WHATEVER I've got knocked me about at the races and distracted my attention from the exquisite fillies of both varieties on parade and I ended up in my sick bed which is where I would still be if it wasn't for that useless creature of ours, Jack the Cat. I asked him to take over this week and though he has been bursting with ambition to fill my empty shoes he now tells me he's too nervous to go it alone. He wants me to help him. Damn cat will kill me. A couple of minutes and I'm back to my bed.......

Jack's Spot

Dear Readers All,

I'm afraid the Guv' really is more than a bit rough because he swears that he has never had a day off through illness since he left school if you ignore the day after Coronation Day and now here he is laid up in his kip and moping like someone out of a Victorian novel. So he reckons it's me for the bigtime this week. This is what he has been training me for – to take over in an emergency. Here, gentle readers, I have to hang my whiskers in shame because I've lost me bottle. And now I suppose I must let you into my secret. My column is not always all my own work. There! Now you know. Occasionally, when I've found myself stuck for something to say, the Guv' has whispered a suggestion or two and, to show that he's not as miserable an ol' bar steward as I sometimes make him out to be, he doesn't even complain about my insults – well, not much anyway.

But, whenever my confidence falters, I know he is there to turn to and despite our mutual antipathy when I was a bit wild we have grown closer together as the columns pass by. You could say, in fact, that in our literary lives we are indivisible which is the word I asked him to get out of his sick-bed to spell for me.

I've got to accept it, I'm not quite ready yet to go it alone. Which is why I'm praying that Harley Street comes up with something cheerful otherwise my days of stardom are over.

He's gone back to bed so that's Jack's Lot for now. He'll be OK next week.

Paws crossed! ***Jack the Cat***

I HAVE CANCER

Dear All,

The medics have discovered, after considerable difficulty, what I have suspected for some time. I have cancer.

You will note the abrupt and possibly brutal way in which I make that announcement which is something I could not possibly have done when I started writing this column more than 30 years ago. Then the very word was taboo. The disease was virtually a death sentence. Today, happily, it is discussed as openly as the common cold. Such has been the advance of medical science that it is now frequently no more than a pesky nuisance and it is curable. We all have friends, and probably relations, who have fought it successfully.

I am in the hands of that marvellous team at Papworth Hospital so I have neither fear nor doubt as to the outcome. I propose simply to look upon the cancer as a gatecrasher, uninvited, unwelcome, unwanted and as such I will treat it with the contempt that it deserves.

However, because I shall be popping into Papworth frequently I won't be able to knock out this column for maybe a couple of weeks which some of you may consider a welcome side-effect. I hope you will manage to get through life without me until we meet again!

Jack the Cat says he looks forward to the break because he has become intellectually exhausted by this writing lark but since he didn't cause my problem will he still get paid?

Off now. Normal service very shortly.

Cheers,

Michael Jeacock

THANK YOU

A VERY quick despatch from the battle zone. As President (and Treasurer) of the British League of Idlers, I find this much the least tiring way of saying a huge "thank you" to all of you who have sent me your best wishes in my current tussle with cancer. Lovely cards, letters and phone calls all – I am deeply moved, immensely encouraged and greatly strengthened by them. I cannot tell you by how much.

If I were to have one tiny speck of doubt about the sincerity of many of the "get well" cards it would be due to the inordinate amount of interest most of you manage to smuggle into your missives about the welfare of Jack the Cat. The flaming cat is perfectly fit and well and apparently lording it over the household when I'm away being medicced so please don't worry about him. He would confirm that if only I knew where the hell he was. I turn my back for a minute and he's off with his mates. Herself assures me he is in the rudest of health just as I propose to be very shortly when I have shrugged off my little problem – with a modicum of help from our splendid local quacks. Meanwhile, my sincerest thanks for your good wishes. I return to the fray much uplifted by them.

Cheers all!

Michael

Jack's Spot

Hi Folks, Fans, Friends All,

What a lovely, loveable crowd you are! I don't particularly want the poor Ol' Clapped-Out Guv' to hear this so keep it quiet please but the subtle way you managed to send your very best wishes to me disguised in all those "Get Well" cards and letters addressed to him was exquisitely organised. I think he still thinks they were meant just for him. But you and I know differently, do we not me hearties? Wink, wink, nudge jolly old nudge.

Anyoldhow, sorry for the breakdown in communications over the past weeks, but to be fair to him he has been a mite rough and I didn't want to steal all the limelight while he was ill. Still, one reason I'm glad to be back in the public eye is because the mates I meet round the back of the dustbins are yowling with glee – they thought I had been given the chop! Another is because I am getting a bit short of the readies. Now it's back to the prawns marinaded in cream and garlic. Tally Ho!!!!!!!!!

Thanks again fans, ***Jack the Unforgettable Cat***

BACKSCRATCHER NEEDED

A PERSONAL matter. One of the side effects of the fierce treatment they have been giving me in Addenbrooke's is a constant and urgent urge to scratch my back. This, of an obvious necessity, requires the occasional aid of Herself who is becoming miffed by this strange, onerous wifely duty. Apparently back scratching was not in the contract. So she slipped into Woolworths.

Herself to shop assistant: "Do you sell back scratchers?"

S.A.: "No, madam. No call for them."

H: "In that case please may I have a lavatory brush."

It is a more than adequate substitute I assure you but there is one major snag. Come the eventide and you can hear Herself half a mile away shouting: "Are you going to bed dear? Don't forget to take your lavatory brush with you."

FEELING AS JOLLY AS THE SHIP'S RAT

LAST week's readers may have noticed a large degree of optimism emanating (good word that) from the quills of your joint servants – M.J. Esq, and Jack the Unforgettable Cat.

Not today, though, shipmates. This ol' cap'n is feeling about as jolly as the ship's rat 'alf way down the plank without so much as a noggin o' Black Ben's rum to fortify his-self. I blame it on my treatment's side effects so I'm off to me hammock.

Here again in full flow next week. Honest.

Cheers,

Mike.

Jack's Spot

Hi. Don't want to upset the 'Guv / Cap'n but I wish he'd make up his flamin' mind, silly 'ol twit. Anyoldhow, I'm back on parade next time, come what may, and if he don't like it he can scuttle his portholes – so there!

Cheers all. ***Jack the Indefatigable Cat***

DOWN THE FEN

IT was just two days after I had finished dangling from a week-long drip on the second highest floor in Addenbrooke's Hospital last week that the startled young roe came bounding across the low, black fen towards Herself and me. Pert little head held high, tail white, rounded and fluffy as an unused powder puff, the deer skipped past within feet of us, totally ignoring us as though we did not exist.

The delicate creature had emerged suddenly, unexpectedly from a long willow thicket close by the River Cam and appeared with all the shock of a disintegrating pillow case, for all the world as though it was sorry for the interruption – or as if it was saying "by your leave gentle folk, this is your world, not mine." It was over in seconds and it was utterly and unbelievably beautiful.

So, you ask? So what? I will tell you. After the previous week high in that medical tower of Babel in the Cambridge sky where those delicious nurses changed my drips with a brilliant insouciance verging on genius Herself knew from her visits to me that in spite of all the medico's magic I was aching for the cleansing air of those fens that seemed just a mirage away.

Thus, two days after I left hospital she drove me into the fen over beyond Swaffham Prior where son Simon was shooting on one estate and grandson Ben was beating. "Next door" on the neighbouring shoot were some of our old friends. Herself and I were distant watchers, standing in the frisky breeze, talking to a couple of old chaps in between drives when the scene with the fearless deer was enacted. Gnarled and grizzled pheasant men they may have been but the sudden, startling appearance of the roe softened them both

And thinking about it afterwards it made me wonder – how much good might a similar scene have done for some of those patients I had left behind in Addenbrooke's? A mad thought, of course, and quite impossible to achieve. But it made me realise how very lucky I have been to experience both.

And that – rather selfishly – is "what".

FINAL FAREWELL

THIS is the last one folks, and these are the final inky scribblings of a very contented man. More than 30 years of writing for you is a long, long time.

It has been a joy to share the ups and downs of 30 years of our lives with you all, and I have met so many of you by letter, by telephone and in person – and what an amazing bunch of readers and friends you have become. Thank you all.

I still don't like antis or enemies of the Crown, but they have had to put up with me exactly as long as I have had to put up with them. Good luck whatever your views. Happily you are too late to force them upon me now.

I am penning this in St Nicholas Hospice, Bury St Edmunds. Wonderful place, everyone here does a marvellous job. Remember them if you have any spare cash left over after Christmas.

When this hard winter I promised finally arrives, please don't throw any snowballs at Jack the Cat. He's a good chap really with a heart of gold, is full of kindness and will be a great comfort to Herself over the coming weeks.

Jack says: "Agreed – I'm one of the nicest cats you could ever meet and it's good to know the Guv' appreciates me. Any mistakes in this are down to Herself to whom he dictated it. She's not very good on the spellings, and long words are very hard for her. He should have asked me to do it."

(By the way, in case you haven't guessed, Jack is illiterate.)

THE OLD SHEPHERD'S PRAYER –

CAMBRIDGE University's Professor Stephen Hawking, the world's foremost cosmologist, is forecasting doom for mankind which, he says, will be caused by some self-inflicted biological disaster. Our only escape route will be by developing space stations whither we can flee to safety. That sounds to me almost as tough as being forced to live in one of Cambridgeshire's new "villages" and if the good Professor doesn't mind I think I'll stay put. Remember the Old Shepherd's Prayer?

"Heavenly Master, I wud like to wake to they same green places where I be know'd for breaking dogs and follerin' sheep.....And if I may not walk in th'old ways and look on th'old faces, I wud sooner sleep."

Michael Jeacock is asleep. He died peacefully on December 14, 2006.

He was English and proud of it and is remembered with love and laughter by his family and all his many friends.